HIDDEN IN PLAIN VIEW

Undesigned Coincidences in the Gospels and Acts

Lydia McGrew is a champion of the argument from undesign—undesigned co-incidences, that is. She is talking about cases in the Gospels and Acts where some event finds its explanation in some other, independent document of the New Testament. Given the relevant independence of the accounts, for which McGrew argues, the coincidence of the accounts cannot plausibly be dismissed as acciden-tal but must be rooted in the actual events which are described in the accounts. Some of McGrew's examples are truly impressive, for example, the independent explanation of the charges brought against Jesus at his trial before the Sanhedrin that he would destroy the Temple and raise it up in three days. Readable and entertaining, as well as instructive, this book is well worth the read.

William Lane Craig, Professor of Philosophy,
Talbot School of Theology; Houston Baptist University

Lydia McGrew thinks outside the box of much contemporary biblical scholar-ship to highlight the ways in which one Gospel completely in passing and there-fore almost certainly inadvertently explains a question that other Gospels raise but leave unanswered by gaps in their narratives. Then she does the same with the Acts of the Apostles and the letters of Paul. She is scarcely the first to have noticed these "coincidences" but is one of the few in the twenty-first century to highlight them. Her work thus forms one more important plank in the ever-growing platform for the reliability of the New Testament, since these connec-tions are far too subtle, consistent and true to what we know of the first-century to be fictitiously created.

Craig L. Blomberg, Distinguished Professor of the
New Testament, Denver Seminary

Given the myriads of challenges that recent critical scholars bring against vari-ous aspects of the New Testament text, different approaches to the reliability of the Gospels and Acts are always welcome. Lydia McGrew has opened a window into Eighteenth and Nineteenth Century apologetics by reintroducing the con-cept of "undesigned coincidences," showing how different passages can comple-ment each other in ways that support their historicity. Like puzzle pieces, these seemingly hidden and often common, everyday pieces of information help to explain each other, thereby providing factual support. I recommend this well-written and exceptionally informative volume for the believer who desires an-other apologetic arrow in their quivers.

Gary R. Habermas, Distinguished Research Professor,
Liberty University and Theological Seminary

Those who defend the reliability of the New Testament Gospels have many argu-ments available. My favorite is to show how admirably the biblical documents find correlation in the established facts of the ancient world. But now Lydia McGrew has unearthed a type of evidence so old that it is new—the evidence of undesigned coincidences. The Gospels interlock with one another, and the book of Acts interlocks with the Pauline epistles, in ways that give evidence that the authors were well informed and truthful. Both those who defend the faith and those who oppose it will have to take these original and welcome insights very seriously.

Paul Maier, Professor emeritus of History,
Western Michigan University; Author of *In the Fullness of Time*

The value of this book's observations is not their novelty but their cumulative effectiveness as an argument. Here then is a valuable and accessible approach for recognizing significant historical information in the Gospels that does not simply repeat arguments that most of us have already heard. ... I have learned much from, and expect McGrew's other readers to learn much from, her revival of this important but neglected argument.

Craig Keener (from Foreword), F. M. and Ada Thompson
Professor of Biblical Studies, Asbury Theological Seminary

Hidden in Plain View is an intriguing, clearly-written argument for the historical claim that the four Gospels and the book of Acts were all written by authors who were eyewitnesses or close associates of eyewitnesses. McGrew points out evidence that is indeed in "plain view" since it requires no special historical or linguistic expertise to understand, though it is subtle enough to require a sharp investigative mind to discern. She shows there are good reasons to believe that the theological and evangelistic ends of these Biblical writers are fully consistent with aims to tell a story that is historically reliable. Although this type of argument goes back at least to William Paley, it has been largely forgotten. McGrew has done us a great service by showing us how to find evidence that is easy to miss even though it is right before the readers' eyes.

C. Stephen Evans, University Professor of Philosophy and Humanities, Baylor University; Professorial Fellow, Logos Institute for Analytic and Exegetical Theology, University of St. Andrews

Often the incidental details in a narrative are what convince modern critics that the ancient writer is telling the truth. When these details exhibit verisimilitude, that is, agree with the realities of the past, we give the ancient source the benefit of the doubt. In *Hidden in Plain View* Lydia McGrew shows that apparent discrepancies often point to independent and reliable contact with the actual events of the Jesus story. What we have here is yet additional evidence of the verisimilitude of the New Testament Gospels.

Craig A. Evans, John Bisagno Distinguished Professor of Christian Origins, Houston Theological Seminary; Houston Baptist University

Typical defenses for the reliability of the Gospels and Acts rely upon manuscript authority, archaeological evidence, and arguments for genuineness of the eyewitness accounts of the respective writers. All these are valid and important. But with the release of *Hidden in Plain View*, Lydia McGrew (re)introduces us to a forgotten but powerful piece of evidence—"undesigned coincidences," as she calls them. Even though I have been teaching and writing in the field of apologetics for nearly two decades, many of her arguments were new to me. And I find them very convincing. This book is not only a must-read for Christians who care about the reliability of the New Testament, but it is a book genuine seekers would benefit from reading as well. My thanks to Lydia for her hard work and important contribution.

Sean McDowell, Biola University; Author of *The Fate of the Apostles*

Keep this book at the ready. It contains some interesting hidden gems, and God may use these overlooked pieces of evidence to persuade someone you know to take the Gospels seriously.

J. Warner Wallace (from Afterword), Cold Case Detective;
Adjunct Professor of Apologetics, Biola University

Hidden in Plain View takes many almost seemingly aside remarks and shows how they are connected to things said elsewhere in Scripture. It is an intriguing concept, executed well. The result is not only a fascinating read but a deeper appreciation for the connections Scripture makes.

Darrell L. Bock, Senior Research Professor of
New Testament Studies, Dallas Theological Seminary

Though I've studied Christian apologetics for almost four decades and have written several apologetic works, I must confess that I never took the argument from "undesigned coincidences" very seriously—*until I read this book.* I was pleasantly surprised by the compelling cumulative case Lydia McGrew makes for the historical veracity of much of the New Testament on this basis. All who want to be prepared to give a rational defense of their hope in Christ (I Pet 3.15) ought to include this well-written and powerfully argued book in their apologetic toolbox.

Greg Boyd, Senior Pastor, Woodland Hills Church (Maplewood MN);
President, ReKnew Ministries (ReKnew.org); Co-Author of *The Jesus Legend*

With her argument from undesigned coincidences, Lydia McGrew revives a long-neglected line of consideration that, taken as a cumulative case, supports the historical reliability of key New Testament documents. Among the reasons for the contemporary neglect of this argument are various conclusions drawn from source, form, and redaction criticism that have fostered a general air of skepticism surrounding these writings. However, these forms of literary criticism were the product of a highly literate, post-Gutenberg world, and all too often have been anachronistically applied to ancient biblical texts born in an orally dominant context. When viewed from a perspective sensitive to the oral dynamics at work within the biblical texts themselves, one can begin to more fully appreciate the insights and cumulative force of McGrew's proposal.

Paul Rhodes Eddy, Professor of Biblical and Theological Studies, Bethel University

I've been looking forward to a book like *Hidden in Plain View.* As a trained trial lawyer, I've seen the the power of multiple, complementary eyewitness accounts in helping us understand what really happened in the past. Lydia McGrew has done us the service of collating and cross-referencing those kinds of accounts in an easily readable and relatable form. I highly recommend this book to anyone who is serious about studying the life of Jesus and the early church.

Abdu Murray, North American Director for Ravi Zacharias International Ministries; Author of *Grand Central Question: Answering the Critical Concerns of the Major Worldviews*

In this engaging book, Dr. McGrew shows that the Gospels and Acts are worthy of our confidence in their historical reliability. In case after case, she demonstrates that these accounts display the features of actual testimony—especially in the way that sources whose authors surely did not collude, nevertheless complement one another. Dr. McGrew explains that she has not pioneered this line of argument, but has reinstated it from 18th and 19th century worthies. She has done more than that, however: with a combination of disciplined imagination and clear thinking, she has brought freshness and vigor to the discussion. She also rightly insists that we do not need to agree with every point she makes to appreciate the force of the cumulative argument. Thanks, Dr. McGrew!

C. John ("Jack") Collins, Professor of Old Testament, Covenant Theological Seminary

The argument from undesigned coincidences, which once was part of the apologetic and exegetical training of almost every British and American minister, has been unjustly neglected by seminaries and churches for over a century. This clearly written book brings the argument back into focus, taking the strongest examples from earlier writers like Blunt and Paley and improving upon their work to build a convincing cumulative case for the historical reliability of the Gospels and Acts. Students and scholars, pastors and laymen, earnest believers and honest doubters—there is something of permanent value here for every reader.

Timothy McGrew, Professor and Chairman, Department of Philosophy, Western Michigan University

What if, aside from conventional historical reasons for crediting the gospels as honest accounts of Jesus' life, these ancient records also hold a series of forensic clues that say, as DNA or fingerprints might announce the presence of some past visitor, 'The Son of God truly walked among us?' Lydia McGrew applies formidable analytical powers to uncovering one especially piquant series of clues preserved in the gospels, like gnats in amber. *Hidden in Plain View* thus helps confirm the intuition even many non-Christians feel when they read the gospels, that their authors are imparting truthful memories of a real person, who spoke and acted as no one else. The most dramatic and significant episode of "CSI-Jerusalem."

David Marshall, Author of *Jesus is No Myth:*
The Fingerprints of God on the Gospels

Lydia McGrew has resurrected the best evidence you've never heard for the historicity of the New Testament. After reading *Hidden in Plain View,* I think you'll not only be amazed by how the accounts inadvertently authenticate one another, but you'll be left with the almost irrefutable impression that you are reading eyewitness testimony from actual historical events (and they happen to be the most important events in human history!). There is simply no other reasonable explanation. Dr. McGrew masterfully shows why.

Frank Turek, CrossExamined

In *Hidden in Plain View* Lydia McGrew enters into the courtyard of New Testament studies and overturns the scholars' tables. McGrew is the anti-redaction critic: Where most scholars argue that one Gospel writer has intentionally altered or even contradicted material from an earlier Gospel, she argues that one Gospel writer has unintentionally complemented and even confirmed material from another Gospel. The accounts differ not because of competing theological or polemical interests but because of the varied perspectives and knowledge of the different eyewitnesses to the reported events. McGrew engages in the same iconoclastic analysis of Acts and the epistles of Paul, contending that Luke and Paul inadvertently corroborate one another despite writing very different sorts of texts. Like an Adrian Monk who compulsively notices things everyone else misses, McGrew draws the reader's attention to apparently undesigned coincidences in statements by different New Testament writers that attest to the factual character of their accounts. Doggedly and fearlessly working through numerous examples, she builds up a cumulative case that the New Testament writers presented largely independent testimonies to the facts about Jesus and the origins of the Christian faith.

Robert M. Bowman Jr., Executive Director,
Institute for Religious Research

Lydia McGrew has accomplished not one but three rare feats in writing *Hidden In Plain View.* She has written a work of Christian apologetics that's truly accessible to everyone; no specialist's knowledge required in archaeology, languages, history, or any other discipline but the words of Scripture itself. She has built a road starting with the study of Christian evidences, leading straight to a deeper appreciation of the intricate beauty of God's word. And she has produced a book that will be enjoyed with equal delight by any student of Scripture, from the lay person to the scholar. *Hidden in Plain View* will help you understand the New Testament as you never have before—and to trust it like never before, too.

Tom Gilson, Senior Editor and Ministry Coordinator, *The Stream*; author of *Critical Conversations: A Christian Parents' Guide to Discussing Homosexuality With Teens*

A very careful, scholarly treatment of a neglected apologetic for the historical soundness of the accounts of our Lord's life. Particularly impressive is the author's avoidance of arguments dependent on commitment to a particular theory of Synoptic priority (e.g., Markan priority).

John Warwick Montgomery, Professor and Director, International Academy of Apologetics, Evangelism, and Human Rights, Strasbourg, France

Hidden in Plain View

Undesigned Coincidences
in the Gospels and Acts

Lydia McGrew

To Tim McGrew

without whom
I would have known nothing about
undesigned coincidences

and

To the late Colin J. Hemer

for his careful and indispensable
scholarship on Acts

and

To William Paley

for obvious reasons.

CONTENTS

Tables and Maps

FOREWORD

In this concise but fascinating work, Lydia McGrew opens up for us a long-neglected consideration for the reliability of the Gospels and Acts: the argument from undesigned coincidences. This is a time-honored argument that was once favored by many Christian apologists of earlier centuries, not least the eighteenth-century thinker William Paley. As she rightly notes, this argument resembles the way that forensic professionals examine testimony. Despite its sensibility, however, it has often been neglected by many biblical scholars, including myself. I first learned of it not from fellow biblical scholars, although some have made use of it, but especially from Lydia's husband Tim, a philosopher.

Some reasons for our neglect are not difficult to fathom. For one, scholars came to dismiss some of earlier apologists' arguments through developments in philosophy. Perhaps most famously, Paley's argument from design (actually adapting an argument already widely articulated by many pre-Christian philosophers) fell on hard times. Yet the argument from undesigned coincidences is a separate matter and one that continues to prove effective, as already noted, in interviewing witnesses. Moreover, even Paley's much-maligned design argument has been resuscitated in some more sophisticated forms (and, for what it is worth, I believe with some very good reasons).

7

Probably a more influential factor in the neglect of the undesigned coincidences argument, at least in biblical studies, has been our appropriate but often myopic focus on single sources. In reaction against popular-level prooftexting that ignores the literary context of verses cited, scholars naturally and rightly emphasize seeing how a passage fits into the larger work in which it appears. We respect the inspired intelligence of the biblical authors and consequently look for design in their work.

But while this disciplined approach is appropriate when considering the meaning of texts, it is easy for us to overlook another commonsense approach when considering the history to which the texts bear witness: we are often dealing with persons or sources that are independent witnesses to events. Information they understood as direct witnesses or reporters of shared sources is not always fully articulated by each of the witnesses, but the interlocking of their respective testimonies bears witness to the common information behind them. Far from imaginatively inventing stories or colluding to tell identical stories, the writers report incidental details that cohere with the larger story behind their works. Paley observes that we would use this method in examining other historical works; I can verify this observation because I have used such criteria when comparing the work of different biographers on some figures of the early Roman empire.

One need not suppose that the Gospels are completely literarily independent—it is, after all, intrinsically unlikely that writers of later Gospels were unaware that earlier Gospels were circulating—to recognize that they draw on prior information. If that is true where we can test them, we have no reason to suspect otherwise where we cannot test them. Obviously the Gospel writers had no way of knowing what sources would survive over the following centuries. McGrew and I gravitate toward different approaches to the chronological sequence of the Gospels, but her argument stands regardless of the sequence.

Although the arguments in this book are not technically new—as noted above, many of these examples circulated already in the eighteenth century—they are new to most of us who read them in the twenty-first century, and it is helpful for us to hear them again with reference to those older sources. The value of this book's observations is not their novelty but their cumulative effectiveness as an argument. Here then is a valuable and accessible approach for recognizing significant historical information in the Gospels that does not simply repeat arguments that most of us have already heard. Instead it complements existing arguments in a persuasive way. Meanwhile, though without intending to answer all the questions, it also turns on its head the frequent anti-Gospel argument that rests on apparent contradictions.

New Testament commentators will be familiar with some of the connections, especially between Acts and Paul's letters, but usually not from this angle and never gathered with this cumulative force. I have learned much from, and expect McGrew's other readers to learn much from, her revival of this important but neglected argument.

Craig Keener
F. M. and Ada Thompson Professor of Biblical Studies
Asbury Theological Seminary
Summer, 2016

GENERAL INTRODUCTION

Just What is an Undesigned Coincidence?

Suppose that two of your friends, Alan and Betty, tell you that they have had a distressing conversation at a coffee shop with a third friend, Carl. They tell you that Carl has confessed to some serious misdoing. Carl denies it all. He says that he never had any such conversation with Alan and Betty and never even met them at the coffee shop. The whole thing is a set-up, he claims. So you sit down with Alan and Betty separately and have them tell you what happened in their own words. At one point in his story, Alan says, "The place was so crowded that we could hardly find a spot for all three of us to sit."

Betty, in telling you her version, mentions, "While we were talking, Alan accidentally knocked his coffee off into my lap."

Alan doesn't mention knocking off the coffee, and Betty doesn't mention that the coffee shop was crowded. But these two bits of detail fit together: If they are both telling about a real meeting, and if the coffee shop really was crowded, they would have been sitting close together with little extra space for themselves and their coffee. This would make an accident with the coffee more likely. And if the coffee were spilled, it would be more likely to spill into someone's lap rather than only onto the table. This dovetailing between Alan's and Betty's stories does not look good for Carl, who is denying that any meeting happened at all.

Notice, too, that these sorts of details are not likely to be the result of collusion. If Alan and Betty are making up a story together to frame Carl, of course they are going to be sure to say the same things about the incriminating admissions he allegedly made. If they are very devious, they might even plot to throw in a few of the same details as part of the set-up. This is why it wouldn't be as good evidence of their truthfulness if they both said, "The coffee shop was so crowded that we could hardly find room for all three of us" while neither of them added the detail about the coffee. Nor would it be as good evidence if Betty alone said, "It was so crowded that we were squished together, and Alan even knocked his coffee into my lap." It's possible that a person doing that is just beefing up the story with extra fictional details. But when one person says that it was crowded and the *other* tells about a minor accident that would be to some degree expected in a crowded café, that is strong evidence that they are both telling about a real meeting at which they were both present.

This, then, is an example of an undesigned coincidence. It's a significant *coincidence* that Alan says that it was crowded and that Betty says that a coffee cup got knocked into her lap. It appears *undesigned* because the details are mentioned casually in a way that would be unlikely if they were colluding.

Here is a broad definition of an undesigned coincidence:

> An undesigned coincidence is a notable connection between two or more accounts or texts that doesn't seem to have been planned by the person or people giving the accounts. Despite their apparent independence, the items fit together like pieces of a puzzle.

An undesigned coincidence provides reason to believe that both (all) of the statements that contribute to it are truthful. Most of the time, the coincidences that I examine in this book will come from different authors, but this isn't always the case. Different passages in a work by the same author can also fit together in this special, puzzle-like way, especially when they are far apart in a document. The concept of an undesigned coincidence will become clearer through the discussion of specific examples.

I will be using the phrase "undesigned coincidences" throughout this book, and I should say at the outset that there are gray areas when it comes to the question of whether something counts as an undesigned coincidence argument. For example, there is an interesting type of evidence for the truth of the Gospels from the consistency of Jesus' character throughout the Gospels, despite their differences of style and emphasis.[1] A similar argument can be made concerning the character of Paul as portrayed in Acts and the epistles.[2] Does this count as an undesigned coincidence? Certainly it is in the same general family and deserves attention, but for my purposes in this book I will not designate it as an undesigned coincidence. Even in the somewhat miscellaneous selection in Chapter IV, I will focus on *particular* events or facts and coincidences related to them.

Similarly, one might well argue that incidental connections between the Biblical texts and external evidence such as archeology and independent information concerning the social and political milieu of the time are, in a sense, undesigned coincidences between the Bible and non-biblical sources. This is a rich vein of evidence that corroborates the Gospels and Acts and deserves to be more widely known. It is certainly a mistake to think that the best external evidence we could have for the Bible is the actual recounting of the same events in some non-biblical text. On the contrary, incidental allusions in Scripture to facts about history and politics are even stronger indications of the reliability of the books than the duplication of specific events. The 19th-century historian George Rawlinson has pointed out the extreme complexity of the period of history to which the Gospels and Acts belong and the remarkable fact that the New Testament "falls into no error in treating of the period."[3]

Coincidences between a text (such as a book of the Bible) and an incidental fact about the history of the time are in a sense a species of undesigned coincidence, but for my purposes in this book I will focus most on *internal* evidence of coincidences within the Biblical text itself, occasionally bolstered by external details, such as (in Chapter II) the time of year when the grass is green in Galilee.

Organization and Argument of this Book

This book is divided into two parts—Part I on the Gospels, and Part II on Acts and the Pauline Epistles. Each part has its own introduction in which I explain in some detail the argument of that section. The big picture is this: The occurrence of multiple undesigned coincidences between and among these documents supports the conclusion that the Gospels and Acts are historically reliable and that they come from people close to the facts who were attempting to tell truthfully what they knew. This picture of the Gospels and Acts stands in sharp contrast to alternatives that would make the Gospels much less reliable.

1) The idea that the Gospels were written at many removes from the events that they chronicle,
2) The idea that they are so full of contradictions that we cannot trust them,
3) The idea that they are full of legendary accretions, or

4) The idea that the Gospels contain statements that are contrary to fact but that were included as literary or theological
embellishments or alterations.

I am suggesting that the reader consider the question of the
historical reliability of the Gospels and Acts from a new angle.
Instead of getting involved in the specifics of alleged contradictions and proposed resolutions to them (not a bad enterprise in
itself), instead of tackling these books from the perspectives of
source and redaction criticism with the assumption that they represent multiple redactors, layers, and "developments," instead of
thinking and speaking of Jesus or Paul as if they are literary characters in fictional works, I suggest that the reader take seriously
the hypothesis that they are what they appear to be *prima facie* and
what they were traditionally taken by Christians to be—historical
memoirs of real people and events, written by those in a position
to know about these people and events, either direct eyewitnesses
or friends and associates of eyewitnesses, who were trying to be
truthful. I suggest that we take this hypothesis for a test drive
while setting aside the apparatus of critical scholarship. Suppose
that these *were* such memoirs. What might they look like? How
does the occurrence of coincidences that appear casual and unre-
hearsed between and among these documents support that hypothesis? When all you have is a hammer, everything looks like a
nail. I suggest that we expand our toolkit.

Casual comments, allusions, and omissions that *fit together*
are not what one would find in different fictional or fictionalized
works written by different people. They are also not to be expected
among different legendary stories that grew up gradually long after the events. They *are* the sort of thing that one gets in real
witness testimony from people close-up to real events. J. Warner
Wallace, a cold-case homicide detective, is one of the only current

writers to discuss the argument from undesigned coincidences; he notes the connection between undesigned coincidences and eyewitness testimony:

> As a cold-case detective, I've experienced something similar to this a number of times. Often, questions an eyewitness raises at the time of the crime are left unanswered until we locate an additional witness years later. This is a common characteristic of true, reliable eyewitness accounts.[4]

> It's my job to assemble the complete *picture* of what happened at the scene. No single witness is likely to have seen every detail, so I must piece together the accounts, allowing the observations of one eyewitness to *fill in the gaps* that may exist in the observations of another eyewitness. ... True, reliable eyewitness accounts are never completely parallel and identical. Instead, they are different pieces of the same puzzle, unintentionally supporting and complementing each other to provide all the details related to what really happened.[5]

The casualness of undesigned coincidences is worth stressing and is also closely connected to the concept of subtlety. In the story I started out with, both Betty and Alan mention the relevant details *in passing*. This is part of what makes the connection between those details so striking. If, for example, Alan were to mention both details and stress the connection between them, going on about how crowded it was and about how he remembered that it was *so crowded* because of the coffee incident, then we might be dealing with a clever liar. Since neither Alan nor Betty appears to be doing that, the connection is a *subtle* one. It is a connection that many people would not notice explicitly and that some might not even notice subconsciously. This is all the more reason to believe that it is not deliberate. If Alan and Betty were making up the story, it is extremely unlikely that they would attempt to get others to believe it by such a roundabout plan: "You say that it was crowded, and I'll say that you knocked your coffee into my lap, okay?" Chances are high that such a plot would not be effective, because many people would not even notice the connection. A trained detective might. Others *might* be subconsciously influenced. But the whole point of the crowdedness/coffee connection would go right over the heads of many listeners. Thus, such a subtle connection is not very useful to a forger or fictionalizer who wants his story to be taken as true. The 19th-century English clergyman J.S. Howson emphasizes this fact. "An intentional and contrived coincidence must be of such a character as to *strike* the reader. Otherwise it fails of its purpose. If it was kept latent for the intelligent … critics of a later age to find out, it has not attained the end for which it was meant at the time of its contrivance."[6]

A further word is in order here about alleged contradictions. It might seem surprising that I do not do more in these pages to address alleged contradictions, including those in the neighborhood of the passages I discuss. For example, since I discuss several undesigned coincidences connected with the accounts of the feeding of the five thousand, and especially since two of them concern the location of the feeding, should I not pause to talk about the alleged discrepancy between John's statement that the disciples took a boat afterwards toward Capernaum (John 6.17)—which would seem to be *away* from Bethsaida—and the statement in Mark 6.45, which, as usually translated, says that after the feeding Jesus sent the disciples in a boat *to* or *toward* Bethsaida?

Entire books have been written on the subject of alleged contradictions in the Gospels, and this is not one of those books. But the decision not to be led into lengthy discussion of that topic is not solely the result of my desire to maintain focus. There is a reason for that focus itself. I believe that an understanding of the case from undesigned coincidences helps us to see the forest and not get lost in the trees. Consider the example of the location of the feeding of the five thousand. Since (as I will discuss) subtle intersections among John, Matthew, and Luke all converge to support the conclusion that this event took place somewhere near the town of Bethsaida, the question of the location of this event is *far* from an embarrassment to the advocate of the Gospels' reliability. Very much to the contrary. That realization, in turn, places in a fairer light the remaining puzzle about how to translate and/or construe the Greek preposition *pros* ("to" or "towards," but also possibly "over against") in Mark 6.45 and whether it is legitimate to translate it in a way that resolves the apparent discrepancy. It is a case of realizing where the weight of the evidence falls. In this case, the weight of the evidence about the location of the feeding is highly *favorable* to the reliability of the Gospels, whereas a focus on the alleged discrepancy creates a false impression that the question of its location is a point *against* their reliability.

Moreover, as I shall often argue, the very existence of variety in detail, up to and including apparent discrepancies between different documents and accounts, is strong evidence of their independence, which is in turn important to the positive force of undesigned coincidences between them.

In short, a view of the positive case from undesigned coincidences gives us a different view of the entire question of alleged contradictions, placing them against a backdrop woven from the intersecting and mutually confirming warp and woof of the documents—the Gospels, in Part I, and Acts and the Pauline Epistles, in Part II.

This issue was well addressed and placed in perspective by William Paley well over two hundred years ago in his *View of the Evidences of Christianity*, originally published in 1794:

> I know not a more rash or unphilosophical conduct of the understanding, than to reject the substance of a story, by reason of some diversity in the circumstances with which it is related. The usual character of human testimony is substantial truth under circumstantial variety. This is what the daily experience of courts of justice teaches. When accounts of a transaction come from the mouths of different witnesses, it is seldom that it is not possible to pick out apparent or real inconsistencies between them. These inconsistencies are studiously displayed by an adverse pleader, but oftentimes with little impression upon the minds of the judges. On the contrary, a close and minute agreement induces the suspicion of confederacy and fraud. When written histories touch upon the same scenes of action, the comparison almost always affords ground for a like reflection.[7]

Paley's dictum should be inscribed upon the office doorposts of every New Testament scholar: "The usual character of human testimony is substantial truth under circumstantial variety." Were we to bear it in mind and weigh evidence accordingly, we could avoid many foolish errors and unnecessary literary and redactive speculations.

Two hundred and twenty years later, Paley's observation is still timely and relevant to the practice of law and the investigation of real-world events, as Wallace attests:

> Unless you've worked a lot with eyewitnesses and have become familiar with the nature of apparent contradictions in eyewitness accounts, it's easy to assume that people are lying (or are mistaken) simply because they don't agree on every detail or have

ignored some facts in favor of others. If nothing else, we have to remember that an eyewitness account can be reliable in spite of *apparent* contradictions. While we might complain about two accounts that appear to differ in some way, we would be even more suspicious if there were absolutely no peculiarities or differences. If this were the case with the Gospels, I bet we would argue that they were the result of some elaborate collusion. ... Human eyewitnesses produce human eyewitness accounts; they are often idiosyncratic and personal, but reliable nonetheless.[8]

I would far rather have three messy, apparently contradictory versions of the event than one harmonized version that eliminated some important detail. I know in the end I'll be able to determine the truth of the matter by examining all three stories. The apparent contradictions are usually easy to explain once I learn something about the witnesses and their perspectives (both visually and personally) at the time of the crime.[9]

Here I must emphasize two important further points about the argument from undesigned coincidences, which are related to each other.

1) The argument is cumulative. While I think that many of the individual coincidences that I bring up here are strong indicators of reliability all by themselves, it is not necessary that any one coincidence carry the weight of the argument for reliability on its own. When, in instance after instance, these documents fit together just as truthful testimony fits together, there is a strong cumulative case for the documents.

2) The argument is varied in strength. Some of the cases I will discuss are easier to explain away than others as sheer coincidence that might arise even if the texts were not truthful or even if the facts were different from those I suggest. Because the case is cumulative, it is not necessary to accept every point as I argue for it

in order to be rationally impressed by the strength of the case as a whole. If you think a particular argument is extremely weak, I will of course disagree with you, or I would not have included it in this book, but I invite you to keep reading.

A Note on My Use of Other Sources on Undesigned Coincidences

The phrase "undesigned coincidence" was coined by the 18th-century Anglican clergyman and apologist William Paley, who used this type of argument extensively in his work *Horae Paulinae* (first published in 1790) to illuminate the intersections between Acts and the Pauline Epistles and among the Pauline Epistles. Paley gave a few examples of the way in which this method could be applied to the Gospels in 1794 in *A View of the Evidences of Christianity* (Part II, Chapter IV). The phrase received further popularity from the work of 19th-century Anglican priest John James Blunt, who began in 1828 to publish a series of lectures that made use of the argument. These came together in 1847 in Blunt's book *Undesigned Coincidences*, which uses this type of argument to support the reliability of the Old Testament as well as the New. Others, such as Thomas R. Birks, who published an edition of Paley's *Horae Paulinae* in 1849, wrote further on the subject. I first learned of undesigned coincidences through the work of my husband, philosopher Timothy McGrew, who has discussed them in numerous lectures.[10]

Of all of the undesigned coincidences, including sub-points, discussed in this book, I claim to have thought of only a few entirely on my own. One of these, as it turns out, was already in Blunt, though I found it independently. Undesigned coincidences are, in a way, like recipes. That is to say, while it certainly helps to have someone else point them out, different people can find

them independently. That is true in the nature of the case for coincidences internal to the Bible, since alert observation, an eye
for detail, and good judgment may suffice, especially if the reader
already knows that such connections do sometimes occur and is
on the lookout for them.

For the most part, then, I do not make a claim to originality
in discovering the *cores* of the various coincidences in this book.
The minimal, necessary texts for most of them, and the fact that
they fit together so as to create such coincidences, have usually
come to my notice from other sources—usually Blunt, Paley, or
McGrew. I have given a reference to a published source for a
coincidence when I am aware of it. Otherwise, if I did not find
the coincidence on my own, I owe the core of the coincidence to
Timothy McGrew, sometimes through his public presentations
and sometimes through personal communication, and I note this
in the endnotes. He wishes me to emphasize that, even when
I have not been able to find any other written source and have
credited him, he does not therefore claim to have discovered the
coincidence on his own. It may well be that at this point we are
simply unable to find the written source that originally inspired
his presentation. In a few cases the coincidence is my own discovery and was not anticipated by the sources I am using, and I have
stated that in the notes when it is the case.

I stress the word "core," because my modifications of the *arguments* for these coincidences are so many and in some cases
so extensive that they cannot be fully specified. *All* of the verbal exposition of the argument in this book, except as expressly
noted and properly cited, is my own. Sometimes the gist of that
exposition follows a line of argument given by Blunt, Paley, or
McGrew, and I strongly encourage readers to read other sources.
(Both Blunt's book and Paley's are in the public domain and are

available in multiple editions for free download.) Often, though, the argument I give for the facts lying behind the coincidence or for the reliability and independence of the texts is different from that in any source. I sometimes de-emphasize or eliminate certain points that I think are less strong, make other points of my own, expound the argument at more length and in more detail, and so forth.

I have also gone beyond my sources time and again in the chapters on the Gospels (I–IV) by listing parallel passages in the Synoptic Gospels and by noting explicitly when some point is found only in a particular account and in none other or when it is found in multiple accounts. At times only one of a number of possible parallel passages is needed to set up a coincidence, and that is usually all that the written sources give, but my argument notes other passages as well. I have also frequently gone into more detail concerning the Greek lying behind the coincidences.

Relatedly, the entire organizational concept of Part I according to the relationships *between* John and the Synoptic Gospels (i.e., Matthew, Mark, and Luke) and the relationships *among* the Synoptic Gospels is my own. So, too, are the arguments (and the coding in the accompanying charts) that a particular coincidence shows that one of the Synoptic Gospels must have had information independent of another—e.g., that Matthew had access to information independent of Mark.

I have sometimes "updated" Blunt silently by choosing not to include a coincidence that relies on a seriously controverted textual reading or on some other point that cannot, in my opinion, be maintained in the light of later scholarship. There were several coincidences that I did not include because of an error that I thought Blunt had made, a plausible alternative explanation that he does not consider, or information to which he did not appear to have access. The reader should not conclude from this that every Gospel coincidence that Blunt gives that I do not was deemed to be faulty. That is not the case. In point of fact, there are additional coincidences from Blunt and others that I think are valuable but that I have not included for various reasons, such as that discussing them would take me afield into issues like the circumstances surrounding Peter's denials of Christ or the various "callings" of Peter in John and the Synoptics.

Most often, coincidences that I did not include from Paley's *Horae Paulinae* were left out because they directly concern an issue that I am not addressing, such as the Pauline authorship of an epistle rather than the reliability of Acts.

There is no doubt that I am standing on the shoulders of giants—a fact that I freely and gratefully acknowledge. In this book I take an argument that has unfortunately and inexplicably fallen out of favor and present it to a new audience, in a new century, in a new voice. I submit it for the reader's consideration in the prayerful hope that it will be of value.

Ad maiorem Dei gloriam.

Lydia McGrew
Kalamazoo, Michigan, 2016

PART ONE

Hidden in Plain View
in the Gospels

INTRODUCTION

Undesigned Coincidences in the Gospels

How can we know that what the Gospels relate about Jesus of Nazareth is true? They are full of miracles. To some, that seems to show that they evolved as legends based on an historical but merely human figure. How can we know that the Gospels are historically reliable? These and similar questions will bother many thoughtful Christians at some point in their lives. Undesigned coincidences provide just one of the many lines of support that help us to answer these questions with confidence, and there are several notable features that make this argument especially useful.

First, it is contained in the text itself and can usually be seen just by reading and making notes. Some of the undesigned coincidences in Acts that I will discuss in Part II also involve the geography of the places discussed, but good maps are readily available. So the appreciation of this argument is not restricted to specialists.[1]

Second, the evidence from undesigned coincidences would be difficult to fake, and it would be even more unlikely to come about by sheer chance in non-factual or manipulated stories. I will explain why this is so as we go along.

Third, undesigned coincidences create an "Aha!" moment for the person who *gets* a particular argument. The evidence is a mark of truth. As I discussed in the general introduction, it is the kind of thing that we find in real human testimony and real human events.

Fourth, in order to appreciate undesigned coincidences in the Gospels, you do not have to decide whether Mark or Matthew was written first or solve the puzzles that surround Matthew, Mark, and Luke, known as the Synoptic Gospels. This evidence gives us reason to trust *all four* Gospels, because undesigned coincidences uniquely confirm the reliability of *each* of them. Even the two that resemble each other the most, Matthew and Mark, have undesigned coincidences that couldn't have arisen from copying between them; this is a reason to believe that that they are reliable and to an important degree *independent.*

Fifth, the argument from undesigned coincidences is bad news for the proposal that the Gospels *developed*, adding more non-factual elements over time. In fact, the number of unique undesigned coincidences does not follow a developmental pattern at all. Which Gospel has the largest number of unique undesigned coincidences? John, which all are agreed is the latest of all! The order of the Gospels according to number of unique undesigned coincidences is 1) John, 2) Luke, 3) Mark, 4) Matthew. This does not fit *any* pattern that treats Mark, the shortest Gospel, as the most factual or that treats later Gospels as literary or redactive alterations of Mark.

I began by mentioning miracles, and it is a fair question whether I am taking the reliability of the Gospels to apply to claims of the miraculous as well as to the non-miraculous. The answer to that question is slightly complex. On the one hand, I do not want to be misconstrued as saying something quite so simple as, "We can see from undesigned coincidences that the Gospels are historically reliable. Therefore, they are reliable when they recount miracles as well as when they give non-miraculous facts. Therefore, probably, all of these miracles happened." On the other hand, I do not want to concede an artificial separation between the miraculous claims in the Gospels and the non-miraculous ones, as though the former were *prima facie* false or dubious. I grant that claims of miracles are legitimately held to a higher evidential standard than non-miraculous claims, for many reasons. If nothing else, there are many ways for honest people to be mistaken about some miracles, especially healing miracles. Mere credulity is not a posture I recommend. It is, however, noteworthy that the internal marks of accuracy in the Gospels cut right across the miraculous/ non-miraculous divide. From a purely evidential point of view, there is no general pattern according to which miracle stories are vague while non-miraculous facts are related with circumstantial detail. Nor do we find that the non-miraculous accounts in the Gospels fit together by way of undesigned coincidences while the miraculous do not. On the contrary, several of the coincidences I discuss relate directly to miracles, and I have noted this in my discussion and coded it in the tables.

Another important point relating this argument to the miraculous is this: If the Gospels are indeed truthful memoirs from those close to the facts, including those who had opportunity to interview the disciples themselves, then they represent not late traditions or "story-telling." Rather, they represent what the alleged eyewitnesses *themselves claimed*, for which they suffered severe, early persecution. This point is presumably why propositions about the dating and authorship of the Gospels are treated by critical scholars as controversial. For if they are early and reliable memoirs of the life and death of Jesus, if they show us what the disciples themselves claimed about his resurrection, if they make it clear that these accounts came from people in a position to know, and if the disciples were willing to face death for their testimony, this pulls the rug out from under a gentle-sounding but skeptical theory that nobody told a lie, *exactly*, but that the miraculous claims about Jesus "grew up" among credulous people telling each other stories. One is instead forced to ask whether the disciples *lied* about these matters, and if so, why they would do such a thing. Even when the undesigned coincidences among the Gospels do not directly support a miracle, they support the argument for their earliness and origins. If the disciples risked their lives to attest that Jesus was risen, not in some vague, spiritual sense but in the robust, bodily sense described in the Gospels, what does this tell us about the truth of those claims?

A note on the use of the names of the Gospel authors: Throughout Chapters I–IV I often refer to Matthew, Mark, Luke, and John without adding the qualifier "the author of." Many times these terms as I use them refer to persons—that is, to the authors of these Gospels—rather than only to the texts of the Gospels, and I will use an expression like, "John…he" in describing what the author of the fourth Gospel has written. I have chosen this convention of wording both for convenience and also because I think that the hypothesis that these Gospels were written by their traditionally ascribed authors is a good explanation for the data found in them, including the undesigned coincidences. In no case do I base the conclusion that an undesigned coincidence exists and is a significant mark of truth on the *assumption* that the author must have been the traditional author, though I will sometimes note when the data fit together especially well with the traditionally ascribed authorship of a particular Gospel.

Chapter I describes instances in which what is given in John, taken by itself, raises questions that are answered by details given in one or more of the Synoptic Gospels (Matthew, Mark, and Luke). This is especially interesting since John is the latest Gospel. One would not expect that John would need to be explained by *earlier* works written by different people. Obviously, John could not have arranged for the earlier authors to write things that would fill in gaps left in his own work. And why would he write deliberately in a way that raises questions, leaving his readers to find the answers to those questions in some other work? Yet the fact is there: Sometimes we find that the Gospel of John does leave out pieces of the puzzle that are supplied by the earlier Gospels, just as a truthful witness will sometimes do.

Chapter II discusses examples where details mentioned casually in John fill in the answers to questions that arise naturally in the Synoptics. Sometimes we have one of each of these in the same passage—that is, one part of the passage where a Synoptic Gospel explains John and a different part of the passage where John explains the Synoptic Gospel.

Chapter III shows how items in the Synoptic Gospels sometimes explain details or omissions in other Synoptic Gospels. And Chapter IV is a grab bag of additional, fascinating undesigned coincidences that cannot quite be described in any of the first three ways—for example, a case involving casually mentioned details in different passages of one Gospel, cases where both John and one of the Synoptics are required to explain something in another Synoptic Gospel, and a case where passages scattered throughout the Gospels all point to the same conclusion.

All of these are marks of the truth of the Gospels hidden in plain view.

I

The Synoptic Gospels Explain John

1. "He was before me"

The prologue to the Gospel of John is a part of the heritage of the Christian church. Read every Sunday as the "last Gospel" in Catholic and Anglican churches, John 1.1–14 shows the author of the fourth Gospel at his theologically most profound.

The prologue is studded with references to John the Baptist, with whom the narrative of the Gospel begins in verse 19. As early as verse 6, the evangelist breaks off his theological discourse to mention a man sent from God whose name was John, who came to bear witness of the light. He then returns in verse 9 to teaching about the true light who lightens all men. John the Baptist comes up again parenthetically in verse 15, immediately after the famous declaration, "The Word was made flesh."

> And the Word became flesh and dwelt among us, and we have seen his glory, glory as of the only Son from the Father, full of grace and truth. (John bore witness about him, and cried out, "This was he of whom I said, 'He who comes after me ranks before me, because he was before me.'") For from his fullness we have all received, grace upon grace. For the law was given through Moses; grace and truth came through Jesus Christ. No

one has ever seen God; the only God, who is at the Father's side, he has made him known. (John 1.14–18)[1]

The words of John the Baptist, emphasized here in an aside, are repeated in due course in the narrative at verse 30.

Why does the evangelist pause and emphasize those particular words at that point in his discourse?[2] Evidently he takes it that those words of John the Baptist support the points he is making. Why those words, rather than, say, John the Baptist's statement that Jesus is the Lamb of God or that Jesus would baptize with the Holy Ghost?

Theologically, the answer does not seem hard to find: John the evangelist seems to be taking John the Baptist's words "he was before me" to be an assertion of, or at least an allusion to, Jesus' pre-existence, which he has been teaching in the prologue. But if one looks at the Gospel of John alone, it is not clear why those words should mean that. Could they not mean that Jesus was literally older than John the Baptist? John's Gospel says nothing to the contrary.

When one looks at the Gospel of Luke, the significance and the almost pun-like nature of John the Baptist's words are made clear. Luke 1.26ff is explicit that John the Baptist, the son of Elizabeth, the cousin of Mary, was conceived six months *before* the angel Gabriel appeared to the virgin Mary to announce that she would conceive and bear the child Jesus. Hence, Jesus came after John the Baptist both in the sense that his ministry began later and also in the human sense that he was six months younger. But he "was before" John the Baptist, if one accepts the doctrine of the Incarnation, in the sense that his existence did not begin with his human conception.

Could the author of John have counted on his audience's familiarity with the point about the ages of Jesus and John the

Baptist? What if some members of his audience had not read the Gospel of Luke? There are two relevant points here, one of which confirms Luke and one of which confirms John: First, John's pointed insertion of those words of John the Baptist at that place in his theological argument supports the conclusion that John knew as a fact that Jesus was biologically younger than John the Baptist. This provides confirmation to Luke. A skeptical scholar might conjecture that Luke made up the respective ages of Jesus and John the Baptist in his narrative, or that it was a legendary addition that he copied down, and that it became accepted on that basis, but that is to add an unnecessary layer of explanation. There is no particular theological reason *in Luke* for making John the Baptist six months older. It simply comes out in the course of the story. The simplest explanation for John's pointed, theological use of the words of John the Baptist that Jesus "was before him" is that the Gospel author knew that Jesus was biologically younger than John the Baptist and hence that these words could not have referred to biological age.

On the other side, the fact that John could not be *sure* that all of his readers would know that John the Baptist was humanly older than Jesus supports at least to some degree the accuracy of his own account of John the Baptist's words. Suppose, instead, that he made up those words, "He was before me," and put them into the mouth of John the Baptist for his own theological purposes. His use of them in the prologue makes it clear that he thinks that they do serve his theological ends. But in that case, why would he leave it to chance as to whether his intended audience would get the point? Why be subtle about it? If one considers only John's Gospel, the point of John the Baptist's words is theologically unclear and leaves the reader wondering why this is being emphasized just here in this way. It is implausible that an author would go to the trouble to *invent* words that John the Baptist never said while leaving their point obscure, requiring for their understanding an historical data point that the inventing author does not even mention in his own account. But if John was recounting what John the Baptist *actually said*, happening to remember it, noting its significance to himself, and mentioning it as a brief aside before getting back to his own theological argument, he may well not have stopped to think about whether all of the relevant background had been fleshed out for his readers.

2. How did John the Baptist know that Jesus was the Son of God?

The Gospel of John tells the baptism of Jesus in an interesting way—by way of a flashback narrated by John the Baptist. By the time the first scene of the Gospel opens, it appears that the baptism has already taken place. John the Baptist, after pointing Jesus out as the Lamb of God, says this,

> "This is he of whom I said, 'After me comes a man who ranks before me, because he was before me.' I myself did not know him, but for this purpose I came baptizing with water, that he might be revealed to Israel." And John bore witness: "I saw the Spirit descend from heaven like a dove, and it remained on him. I myself did not know him, but he who sent me to baptize with water said to me, 'He on whom you see the Spirit descend and remain, this is he who baptizes with the Holy Spirit.' And I have seen and have borne witness that this is the Son of God." (John 1.30–34)

The detail of the Holy Spirit descending like a dove, familiar from Christian art throughout the ages, is also found in Matthew, Mark, and Luke. John the Baptist as quoted in John is explicit: He discovered who Jesus was at the time of his baptism because of a combination of factors—an interior revelation to himself from God and the visible sign of the Spirit descending like a dove. So far, so clear.

Those of us who are familiar with the baptismal accounts in Matthew, Mark, and Luke are apt to overlook, however, what John the Baptist leaves *unexplained* in this account of the baptism. He does not say why he bore witness that Jesus is the Son of God.[3] There is no statement here that John the Baptist received a revelation that the one he was waiting for was the Son of God. One can infer that John knew something "heavy" about the one he foretold from his cryptic reference to him as "being before him," discussed in the previous section. But this certainly is not a clear statement that the one to come is the Son of God.

In any event, John the Baptist seems to be referring to some further knowledge that he gained at the time of the baptism from something specific that occurred then. He says that he has "seen and borne witness that this is the Son of God." But why would the sight of the Spirit descending like a dove tell him that? What he recounts as a personal revelation is that the person on whom the Spirit descends is the one who will baptize with the Holy Spirit. Nothing about being the Son of God.

The answer is found in a well-known detail of the baptism of Jesus, but one that is not told in the Gospel of John. Here it is from Matthew:

> And when Jesus was baptized, immediately he went up from the water, and behold, the heavens were opened to him, and he saw the Spirit of God descending like a dove and coming to rest on him; and behold, a voice from heaven said, "This is my beloved Son, with whom I am well pleased." (Matt 3.16–17)

Mark 1.11 and Luke 3.22 are similar. Now John's words are explained: John the Baptist and all who witnessed the scene at the baptism had reason to think that Jesus was the Son of God because a voice from heaven *said* that he was the Son of God. If we take it that the events recounted in the other Gospels actually occurred, this explains the words of John the Baptist in the Gospel of John.

The fit between John the Baptist's words and the voice from heaven also confirms John. Suppose for a moment that John the evangelist were *not* giving a reliable, partly independent, factual account of events, including the testimony of John the Baptist. Suppose that, for example, he were putting words in John the Baptist's mouth, telling about the baptism partly fictionally and partly based on accounts in the earlier Gospels. That hypothesis does not explain the *omission* of the voice from heaven from John the Baptist's words in John. If the Gospel author were inventing a speech for John the Baptist based upon other accounts of events, he would at least be expected to make the speech complete, not to write it in a way that raises unnecessary questions. John the Baptist's account would also be even more dramatic and theologically profound if it included the voice from heaven, and it would have been simple to include the voice in a single additional sentence. John the Baptist could have been made to say, "I saw the Spirit descend from heaven like a dove, and it remained on him. And I heard the mighty voice from heaven that said, 'This is my beloved Son.'"

As discussed in the previous section, the Gospel of John begins by affirming at length and with much theological depth that Jesus is the only Son of the Father (John 1.14). John certainly wishes to teach that Jesus is the Son of God. But in all of this, neither in the preface nor in the narrative account of the words of

John the Baptist does he ever mention the voice from heaven. In a fictionalized account, especially one from so theological a writer as John, this is an astonishing omission.

In a truthful account, it is not surprising at all. In fact, the hypothesis that provides the best explanation of the coincidence noted in this section (and the one in the previous section) is the most simple-minded, the one that might seem the most naïve—namely, that the author of the Gospel recorded these words and attributed them to John the Baptist because that is the way that John the Baptist actually told the story, and the author of the fourth Gospel knew what he said, perhaps even from hearing it himself. John the Baptist's words, including their inclusions and omissions, are readily explicable in the context in which they are set. Jesus' baptism has occurred, we can guess, about six weeks previously. Based on the Synoptic Gospels we can conjecture that Jesus went away to be tempted in the wilderness and has recently returned. John the Baptist sees him upon his return and begins talking about him, either to the crowds or to his own disciples or to both.

Like most eyewitnesses, John the Baptist does not tell everything. He selects details. His focus at this point is on his own partial knowledge prior to the baptism and his progressive understanding of who Jesus is. He is telling his audience, perhaps consisting mainly of people who were present at the baptism, how his interior revelations concerning the descent of the Holy Spirit were fulfilled in what he saw at the baptism. He marvels and goes over, again and again, the fact that he *did not even know* before that Jesus was the one to come. This may have been all the more striking to him if he had known Jesus previously as a kinsman. Now, in light of the knowledge that Jesus is the Son of God, his own earlier words, "He who comes after me ranks before me, because he was before me" take on a profound meaning, since John the Baptist knows that his cousin is younger than he is by several months. So he repeats that, too, with emphasis, and makes his own avowal, based on what he saw and heard at the baptism, that Jesus is the Son of God. In all that he has to say, he simply happens to leave out the voice from heaven, and that is how his words are reported in the Gospel of John.

It should not be assumed that, because the Gospel writer emphasizes certain aspects of the narrative for his own theological purposes, he therefore treats John the Baptist as a malleable character into whose mouth he puts his own ideas. Nor is that the picture that emerges from a careful examination of the text.

3. Why were the water pots empty?

The account in John of the wedding at Cana where Jesus turns water into wine begins like this:

> On the third day there was a wedding at Cana in Galilee, and the mother of Jesus was there. Jesus also was invited to the wedding with his disciples. When the wine ran out, the mother of Jesus said to him, "They have no wine." And Jesus said to her, "Woman, what does this have to do with me? My hour has not yet come." His mother said to the servants, "Do whatever he tells you." Now there were six stone water jars there for the Jewish rites of purification, each holding twenty or thirty gallons. Jesus said to the servants, "Fill the jars with water." And they filled them up to the brim. (John 2.1–7)

John says that the water jars were there "for the Jewish rites of purification." But in that case wouldn't they be expected to be full of water? Empty water jars aren't very useful for purification rites. John doesn't bother to give any further explanation of those rites or of the empty jars. He wants to get on with telling his story, and the crucial point for the story is that Jesus told the servants to fill the jars with water.

The miracle of water into wine doesn't come up in any of the other Gospels, so the explanation of the empty water pots is not to be found in another Gospel's account of the same incident. Both Mark (7.1–5) and Matthew (15.2), however, mention a separate incident in which the Pharisees challenge Jesus because his disciples are insufficiently ritually pure. They do not follow the tradition of the elders; they eat their food with unwashed hands. Mark, apparently with a Gentile audience in mind, goes into detail about the reason for this accusation:

> Now when the Pharisees gathered to him, with some of the scribes who had come from Jerusalem, they saw that some of his disciples ate with hands that were defiled, that is, unwashed. (For the Pharisees and all the Jews do not eat unless they wash their hands properly, holding to the tradition of the elders, and when they come from the marketplace, they do not eat unless they wash. And there are many other traditions that they observe, such as the washing of cups and pots and copper vessels and dining couches.) And the Pharisees and the scribes asked him, "Why do your disciples not walk according to the tradition of the elders, but eat with defiled hands?" (Mark 7.1–5)

The empty water pots at Cana are now explained.[4] The pots had already served their purpose and had been emptied in the process; the wedding guests had already ritually washed *before* eating and drinking at the wedding feast.

This detail does not, of course, *prove* that the story of the miracle at Cana is true. It's important to realize that the argument from undesigned coincidences is a *cumulative* argument, and I will come back to this point from time to time. What the empty water pots do tell us is that John is telling the story in the way that a truthful witness reports—namely, without stopping to give unnecessary explanations. He is getting on with the story, mentioning or implying details in passing that make sense when they are understood against a backdrop of independent information. That independent information comes here from the Gospel of Mark, written earlier.

4. "Unless you eat the flesh of the Son of Man and drink his blood…"

I have hesitated about including the following coincidence in this book, because the interpretation of the passage in John's Gospel, not to mention the interpretation of the passages with which I compare it in the Synoptic Gospels, is highly controversial along denominational lines. My intent in this book is that Christians from a variety of denominations will be able to see that these coincidences support the reliability and eyewitness nature of the texts, so I prefer that no item should depend crucially upon an interpretation that is hotly contested among orthodox theologians or is regarded as "belonging" to a particular denomination.

But undesigned coincidences are data, and the data in this case reveal a coincidence between John and the Synoptic Gospels, which I present for the reader's consideration. It will emerge from the discussion that the coincidence is durable in the sense that it supports the reliability of John despite different possible interpretations of the relevant passages.[5]

There is a striking similarity between the language Jesus uses concerning eating his flesh and drinking his blood in what is known as the bread of life discourse, found only in John 6, and in the institution of the Lord's Supper, found in all three of the Synoptic Gospels but not in John.

So Jesus said to them, "Truly, truly, I say to you, unless you eat the flesh of the Son of Man and drink his blood, you have no life in you. Whoever feeds on my flesh and drinks my blood has eternal life, and I will raise him up on the last day. For my flesh is true food, and my blood is true drink. Whoever feeds on my flesh and drinks my blood abides in me, and I in him." (John 6.53–56)

Compare this passage to, for example, the words of institution in the Gospel of Luke:

And he took bread, and when he had given thanks, he broke it and gave it to them, saying, "This is my body, which is given for you. Do this in remembrance of me." And likewise the cup after they had eaten, saying, "This cup that is poured out for you is the new covenant in my blood…." (Luke 22.19–20)

Mark and Matthew also refer to eating Jesus' body and drinking his blood in parallel passages (Mark 14.22–24 and Matt 26.26–29).

There is a well-known tradition of interpretation that insists that John 6 is absolutely not about Communion in any sense *at all* but only about believing in Jesus by faith, whether or not in connection with receiving Communion. Perhaps the most famous proponent of this view was Martin Luther,[6] who insisted that "the sixth chapter of John does not refer at all to the Supper."[7] Luther, as it happens, was a sacramentalist, holding to consubstantiation (the view that in some sense the body and blood of Jesus are "in, with, and under" the elements of bread and wine in Communion), but many non-sacramentalists have, quite understandably, adopted Luther's interpretation of John 6 as having nothing whatsoever to do with Communion.

I should admit frankly that this insistence that Jesus' words in John 6 do not have *anything* to do with the Lord's Supper seems to me extreme and implausible. Assuming that Jesus spoke the words in John 6 at all (a point to which I will return shortly), it would seem that such an insistence means that the exact similarity of the wording between the passages is at most the result of Jesus' general fondness for the metaphor of eating his flesh and drinking his blood. Moreover, this view would seem to mean that in John 6 the metaphor refers to believing in him by faith at *any* time and in *any* context but that in the words of institution it refers more specifically to believing on him and remembering his death when one partakes of Communion. Despite the similarity of wording, the disciples, apparently, were not expected to recognize his words at the institution as connected in any special way to the discourse which made such a stir, recorded in John 6, but were to have understood both teachings merely to use a striking and even disturbing metaphor for faith in Jesus in some context or another. All of this seems to me quite strained, perhaps motivated in part by the idea that Jesus could not have been speaking in John 6 about a rite that he had not yet instituted. My own interpretive conclusions notwithstanding, however, the claim that John 6 is not at all about Communion cannot be entirely set aside, if for no other reason than that (I suspect) a fair number of the readers of this book accept that interpretation.

Alternatively, one can hold that Jesus was speaking of the Lord's Supper in John 6, not in the sense that the crowds were expected to understand this at that time by his teaching, but in the sense that he was alluding cryptically to something that he would make clearer later to those who continued to follow him. This sort of veiled allusion would hardly be uncharacteristic of Jesus' teaching as we find it elsewhere. For example, his words to Nicodemus about the Holy Spirit in John 3 would not have been clear to Nicodemus at the time but would have become much clearer in the light of Pentecost. The statement, "Destroy this Temple, and in three days I will raise it up" recorded in John 2.19 is glossed by John, in hindsight, as referring to the resurrection, but Jesus himself apparently did not explain it at the time.

If one takes Jesus to be teaching in John 6 in anticipation of his own later institution of the Lord's Supper, there is a further division that can be made: One can hold a memorialist view and take it that Jesus was alluding in advance to the Lord's Supper and that the disciples would have understood only later that he was urging the importance of *remembering* his death by means of that commanded rite. Or one can hold some version of sacramentalism, whether it be transubstantiation, consubstantiation, or a spiritual Real Presence view.

What does all of this have to do with undesigned coincidences? Can one agree that there is an undesigned coincidence between John 6 and the words of institution if one holds Luther's view on the interpretation of John 6?

If one holds that Jesus was foreshadowing the Lord's Supper in John 6, regardless of whether or not one holds a sacramental view of Communion, one can view the similarity of language (rightly, I believe) as a straightforward, familiar type of undesigned coincidence between the passages. The passage in John 6 raises the question, "Why did Jesus talk to the people about such an odd thing as eating his flesh and drinking his blood?" and this question is answered by the institution of the Lord's Supper. The institution is recorded o*nly* in the Synoptics, and Jesus' discourse on himself as the bread of life and on the necessity of eating his flesh and drinking his blood is recorded *only* in John. The answer to the question is that he spoke this way in John 6 in anticipation of instituting the Lord's Supper at the end of his ministry, expecting his followers to put it all together later if they persevered in discipleship (as contrasted with those who fell away in John 6.66–67). This is the kind of undesigned coincidence we have seen already, in which a question is raised by one Gospel and the answer found only in one or more of the other Gospels. Such a coincidence confirms both accounts by means of the fit between question and answer.

But what if one is insistent that John 6 is not about the Lord's Supper at all? In that case, the following argument still applies: Suppose, hypothetically, that Jesus did not give the bread of life discourse at all. Suppose, for example, that John made it up and inserted it into the Gospel for theological reasons. In that case, where did he get the language about eating Jesus' flesh and drinking his blood? Even someone who thinks that there is no actual teaching about Communion in the passage should recognize that, *if* the passage were *not* genuine, the language put into Jesus' mouth *almost certainly* would have been borrowed from the words of institution in the Synoptic Gospels. But in that case, a critic who denies the authenticity of the discourse in John 6 faces a conundrum. Why did John not include the institution of Communion in his own Gospel? Why does he leave the odd and difficult bread of life discourse dangling, using eucharistic-sounding language but without making any connection to the very passage from which he borrowed that language? Indeed, even if John had included the institution of the Lord's Supper, the connection would be inexplicit, as the two passages would come far apart in the Gospel without any obvious connection. One might have expected even more than mere inclusion of the Lord's Supper if the bread of life discourse is an invention. Just as John pauses to inform the reader that Jesus spoke of the temple of his body in John 2, one might expect John to pause after noting the disgust and puzzlement of the crowd in John 6 and gloss Jesus' words as referring to his body given in the Lord's Supper.[8] That, at any rate, would not be an unreasonable expectation if he had gone to the trouble to invent the discourse. But *at least* we would expect that he would include the institution of the Lord's Supper itself. This is all the more likely since the purpose of such an invention of the discourse would presumably be theological, but including the words about eating his flesh and drinking his blood without any connection to the Supper or to any other passage on the same theme does little to serve a theological agenda.

Here it should be noted that the argument from undesigned coincidences often gives us evidence that the Gospel writers saw themselves first and foremost as *witnesses* to the deeds and words of Jesus Christ, not primarily as authors of literary and/or theologically sculpted works. Those two roles are not *necessarily* in conflict, so long as the author of the literary or theological work is always scrupulous about his role as a witness—for example, so long as he does not ever "make" things happen in a way contrary to the way that, to the best of his knowledge, they actually happened. But it is particularly noticeable that the Gospel authors often seem to write with the lack of affectation that we find in a person whose primary purpose is getting important information out there, getting down what happened, making it available, rather than in one whose primary purpose is to fit together what he writes in a polished manner. The author of the Gospel of John is certainly theological, perhaps more so than any of the other Gospel writers. But again and again we find him including items in his Gospel without their full explanations, apparently just because he wanted his readers to know that they happened. That sort of approach on John's part is a perfectly good explanation of the presence of the John 6 discourse and the absence of the account of the institution of the Lord's Supper in John. The fact that we find John apparently doing this type of thing repeatedly argues for the priorities of the witness rather than the priorities of the theologian or literary craftsman, and it fits well with statements within the Gospel itself, most notably John 19.35: "He who saw it has borne witness—his testimony is true, and he knows that he is telling the truth—that you also may believe."

One does not need to hold that Jesus' words in John 6, taken as genuine, are *actually* about the Lord's Supper to see the force of this argument. If John had faked the discourse, it is highly unlikely that he would not include the institution. Since he does not include the institution but does include the discourse, leaving it as a puzzle over which theologians have argued down the ages, the better explanation is that he includes the discourse because it *actually happened* and because he knows that it actually happened and wants to tell about it. He doesn't include the Lord's Supper when he tells about the Last Supper because he has other things he wants to include at that point in his Gospel instead that are not found in the Synoptic Gospels—things like Jesus' washing the disciples' feet (John 13), the high priestly prayer (John 17), and several chapters of additional teachings of Jesus found only in John's account of Jesus' last night with his disciples. Since his purpose is to be a witness to Jesus more than the crafter of a unified theological and literary work of art, and since he is in all events testifying to what he knows is true, he does not worry about the fact that the bread of life discourse with its surprising language is not particularly connected to anything else in his own Gospel.

If you take the discourse in John 6 to be about the Lord's Supper, you will take the undesigned coincidence to be of one kind: What lies behind both it and the words of institution is the reality that Jesus said both of them and that Jesus wanted in both of them to teach about the Lord's Supper. On the other hand, if you take the discourse in John 6 to be about believing on Jesus and not about the Lord's Supper at all, you will take the undesigned coincidence to be of a somewhat different kind: On that view, the coincidence of language is explained by Jesus' preference for that particular metaphor, which he used in both places as a way of teaching about believing in him in various contexts. For a similar explanation in terms of Jesus' use of language, see #6, below, on Jesus' use of the metaphor of "the cup."

In either case, the coincidence supports the reliability of John in his unique material.[9]

5. Why did Jesus wash the disciples' feet?

The Gospel of John says that, on the night in which Jesus was betrayed, he did something unusual: He washed the disciples' feet, and he did so in an extremely deliberate and even formal manner, taking upon himself a servant's garb and role.

> During supper, when the devil had already put it into the heart of Judas Iscariot, Simon's son, to betray him, Jesus…rose from supper. He laid aside his outer garments, and taking a towel, tied it around his waist. Then he poured water into a basin and began to wash the disciples' feet and to wipe them with the towel that was wrapped around him. He came to Simon Peter, who said to him, "Lord, do you wash my feet?" Jesus answered him, "What I am doing you do not understand now, but afterward you will understand." …When he had washed their feet and put on his outer garments and resumed his place, he said to them, "Do you understand what I have done to you? You call me Teacher and Lord, and you are right, for so I am. If I then, your Lord and Teacher, have washed your feet, you also ought to wash one another's feet. For I have given you an example, that you also should do just as I have done to you." (John 13.1–15)

It is certainly possible that Jesus did this on that particular night for no special reason. Perhaps he simply wanted to teach this lesson about mutual service and humility before his death, as he instituted the Lord's Supper on that same night. Still, one cannot help wondering why he washed their feet and drew the moral from it *just then*. If we could find an explanation in another Gospel, this would be interesting and satisfying.

As it happens, there is such an explanation. Better still, it comes up in a Gospel that does not mention the foot-washing at all, though it is describing the same night:

> A dispute also arose among them, as to which of them was to be regarded as the greatest. And he said to them, "The kings of the Gentiles exercise lordship over them, and those in authority over them are called benefactors. But not so with you. Rather, let the greatest among you become as the youngest, and the leader as one who serves. For who is the greater, one who reclines at table or one who serves? Is not the one who reclines at table? But I am among you as the one who serves." (Luke 22.24–27)

Once this piece of information is in place, it is difficult to doubt that this is the explanation for Jesus' object lesson.[10] Like competitive siblings, the disciples were arguing, not for the first time, about which of them was the greatest—probably about which was to be the most important when he established his kingdom. (Compare Mark 9.34 and Matt 20.21.) In response to their dispute, Jesus rose from supper and served them by washing their feet as a servant would do, then explained to them what they were supposed to understand from what he had done.

This coincidence illustrates an important point. While the strength of a coincidence will indeed be greater if an event that prompts a question is highly improbable, it does not follow that a coincidence is valueless if the events involved might have other explanations. In this case, while we *could* envisage Jesus as washing the disciples' feet "out of the blue," simply to teach a lesson, the further information that they had been bickering fits together in such a satisfying way with Jesus' action that the conclusion that the bickering explains the foot-washing on that particular night is quite well-supported when all data are taken into account. I note, too, that the Gospels of Mark and Matthew already give an example in which Jesus used an object lesson to reprove the disciples for one-upmanship. In Mark 9.33–37 the disciples have been debating which of them is the greatest. There, Jesus takes a child and places him in the midst of them after telling them that whoever wants to be the first among them must be the servant of all. (Compare Matt 18.1–4.)

Alert readers may have noticed that there is also an undesigned coincidence in the opposite direction between the passages in Luke and John concerning the disciples' dispute and the foot-washing. Luke explains John; John explains Luke. But I will leave a discussion of the way that John explains Luke for the next chapter. This is not the only case where John and Luke fit together in such a way that each explains the other within the space of a few verses.

John does not mention the dispute among the disciples. Luke does not mention the foot-washing. Put together, they give us a more complete picture than either gives alone. The fact that each Gospel gives different details is a reason to believe that they represent independent accounts of the same night.

This mention of the dispute on the night of the Last Supper is found *only* in Luke. It is thus evidence of Luke's independent access to the events, not only independent of John but also independent of Matthew and Mark.[11] If the author of Luke was indeed a companion of the Apostle Paul, he may, for example, have interviewed a different disciple about the events of that night. That person might have mentioned the dispute but not the foot-washing. The author of the Gospel of John apparently remembers the story in his own way and chooses to describe the foot-washing but not the dispute. He doesn't particularly feel a need to tell why Jesus washed their feet. His interest lies in telling about what Jesus did. Both are accurate, but their emphases are different, and they complement each other. This, again, is a mark of testimony to real events.

6. "Shall I not drink the cup?"

John's account of Jesus' arrest says that Simon Peter cut off the ear of one of the high priest's servants, and this event will play an important role in several of the undesigned coincidences I will be discussing. John says that Jesus rebuked Peter, and so do Matthew and Luke, but the words of rebuke in each Gospel are different. In John, Jesus uses a vivid metaphor for his coming death:

> Then Simon Peter, having a sword, drew it and struck the high priest's servant and cut off his right ear. (The servant's name was Malchus.) So Jesus said to Peter, "Put your sword into its sheath; shall I not drink the cup that the Father has given me?" (John 18.10–11)

This expression, "Shall I not drink the cup that the Father has given me?" appears in no other Gospel's account of this event. Even more striking, the Gospel of John *never anywhere else* portrays Jesus as using the metaphor of the cup to describe his crucifixion. So why does he use it here?

The Synoptic Gospels give the answer. In their accounts of Jesus' agonized prayers to his Father in the Garden of Gethsemane, the Synoptics all show Jesus using this very metaphor.

> And going a little farther he fell on his face and prayed, say-
> ing, "My Father, if it be possible, let this cup pass from me; nev-
> ertheless, not as I will, but as you will." And he came to the
> disciples and found them sleeping. And he said to Peter, "So,
> could you not watch with me one hour? Watch and pray that
> you may not enter into temptation. The spirit indeed is willing,
> but the flesh is weak." Again, for the second time, he went away
> and prayed, "My Father, if this cannot pass unless I drink it, your
> will be done." (Matt 26.39–42)

Luke 22.42 and Mark 14.35–36 are similar.[12] Though John gives
no version of this prayer at all, the Synoptics state that Jesus
prayed that night in these very terms, asking that the Father
would take from him the necessity of suffering crucifixion, calling it "the cup." When Judas and the guards came to arrest him,
Jesus accepted this as the Father's decision to give him the cup, as
shown by the words in John, "Shall I not drink the cup that the
Father has given me?"

Matthew and Mark tell of a different incident, also not recorded in John, in which Jesus used the same metaphor. When the
mother of James and John asked that her sons might be allowed to
sit on Jesus' right and left hands when Jesus eventually came into
his kingdom, he answered them, "You do not know what you are
asking. Are you able to drink the cup that I drink, or to be baptized with the baptism with which I am baptized?" (Mark 10.38),
an allusion to his coming death. This makes it clear that this was
a metaphor Jesus tended to use, though one would never draw that
conclusion from reading John alone.

This point strengthens the case for the historicity and eyewitness sources of the Synoptics, on the one hand, and John, on the
other. They tell of different incidents in which Jesus used this
metaphor of the cup for his death. Moreover, John's account of

Jesus' specific words to Peter dovetails especially beautifully with the Synoptics' account of Jesus' anguished request to the Father on that very night. Yet John, though later than the Synoptic Gospels, made no attempt to include that prayer that the cup might pass, though it would help to explain his own account of what Jesus said when he was arrested. What we have here are different, interlocking details of the night of Jesus' betrayal and arrest as told truthfully from different perspectives.

7. "Are you the king of the Jews?"

When John describes the transfer of Jesus as a prisoner from the custody of the Jewish leaders to Pilate, he paints a vivid scene. The Jewish leaders take Jesus to the Praetorium early in the morning and rouse Pilate to judge his case. They refuse to enter the Praetorium lest they be ceremonially defiled, so Pilate (no doubt annoyed by being awakened to deal with a disturbance from his difficult subjects) goes out to them. He asks them what accusation they bring against Jesus, and they answer unhelpfully, "If this man were not doing evil, we would not have delivered him over to you." (John 18.30) Pilate urges them to judge Jesus according to their own law, since (he suspects) the matter concerns only some violation of Jewish law. They reply, in a frankly bloodthirsty manner, that they are not authorized to put anyone to death, whereupon Pilate reluctantly re-enters the Praetorium and questions Jesus.[13] Not a word is said in the account John gives of an accusation of sedition or any other political accusation against Jesus. But when Pilate confronts Jesus, the first thing he asks is, "Are you the king of the Jews?" (v 33) Why does Pilate ask this, if John's account tells us all that the Jewish leaders have said against Jesus? Why would Pilate even *think* that Jesus claimed to be the king of the Jews?

Luke alone among the Gospels answers this question.[14] Luke tells of the original accusation like this:

> Then the whole company of them arose and brought him before Pilate. And they began to accuse him, saying, "We found this man misleading our nation and forbidding us to give tribute to Caesar, and saying that he himself is Christ, a king." And Pilate asked him, "Are you the King of the Jews?" And he answered him, "You have said so." (Luke 23.1–3)

So Luke's sources evidently indicated that the Jewish leaders made an accusation of sedition against Jesus, forcing Pilate to intervene in the case.[15] It is worth emphasizing the uniqueness of Luke in this respect, since both Matthew and Mark do have a *generally* similar scene in which Jesus is turned over to Pilate and Pilate asks Jesus whether he is the king of the Jews (Mark 15.1–3, Matt 27.11–12). They do not, however, record that the Jewish leaders accused Jesus of sedition when they brought him to Pilate. They merely mention unspecified charges and accusations. Luke is therefore adding details to this part of the story in some way independently of the earlier Gospels, even if we consider him to have been relying in some measure on Mark and/or Matthew. Luke is reporting independently, moreover, not only in *whole passages* that are unique but even in passages that cover the same events and contain similar wording.[16]

A skeptic might try to say that John's and Luke's accounts are in contradiction to one another, but there is no reason to think so unless one insists on taking them both to be *complete* accounts of everything that was said between Pilate and Jesus' accusers. But why should we think that? Witnesses do not always give complete accounts. Rather, they often give accounts of what struck them or what they consider most interesting to mention at the time. It is entirely possible that the accusers said both what John gives and what Luke gives—that at first they grumbled to Pilate that they would not have brought Jesus if he were not an evildoer but that, upon Pilate's trying to refuse the case and give it back to them to judge according to Jewish law, they made the incendiary accusation of sedition, which would bring a sentence of death from the Roman authorities if upheld. The fact that Luke does not tell about the initial slight insouciance toward Pilate and that John does not tell about the accusation of sedition shows the independence of the accounts from each other. The fact that the accounts fit together, with Luke explaining John, is both evidence of the truthfulness of the accounts and evidence that the sources of the accounts were very close to the facts.[17]

8. What happened to Malchus's ear?

Let's return to the incident in John 18 in which Peter cuts off the ear of the high priest's servant. John alone gives the name of the servant, Malchus, a point I will return to in a later chapter. For right now, consider the fact that John does not say anything further about what happened to the servant's ear. For all one could tell from John (or from Matthew or Mark, for that matter), one might have thought that the servant went away bleeding from the fray and was left without one ear for the rest of his days.

This makes the following detail, recounted in John, quite curious. Jesus assures Pilate that his kingdom is not of this world (another point I will return to in a later chapter), and he gives the following argument for the unworldly nature of his kingdom:

> Jesus answered, "My kingdom is not of this world. If my kingdom were of this world, my servants would have been fighting, that I might not be delivered over to the Jews. But my kingdom is not from the world." (John 18.36)

But the careful reader of John knows from a scene earlier in the same chapter that one of Jesus' servants, Simon Peter, *did* fight, maiming someone, to prevent Jesus from being delivered over to the Jews. Had Pilate inquired into Jesus' claim of unworldly peacefulness, wouldn't Malchus have been produced, bloody and earless, as evidence for the belligerence of Jesus' disciples and of his movement? Why (based only on John) would Jesus make this argument, knowing that such evidence could be produced against him?

Once again, it is the Gospel of Luke that supplies the answer.[18] Describing the scene in the garden, Luke says,

> While he was still speaking, there came a crowd, and the man called Judas, one of the twelve, was leading them. He drew near to Jesus to kiss him, but Jesus said to him, "Judas, would you betray the Son of Man with a kiss?" And when those who were around him saw what would follow, they said, "Lord, shall we strike with the sword?" And one of them struck the servant of the high priest and cut off his right ear. But Jesus said, "No more of this!" And he touched his ear and healed him. Then Jesus said to the chief priests and officers of the temple and elders, who had come out against him, "Have you come out as against a robber, with swords and clubs? When I was with you day after day in the temple, you did not lay hands on me. But this is your hour, and the power of darkness." (Luke 22.47–53)

Only Luke says that Jesus healed the servant's ear, though Matthew and Mark also recount that the ear was cut off. Here again, Luke supplies a unique detail within a passage that is in some respects similar to the other Synoptic Gospels. And here, too, this detail is confirmed by an undesigned coincidence. If it is true that Jesus healed the servant's ear, it explains Jesus' words to Pilate, though those words are given only in John. Jesus could confidently declare that his kingdom is not of this world and even say that his servants would be fighting if his kingdom were not peaceful. If anyone tried to say that Peter cut off a servant's ear, the wounded servant himself could not be produced to show this, and an admission that Jesus healed the ear would be further evidence of Jesus' non-violent intentions, not to mention evidence of his miraculous abilities. This undesigned coincidence thus confirms John's and Luke's separate accounts of the events of Jesus' passion and trial.

I note here that the way in which Luke explains John involves a miracle; therefore, this undesigned coincidence is some confirmation of the occurrence of that miracle. As I mentioned in the introduction to Part I, it would be a mistake to think that the accounts of miracles in the Gospels are notably different from the accounts of non-miraculous events. In the previous section I argued that an undesigned coincidence confirms two different accounts of the way in which Jesus was first delivered to Pilate, neither of which is miraculous in any way. Here I am pointing out a coincidence that involves, among other things, Jesus' healing the servant's ear, which is a miracle. The coincidence concerning the empty water pots also involved the circumstances surrounding a miracle—turning water into wine at Cana. In the next section I will discuss an undesigned coincidence directly related to Jesus' resurrection, and in the chapters that follow I will discuss several coincidences surrounding the feeding of the five thousand, recounted in all four Gospels. The Gospels tell of miracles in the same way in which they tell of other events.

9. Why is Jesus being so mean?

John's Gospel tells about a long encounter between Jesus and his disciples after his resurrection. As John tells it, Jesus meets the disciples by the Sea of Galilee, shares a meal with them, and has an entire conversation with them. There is even more to the story, involving a miraculous catch of fish (which I will discuss in a later chapter), but for this undesigned coincidence I want to focus on the conversation between Jesus and the disciples. As they are sitting together after breakfast, Jesus turns to Peter with a question:

> When they had finished breakfast, Jesus said to Simon Peter, "Simon, son of John, do you love me more than these?" He said to him, "Yes, Lord; you know that I love you." He said to him, "Feed my lambs." He said to him a second time, "Simon, son of John, do you love me?" He said to him, "Yes, Lord; you know that I love you." He said to him, "Tend my sheep." He said to him the third time, "Simon, son of John, do you love me?" Peter was grieved because he said to him the third time, "Do you love me?" and he said to him, "Lord, you know everything; you know that I love you." Jesus said to him, "Feed my sheep." (John 21.15–17)

This seems almost cruel of Jesus. No doubt he is alluding to Peter's denial of him, which is told in John 18.15–27. But why, specifically, does he ask Peter if he loves him *more* than the other disciples love him? That seems to be what is meant by, "Do you love me more than these?"[19] Peter answers, "Yes, you know that I love you" but does not actually claim to love Jesus more than the other disciples do. Jesus himself has repeatedly urged the disciples not to have a spirit of competition among themselves (for example, in Luke 22.24–26), so why would he encourage Peter to compare his love to the love of the other disciples?

Although John does say that Peter asked to go with Jesus and said that he was willing to die for him (John 13.37–38), in response to which Jesus foretold that Peter would deny him, John never portrays Peter as comparing his own love for Jesus with the love of the other disciples. So this detail of Jesus' post-resurrection probing is unexplained in John.

The explanation is found in Matthew and Mark (not in Luke this time).[20.] They both say that Peter stated not merely that he was willing to die for Jesus but, further, that even if all the other disciples forsook Jesus (as Jesus foretold), *he* never would do so:

> Then Jesus said to them, "You will all fall away because of me this night. For it is written, 'I will strike the shepherd, and the sheep of the flock will be scattered.' But after I am raised up, I will go before you to Galilee." Peter answered him, "Though they all fall away because of you, I will never fall away." Jesus said to him, "Truly, I tell you, this very night, before the rooster crows, you will deny me three times." Peter said to him, "Even if I must die with you, I will not deny you!" (Matt 26.31–35)

It seems that Jesus singles Peter out for questioning in these terms later not only because he denied him but also because he boasted that his love for Jesus was greater than the other disciples' love. Mark 14.26–30 is similar to the passage in Matthew.

Suppose that Jesus never rose from the dead and that the story of the breakfast by the Sea of Galilee were invented. Why, if that were the case, would the Gospel of John contain this bit of conversation that alludes to an earlier event, though John's Gospel does not include the earlier story? Such an omission serves no literary purpose. Someone writing a literary work containing back-references and foreshadowings includes all of those aspects in the work. Similarly, if the author of John were careless about historicity and were including a legend that had grown up in some way in the Christian community, it seems that he would be more likely at least to include the story of Peter's boast which explains this aspect of such a legend. He might even go so far as to make an explicit connection between the two passages. If, on the other hand, the author of John was a disciple and *remembered* the conversation, his intent in writing was not to produce a literary work or even a connected series of legendary stories. Rather, as a witness, he put down what was said because that was how he remembered it, casually, without bothering about including everything necessary to explain precisely why Jesus said this or that.

It's also interesting that this story is of a *lengthy* encounter between Jesus and the disciples after the resurrection. It is not a brief vision; it is not ambiguous. It is resolutely physical. Jesus has been cooking fish (John 21.9), and he shares bread and fish with them. He has an entire conversation with a group of his closest friends, covering more than one topic. If this represents accurately what the disciples were claiming happened, then they either lied, had the most improbable, polymodal hallucinations that just happened to fall upon all of them as a group in the same way at the same time, or told the truth. This is not the sort of event that a group of people could be merely mistaken about!

Conclusion

Throughout this chapter I have been emphasizing the significance of the fact that John is explained by earlier Gospels. Here I want to look at that significance from a slightly different angle: John is universally agreed, by conservative and liberal New Testament scholars alike, to be the last Gospel. It is entirely possible that the author of John had read the earlier Gospels. He may have had access to them while writing his own work. But this fact does very little to help a skeptic to account for the undesigned coincidences I have noted here. Think what a subtle and almost pointless form of deception it would be for the author of a non-factual book of John to *leave out* information in his own account, to *raise questions* by his own somewhat incomplete stories, in order that his stories might appear truthful because a really alert reader *might* find the explanations in *earlier* Gospels. That would be an extremely strange form of fakery. Many readers will not notice such coincidences at all.

That the author of John was not attempting to fake correspondences between his own book and the earlier Gospels is also shown by the fact that there are, in fact, places where it is necessary to harmonize John with the other Gospels and even where we find apparent contradictions. For example, in John 6.3–5, Jesus goes up onto a mountain apparently *before* seeing the multitude coming, just before the feeding of the five thousand. But in Mark 6.34, in the account of what is clearly the same event, the Gospel states that Jesus first saw the multitude when disembarking from a boat, which would not be on the top of a mountain. The point here is not that such allegations of contradiction are unanswerable. For example, in this case one should note that Jesus does not feed the crowd immediately when he sees them in Mark 6 and that he is moving about amongst the crowds all day. So he might well have gone higher up the mountain and sat down shortly before the feeding, as recounted in John, meaning that the account in John is simply not exhaustive. The point is that, however one harmonizes the accounts, the Gospel of John definitely does not appear to be the work of someone contriving *agreement* between his own document and the earlier documents. Very much to the contrary. A skeptic who attempts to explain the undesigned coincidences in which the Synoptic Gospels explain John by hypothesizing a subtle, cunning deception must explain why the same author is so careless about connections with the earlier Gospels that he does not avoid simple, surface-level appearances of contradiction. A similar consideration applies to the undesigned coincidences I will discuss in the next chapter: "John Explains the Synoptics."

Table 1: The Synoptic Gospels Explain John

Coincidence	Matthew	Mark	Luke	John
†L 1. "He was before me."			**1.26,36**	1.15, 30
* 2. How did John the Baptist know that Jesus was the Son of God?	**3.17**	**1.11**	**3.22**	1.32–34
†* 3. Why were the water pots empty?		**7.1-5**		2.6–7
4. "Unless you eat the flesh of the Son of Man and drink his blood…"	**26.26-29**	**14.22–24**	**22.19–20**	6.53–56
†L 5. Why did Jesus wash the disciples' feet?			**22.24–27**	13.1–15
6. "Shall I not drink the cup?"	**26.39–42**	**14.35–36**	**22.42**	18.10–11
†L 7. "Are you the king of the Jews?"			**23.1–3**	18.28–33
†*L8. What happened to Malchus's ear?			**22.51**	18.36
* 9. Why is Jesus being so mean?	**26.31–35**	**14.26–30**		21.15–17

† Indicates a coincidence that uniquely confirms one or more of the Synoptic Gospels.

*Indicates a coincidence connected with a miracle.

L indicates a coincidence that shows Lukan independence from both Mark and Matthew and that supports Luke's reliability in matters on which he is independent.

Bold font indicates a passage that provides an explanation. Plain font indicates a passage that raises a question.

Note: *All* coincidences in this table confirm John, specifically, because all involve material unique to John in what is explained.

II

John Explains the Synoptic Gospels

1. "Many were coming and going"

The Gospel of Mark introduces the feeding of the five thousand by telling of Jesus' attempt to get away from the crowds with his disciples after the twelve returned from a preaching mission.

> The apostles returned to Jesus and told him all that they had done and taught. And he said to them, "Come away by yourselves to a desolate place and rest a while." For many were coming and going, and they had no leisure even to eat. (Mark 6.30–31)

One might at first guess that the reference to many "coming and going" is merely another allusion to the fact that Jesus was often pressed and followed by crowds. And indeed, as the passage goes on, Mark does say that the crowds found a way to follow Jesus (vv 34–35). But the phrase "many were coming and going" is slightly odd as a description of Jesus' popularity alone and suggests that there was some other reason for a general bustle of crowds in their vicinity. But Mark gives no further explanation for the busyness surrounding them.

John does, though without any appearance of *intending* to explain anything at all. John introduces the feeding of the five thousand like this:

> After this Jesus went away to the other side of the Sea of Galilee, which is the Sea of Tiberias. And a large crowd was following him, because they saw the signs that he was doing on the sick. Jesus went up on the mountain, and there he sat down with his disciples. Now the Passover, the feast of the Jews, was at hand. (John 6.1–4)

John notes that the crowd followed Jesus when he went to the other side of the Sea of Galilee, but he does not mention that there were "many coming and going" in the location from which Jesus came. What John does mention in passing is the time of year—namely, just before Passover.[1]

Josephus (*War of the Jews* 6.9.3) tells of an estimate of almost three million Jews in Jerusalem for Passover during the reign of Nero. Josephus also mentions difficulties caused by the Galileans' habit of passing through Samaria on the way to Jerusalem for festivals (*Antiquities* 20.6.1). The biblical texts themselves speak often of the practice of traveling to Jerusalem for the festivals. (See, among others, Luke 2.41, John 2.13, John 7.1–8, Acts 2, Acts 20.16.) There is no doubt that Jews would have been on the roads in large numbers when the Passover was coming up.

J. J. Blunt conjectures that Jesus was in Capernaum when he and his disciples were first troubled by the crowds, but Mark does not actually say so, and there is no need to assume that he was specifically in Capernaum.[2] There was a Roman road that ran over the top and along the western edge of the Sea of Galilee.[3] Jesus was evidently on the western side of the Sea of Galilee (see Mark 6:1-6) to begin with and took ship somewhere on that shore to try to get away from the crowds by going to a deserted area on the northeastern side of the Sea of Galilee near Bethsaida (see Luke 9.10, Matt 14.13). The major population centers of Tiberias and Capernaum were both on the west of the Sea, with the road between them, and things would have been busy indeed in that vicinity just before the Passover.

But the correspondence here is so indirect that there can be no question that it is undesigned. Mark does not mention the Passover, and John does not mention the general bustle on the western side of the Sea of Galilee. Mark, being earlier, could not have coordinated deliberately with John. John, so far from attempting to coordinate with Mark, actually leaves himself open to the charge of contradicting Mark, as discussed at the end of the previous chapter. It is implausible enough to begin with that the author of John would have planted a hyper-subtle correspondence between his own Gospel and Mark's by stating that Passover was at hand, without bothering to repeat Mark's comment about the crowds on the eastern side of the sea. But it passes beyond implausible to bizarre to suggest that he would make so clever a connection while *at the same time* leaving apparent discrepancies on other matters of detail between his own account and Mark's. The author of John, imagined as a deceiver, cannot be both extremely subtle and clever and extremely bumbling at the same time! The fact is that John gives the strong impression of writing an independent account of the feeding of the five thousand, so much so that one might even suspect that he had not recently heard or read the account in Mark.

The best explanation for this correspondence (and for that matter, for the differences) between Mark's and John's account is that both are attempts, by someone close to the facts, to tell a truthful story. It is just so that honest witnesses both casually corroborate and differ from each other.

2. The green grass

I mentioned in the previous chapter that there are quite a number of undesigned coincidences related to the feeding of the five thousand. Here is another, connected to the same verse in John concerning the time of year.

Three different Gospels mention the fact that there was grass in the place where the feeding of the five thousand took place (Mark 6.39, Matt 14.19, John 6.10), but only Mark emphasizes its color: "Then he commanded them all to sit down in groups on the green grass." (Mark 6.39) Why does Mark specifically mention that the grass was green?

It will come as no surprise to a reader who has followed the previous coincidence that I turn at this point again to John 6.4— "(T)he Passover … was at hand." Passover, of course, falls in the spring. The grass is not *generally* green in that region, but it *is* green in the spring after the winter rains, around the time of Passover.[4] There would have needed to be quite a lot of green grass to make Mark's statement true, since he implies that more than 5,000 people sat down on it. At that time of year, but not at others, such a quantity of green grass would be possible. So here we have a perfect fit between John's casual reference to the time of year and Mark's specification of the detail of the green grass.

J. J. Blunt discusses several fascinating contrasts between the feeding of the five thousand and the feeding of the four thousand and notes, among other things, that the accounts of the former emphasize the grass whereas the accounts of the latter say instead that the people sat down on the ground.[5] His comment is applicable both to that point and to Mark's reference specifically to the green grass:

> It should seem … that the abundance of the grass was a feature
> of the scene of the miracle of the five thousand, which had im-

pressed itself on the eye of the relator, as peculiar to it. It was a graphic trifle which had rendered the spectacle more vivid[.] [6]

What one sees in undesigned coincidences, again and again, are points which "impressed themselves upon the eye" of the spectator and came thus into the accounts we now have.

3. "I am among you as the one who serves"

In the last chapter I mentioned that there are instances in which one of the Synoptic Gospels explains John and, in the same passages, John explains the same Synoptic Gospel. I suggested that one such instance occurs in connection with the foot-washing at the Last Supper.

The reader will recall that Luke explains John in that passage because, though Luke never mentions the foot-washing, Luke says that there was a dispute among the disciples about who would be the greatest and that Jesus taught the disciples on that occasion that they must be willing to be humble and to serve one another. The dispute and Jesus' desire to illustrate humility provide the occasion for the foot-washing, which is recounted in John, though John says nothing about the dispute.

The same passage contains a coincidence in the opposite direction, so that John explains Luke while Luke explains John. Jesus' teaching to the disciples in Luke, in response to their dispute, is this:

> And he said to them, "The kings of the Gentiles exercise lordship over them, and those in authority over them are called benefactors. But not so with you. Rather, let the greatest among you become as the youngest, and the leader as one who serves. For who is the greater, one who reclines at table or one who serves? Is it not the one who reclines at table? But I am among you as the one who serves." (Luke 22.25–27)

Here is Jesus' teaching after the foot washing as recorded in John:

> When he had washed their feet and put on his outer garments
> and resumed his place, he said to them, "Do you understand
> what I have done to you? You call me Teacher and Lord, and
> you are right, for so I am. If I then, your Lord and Teacher, have
> washed your feet, you also ought to wash one another's feet. For
> I have given you an example, that you also should do just as
> I have done to you. Truly, truly, I say to you, a servant is not
> greater than his master, nor is a messenger greater than the one
> who sent him. If you know these things, blessed are you if you
> do them...." (John 13.12–17)

John does not mention Jesus' statement, "I am among you as the
one who serves." John does not give the almost pun-like questions
and answers Jesus gives in Luke: Who is greater, the one who
reclines at table or the one who serves? In one sense, the earthly
sense, the one who reclines at table is greater than a mere servant,
but Jesus is teaching that the one who serves is, in the eyes of
heaven, greater than the one who is served. He illustrates this
spiritual teaching by the fact that he, their teacher and master,
takes the part of the one who serves.

But Luke leaves something unclear about the statement, "I am
among you as the one who serves." To what, specifically, does that
statement refer? In Luke's account, Jesus does not do anything
conspicuously servant-like, so how is he among them as the one
who serves? John's account of the foot-washing fills in this lacuna
and explains Luke.[7] When Jesus said, "I am among you as the
one who serves," he was not merely making some generic statement about his being a servant-like leader. He was referring to his
concrete act of having taken on the garb of a servant and having
washed their feet. John's description is vivid:

Jesus, knowing that the Father had given all things into his hands, and that he had come from God and was going back to God, rose from supper. He laid aside his outer garments, and taking a towel, tied it around his waist. Then he poured water into a basin and began to wash the disciples' feet and to wipe them with the towel that was wrapped around him. (John 13.3–5)

No doubt it was because of the symbolism of this act, in which Jesus was "among them as the one who serves," that Peter objected to Jesus' washing his feet (John 13.8). It is after this concrete demonstration of humility, in which Jesus takes upon himself the form of a servant (compare Philippians 2.7), that Jesus teaches the disciples that they ought to do likewise.

John could not, of course, have arranged matters so that Luke's earlier account would leave this gap for him to fill in. And if John *made up* the foot-washing to fill in the gap, why not include Jesus' statement, "I am among you as the one who serves" as well, to complete the literary effect? Moreover, if John was influenced to *invent* the foot-washing scene by access to Luke (or to stories similar to Luke's), why did John leave out the dispute in Luke that, it is natural to conclude, gave rise to the foot-washing? But if John was a disciple himself and told what he remembered, and if Luke's sources told what they remembered, exactly this sort of situation could arise in which partial accounts fit together and explain each other.

There is an interesting point here, too, concerning Luke's independence from Mark and Matthew. As it happens, Luke 22.24–26 is extremely similar in wording to Mark 10.42–44 and Matthew 20.25–28. But those passages occur in a different context, when the mother of the sons of Zebedee comes to ask if her sons may sit on Jesus' right and left hands in the kingdom, and the ten resent the request. It might be thought, then, that at just this point Luke's information is *not* independent and that he has for some reason of his own merely copied (from Mark, presumably) and transferred these sayings of Jesus about servanthood and competition to a different setting—the night of the Last Supper. Yet from the point where Jesus says, "For who is the greater, one who reclines at table or one who serves?" Luke's wording is unique, and it is precisely in that uniqueness that Luke's verses are confirmed by the foot-washing account in John. For it is only at the Last Supper that Jesus ceases for a time to be the one who reclines at the table and becomes, literally, the one who serves. Further, the argument that Jesus is making, beginning by contrasting the social structures of the Gentiles with the behavior he expects from his own disciples, leads seamlessly into the unique verses in Luke. Whether Luke saw himself as correcting Mark and Matthew concerning when Jesus uttered those words, based on his own independent sources, or whether Luke thought that Jesus said something like this twice, one thing seems to be supported by this coincidence: Luke believed that Jesus said those words about leadership and servanthood *on that night*, whenever else he may or may not have said them. And that he actually did say them on that night (whenever else he may have also said them) is confirmed by the perfect fit with the foot-washing in John.

Again, these questions and answers, these gaps and the details that fill them, fit together not as designed tales, nor as literary tales, nor as redaction of earlier documentary sources, nor as legends. They fit together as eyewitness testimony fits together.

4. Gossip, gossip

Both Matthew and Mark recount, in similar terms, an accusation that was made against Jesus in his show trial before the Sanhedrin after his arrest.

And some stood up and bore false witness against him, saying, "We heard him say, 'I will destroy this temple that is made
with hands, and in three days I will build another, not made with
hands.'" (Mark 14.57–58)

At last two came forward and said, "This man said, 'I am able
to destroy the temple of God, and to rebuild it in three days.'"
(Matt 26.60–61)

It is certainly true that such an accusation was likely to inflame
feelings against Jesus. Jewish feelings about the Temple ran high,
and the suggestion that one would destroy the Temple would be
inflammatory. We are familiar with such taboos in our own day.
The wise elementary or high school teacher would never use a
mass school shooting as a teaching example in the 21st century.
Job loss or worse might follow. One does not mention the word
"bomb" while going through a TSA airport screening. There are
some things one does not even joke about in a given culture, and
Temple destruction was one of them in first-century Judea.

But if this were merely a story that the witnesses made up out
of whole cloth as an attack against Jesus, it could easily have been
made even *more* inflammatory. For example, why did the witnesses say that Jesus said that he would rebuild the Temple? Why not
just accuse him of threatening to destroy it? And why the detail
about three days?

What this testimony sounds like to the unbiased ear is not a
pure fabrication but rather a twisted or garbled version of something the accused person *actually said*. In our own day, such a report would have curious, fair-minded people rushing to search the
Internet and find out the exact wording of the original statement
and its context in order to understand the origin of the inflammatory report.

Yet none of the Synoptics, including Matthew and Mark, contain any such statement by Jesus. Nothing about destroying the Temple. Nothing about rebuilding it in three days. Nothing at all to explain the origin of this accusation.

One must turn to John to find the explanation, in a completely different passage concerning a completely different time period in Jesus' ministry:

> The Passover of the Jews was at hand, and Jesus went up to Jerusalem. In the temple he found those who were selling oxen and sheep and pigeons, and the money-changers sitting there. And making a whip of cords, he drove them all out of the temple, with the sheep and oxen. And he poured out the coins of the money-changers and overturned their tables. And he told those who sold the pigeons, "Take these things away; do not make my Father's house a house of trade." His disciples remembered that it was written, "Zeal for your house will consume me." So the Jews said to him, "What sign do you show us for doing these things?" Jesus answered them, "Destroy this temple, and in three days I will raise it up." The Jews then said, "It has taken forty-six years to build this temple, and will you raise it up in three days?" But he was speaking about the temple of his body. (John 2.13–21)

So John says that, several years earlier, Jesus had said that he would raise up the temple in three days if it were destroyed. John gives this saying as an answer to those asking for Jesus' authority to drive money-changers and others out of the Temple, and he takes it to be a prophecy of Jesus' resurrection.[8]

I must stress here that John *nowhere* includes in his Gospel the story of the witnesses who said that Jesus threatened to destroy the Temple. I have already mentioned that none of the Synoptic Gospels contain the earlier scene in which Jesus says, "Destroy this temple, and in three days I will raise it up." It is only by putting the two together that one gets the whole story: Jesus makes a cryptic statement about his own ability to raise up the Temple in three days if it is destroyed. He intends it as a prophecy of his resurrection, though he doubtless knows that it will be confusing and annoying to his interlocutors. It is remembered against him, garbled somewhat in the retelling, and brought back up at his trial later as an accusation that he was making the equivalent of terrorist threats against the Temple.

This picture is realistic and believable, but it comes to us only by way of the *combination* of John and the account in Mark/Matthew. Nothing could be less like design or more like truthful testimony.

5. "So you're a king? No problem!" [9]

In the previous chapter I discussed an undesigned coincidence concerning Jesus' appearance before Pilate. That coincidence showed that John's account raises the question, "Why does Pilate ask whether Jesus is the king of the Jews?" The question is answered by Luke's account in which the Jewish leaders accuse Jesus of sedition against Rome. In that respect, Luke explains John. But that is by no means all. Just as there are two complementary coincidences between John and Luke concerning the foot-washing at the Last Supper, there are two complementary coincidences here.

Luke's Gospel raises quite a pointed question when Pilate questions Jesus:

> Then the whole company of them arose and brought him before Pilate. And they began to accuse him, saying, "We found this man misleading our nation and forbidding us to give tribute to Caesar, and saying that he himself is Christ, a king." And Pilate asked him, "Are you the King of the Jews?" And he answered him, "You have said so." Then Pilate said to the chief priests and the crowds, "I find no guilt in this man." (Luke 23.1–4)

Here in Luke is the accusation of sedition, and here is Pilate's natural question to Jesus, "Are you the King of the Jews?" But what follows is quite surprising. Jesus does not reject the charge. His answer is variously translated. The New American Standard Bible (NASB) translates his answer, "It is as you say," treating it as an idiom rather like our American expression, "You said it." [10] The English Standard Version (ESV), quoted above, translates his words strictly literally, allowing the expression to be taken as an ambiguous refusal to reply to the charge. Such ambiguity by itself was cheeky, at a minimum, in response to an accusation of a kind that Pilate, as the Roman governor, was bound to treat seriously. In neither case is there any explanation for Pilate's going back to the crowd and stating that he finds Jesus innocent. Why does Pilate not even question Jesus further? Why does he seem so unfazed by Jesus' reply? Why does he go so far as to declare Jesus free of all guilt concerning the charge?

The explanation is found in John's account of the same scene:

So Pilate entered his headquarters again and called Jesus and said to him, "Are you the King of the Jews?" Jesus answered, "Do you say this of your own accord, or did others say it to you about me?" Pilate answered, "Am I a Jew? Your own nation and the chief priests have delivered you over to me. What have you done?" Jesus answered, "My kingdom is not of this world. If my kingdom were of this world, my servants would have been fighting, that I might not be delivered over to the Jews. But my kingdom is not from the world." Then Pilate said to him, "So you are a king?" Jesus answered, "You say that I am a king. For this purpose I was born and for this purpose I have come into the world—to bear witness to the truth. Everyone who is of the truth listens to my voice." Pilate said to him, "What is truth?" After he had said this, he went back outside to the Jews and told them, "I find no guilt in him...." (John 18.33–38)

John fills out the dialogue given only briefly in Luke. Jesus affirms that he was born to be a king. But he makes it clear that his kingdom is not of this world and that he is not encouraging the use of physical force to achieve his aims. Pilate evidently concludes that he is a harmless religious crank of some sort, and it is in this fuller context that Pilate tells the Jewish leaders that he finds no guilt in Jesus.

We saw before that John's account is incomplete just a few verses earlier concerning the charges against Jesus. Now we see that Luke's account is incomplete as regards Jesus' answer. Together they present a complete picture—an accusation of sedition, Pilate's question, Jesus' answer that he is a king, but not a king of this world, and Pilate's conclusion that he is not guilty in the eyes of Roman law.

How tempting it would be for a skeptic to attempt to make the various omissions in Luke and John at this point into contradictions. The independence of the accounts is certainly clear from the dual omissions and explanations, but so far from being contradictory, the two partial accounts are complementary—an important lesson in the limitations of the argument from silence.

This complementarity of accounts, again, manifests the eye of the spectator. Since the author of Luke himself was probably not a disciple, we don't know who his source or sources would have been for this scene, but it appears that they were not the same as John's. It is even possible that the author of the Gospel of Luke got his information from Mary, the mother of Jesus. (The earliest chapters of the Gospel of Luke show a decided bent towards Mary's perspective.) If the author of the Gospel of John was the beloved disciple John himself (and all of the undesigned coincidences concerning John tend to support that conclusion, which is also supported by independent evidence), then it may be that John is his own source and reports the scene as a witness, as he remembers it, with his own emphases and details.[11]

6. The courage of Joseph of Arimathea

All four Gospels say that, after Jesus died, a man named Joseph of Arimathea requested and buried his body. There will be one other undesigned coincidence about Joseph of Arimathea in a later chapter, and in general the Gospels' varied treatment of him is quite interesting. The particular point for this coincidence arises from the Gospel of Mark:

> And when evening had come, since it was the day of Preparation, that is, the day before the Sabbath, Joseph of Arimathea, a respected member of the council, who was also himself looking for the kingdom of God, took courage and went to Pilate and asked for the body of Jesus. Pilate was surprised to hear that he should have already died. And summoning the centurion, he asked him whether he was already dead. And when he learned from the centurion that he was dead, he granted the corpse to Joseph. (Mark 15.42–45)

The word translated "took courage" in this verse is translated elsewhere as "dared" or "ventured" (see, e.g., Mark 12.34 and Acts 7.32).

Pilate was not likely to balk at a request for the body, since burial was important to Jews. At the same time, Joseph's "sticking his neck out" in this way is not terribly probable. The fact that he was a respected member of the council might well make him reluctant to bring his name into association with that of Jesus, who had been condemned for blasphemy. Mark's reference to courage is somewhat explicable on the basis of general knowledge about Jesus' trial and death.[12] Nonetheless the reference to Joseph as "taking courage" is rather emphatic, and some further explanation for Mark's emphasis would be satisfying.

Such an explanation for an emphasis on Joseph's boldness is forthcoming in the Gospel of John, which does not speak quite so positively about Joseph of Arimathea.

> After these things Joseph of Arimathea, who was a disciple of Jesus, but secretly for fear of the Jews, asked Pilate that he might take away the body of Jesus, and Pilate gave him permission. So he came and took away his body. Nicodemus also, who earlier had come to Jesus by night, came bringing a mixture of myrrh and aloes, about seventy-five pounds in weight. (John 19.38–39)[13]

John does not emphasize Joseph's courage, but what he does say explains why someone else writing about him might be moved to note it. According to John, Joseph had previously been a secret disciple for fear of the Jews; John implies that this was the first time that he had openly shown himself to be sympathetic to Jesus. As if to emphasize the point still further, John states that Joseph was joined in the work of burial by Nicodemus, who had previously come to Jesus by night (John 3), presumably out of a similar fear.

What we have in the two accounts is an interesting case of two reporters with the same facts giving those facts a different spin. Mark accentuates the positive. He speaks of Joseph as "looking for the kingdom of God" (always considered a good thing in the New Testament) and calls him courageous for asking for Jesus' body. Yet this very praise of Joseph raises the question I have already noted—why Mark's emphasis upon "taking courage"? Does this imply that it was unlikely that Joseph would take courage to ask for the body? John's report tells of Joseph's previous *lack* of boldness (not mentioned in any of the Synoptic Gospels), which the twelve disciples may well have known about and had different opinions about. John respects Joseph and Nicodemus only insofar as they *finally* step forward and make their discipleship known, which John may consider to be the least they could do. Mark, on the other hand, is more sympathetic and inclined to praise Joseph for "taking courage."

One may even conjecture (though I would not lean heavily on this) that, if Peter were the eyewitness source for much of Mark (as Christian tradition says), Peter would be inclined not to be too hard on one who was at first afraid but later "took courage," since Peter himself denied Jesus out of fear. If John the beloved disciple were the author of John, he would have no such motive to mercy, much less praise, since he never denied Jesus. According to the Gospel of John, the beloved disciple even followed Jesus to the cross.

In general, the Gospels' varying treatment of Joseph of Arimathea is a fascinating example of their independence of perspective and to some extent their independence of information. In Chapter IV, I will examine one aspect that is unique to Matthew, so I will not mention it here, but here are a few other details that differ from one account to another: Matthew alone says that Joseph was rich (Matt 27.57). Matthew says that Joseph was a disciple of Jesus, while Mark and Luke do not say this. Matthew does not mention that Joseph was a member of the council or that he was looking for the kingdom of God; these are mentioned in both Mark (see above) and Luke 23.50–51. Mark alone says that Joseph "took courage." Luke heaps the highest praise of any of the Gospels on Joseph. He calls him a "good and righteous man" (Luke 23.50). Luke also, alone among the Gospels, is careful to say that Joseph of Arimathea had "not consented" to the "decision and action" of the rest of the council, though he does not give any further details about exactly what happened. (Is he implying that the night-time meeting of the Sanhedrin was called in Joseph's absence? Or does Luke believe that Joseph spoke up for Jesus and got out-voted? Or had Luke simply heard, without detail, that Joseph was not involved in Jesus' condemnation by the council?) John alone, as I have already pointed out, mentions Joseph's previous secrecy and the involvement of Nicodemus.

The miscellaneously varied accounts in the four Gospels of Jesus' burial by Joseph of Arimathea provide an especially good opportunity to see that the relationship among the Gospels is not one of gradual accretion or development. Nor is it easy to find any sort of pattern in the inclusions and omissions, which is very much what one expects from varying testimonies. The different Gospel writers show independence of judgment and of detail in their portraits.

Conclusion

In the last chapter we saw that the Synoptic Gospels explain John, though they were written earlier. Here I have shown that John explains various aspects of the Synoptic Gospels but does it in so casual a way and with so little appearance of attempted harmonization between his own accounts and the earlier accounts that any theory of design on the part of the author of John is overwhelmingly implausible. Sometimes both types of explanation (John explains the Synoptics and the Synoptics explain John) occur in the same passage. Sometimes an explanation in John comes in an account that is quite separate from the scene in the Synoptics, as when John's account of Jesus' words about raising up the Temple explains the later accusation against him before the Sanhedrin. The sheer variety of undesigned coincidences creates a tight web of connections between John, on the one hand, and the various Synoptic Gospels, on the other hand, giving us good reason to believe that they came from truthful people close to the facts.

Note that, with the possible exception of coincidence #7 in the previous chapter (see note 14 in that chapter), *every single one* of the coincidences discussed in these two chapters confirms unique material in the Gospel of John. For that reason I have not bothered to use a special code in Table 1 and Table 2 for coincidences that involve material unique to John. Only John gives John the Baptist's version of the baptism of Jesus. Only John tells of the miracle of water into wine, so John's unique material is confirmed through the coincidence about the emptiness of the water pots. Only John tells of the foot-washing, so John's unique material is involved both when Luke tells of the dispute that apparently occasioned the foot-washing and when the foot-washing explains how Jesus was "among them as the one who serves." Only John tells of the meeting by the Sea of Galilee after the resurrection, so his unique material is confirmed by the coincidence concerning Jesus' question to Peter. Only John tells of Jesus' statement, "Destroy this temple, and in three days I will raise it up," which dovetails with the account in Matthew and Mark of the accusation at Jesus' trial. Only John says that Jesus told Pilate, "My kingdom is not of this world" and that Jesus went on to say that his servants would otherwise fight to protect him—a portion of the trial that is involved in two different undesigned coincidences in these chapters. And so forth. These chapters constitute one long list of ways in which John's own material, not found in the Synoptics, is confirmed by its interlocking with information in the Synoptics. In other words, when John, the latest Gospel, contains material not found in the earlier Gospels, the evidence does *not* indicate that this material represents fictional, literary, or redactive additions to some shorter, purer, more primitive narrative. On the contrary, the rich store of additional information in the Gospel of John provides more opportunities for confirmation of John by its indirect intersection with the earlier accounts of Jesus' life.[14]

In the next chapter I will argue that the Synoptic Gospels, despite their similarities, sometimes explain each other.

Table 2: John Explains the Synoptic Gospels

Coincidence	Matthew	Mark	Luke	John
†* 1. "Many were coming and going."		6.30–31		**6.4**
†* 2. The green grass		6.39		**6.4**
†L3. "I am among you as the one who serves"			22.27	**13.2ff**
4. Gossip, gossip	26.60–61	14.57–58		**2.13–21**
†L5. "So you're a king? No problem!"			23.1–4	**18.36**
† 6. The courage of Joseph of Arimathea		15.42–45		**19.38–39**

† Indicates a coincidence that uniquely confirms one or more of the Synoptic Gospels.

*Indicates a coincidence connected with a miracle.

L indicates a coincidence that shows Lukan independence from both Mark and Matthew and that supports Luke's reliability in matters on which he is independent.

Bold font indicates a passage that provides an explanation. Plain font indicates a passage that raises a question.

Note: *All* coincidences in this table confirm John, specifically, because all involve material unique to John when John explains the Synoptics.

III

The Synoptic Gospels Explain Each Other

Introduction

It is widely understood that the Gospels designated as the Synoptics—Matthew, Mark, and Luke—have many similarities in contrast to John, which contains a great deal of material not found in any of them. Moreover, there appears to be some degree of literary dependence among them, though the nature of this is hotly debated, and drawing definite conclusions is incredibly difficult. I take it as a given that either Matthew or Mark was written first; I am open to John Wenham's thesis of Matthean priority, but I realize that it is in the minority among New Testament scholars and do not take a definite stand on the question.[1] Luke appears to have some dependence on either Matthew or Mark or (more probably) on both, though Luke also has a good deal of entirely unique material.

However, acknowledging some degree of literary dependence among the Synoptic Gospels is by no means the same thing as granting that the later ones tack on non-factual material as they go. Nor does it mean that the differences among them are due to redactive manipulation of earlier material as opposed to differences in eyewitness perspective.

I want to stress that this chapter is not the only one that shows independence among the Synoptic Gospels. The earlier chapters have already shown their independence at various points. The Synoptic Gospels rarely *all* contain the information that creates an undesigned coincidence with John (whether as the explanation or as that which is explained), and in several cases, which I noted as I went along in Chapters I and II, the information that dovetails with John is unique to a single Synoptic Gospel, thereby confirming the independence of the Synoptics at that point from one another.

In this chapter I show that the Synoptic Gospels explain each other in several undesigned coincidences.

The argument from undesigned coincidences therefore swings free, as I pointed out in the introduction to Part I, of the vexed issues surrounding the so-called "synoptic problem." By showing that the Synoptic Gospels have clear signs of independence from each other in information and perspective, while being reliable in those areas where they are independent, the argument from undesigned coincidences allows us to treat the "synoptic problem" instead as a "synoptic puzzle"—of interest to scholars but lacking the power to undermine our confidence in the truth of the events related. In short, it doesn't matter to the historicity of the Gospels whether (for example) Mark was written first and Matthew and Luke got some of their material from Mark. Even if that is true, it doesn't mean that Matthew and Luke *developed* from Mark in an evolutionary fashion or that Matthew and Luke did not have reliable, independent information of their own. Moreover, as I note in several passages, some of that independent information appears precisely at those points where Matthew and Luke seem in many respects similar to Mark.

1. The paired disciples

All three Synoptic Gospels list the names of the twelve disciples. The names are all identical in Matthew and Mark, though the order differs slightly between them. Luke 6.14–16 has other variations in that Luke omits the name "Thaddeus," includes the name "Judas the son of James" (not in Matthew and Mark) and orders the names slightly differently toward the end of the list. A noticeable point in Matthew (found in some texts in Luke as well) is that the names of the twelve are given in pairs. Since this pairing is found with only one extra "and" in Matthew regardless of the text family one follows, I will illustrate the point from Matthew rather than from Luke:

> The names of the twelve apostles are these: first, Simon, who is called Peter, and Andrew his brother; James the son of Zebedee, and John his brother; Philip and Bartholomew; Thomas and Matthew the tax collector; James the son of Alphaeus, and Thaddaeus; Simon the Zealot, and Judas Iscariot, who betrayed him. (Matthew 10.2–4)

The punctuation, of course, would not have been in the original manuscript, but the "ands" are there in the Greek. There is one extra "and" in some texts of Matthew that is not represented in this translation, though the NASB shows it. This extra "and" comes between Andrew and James. Other than that, Matthew's list in the Greek consistently and precisely sorts the disciples into pairs using the word "and."[2] That is to say, with that one exception, there are "ands" between the members of each pair but no "ands" between the pairs.

This point concerning the listing in pairs in Matthew might not seem to call for much explanation. Twelve is an even number, and perhaps grouping the names into pairs was done simply because it sounded good and made the list easy to remember.

But a more satisfactory explanation is forthcoming if we turn to a passage in Mark—not, I note, to Mark's list of the disciples. All of the Synoptic Gospels state that Jesus sent forth the twelve disciples on a mission to go from city to city preaching repentance. Mark's account, which does not occur in the same passage as his list of the names of the disciples, contains a unique detail:

> And he called the twelve and began to send them out two by two, and gave them authority over the unclean spirits. (Mark 6.7)[3]

While Luke 10.1 says that a larger group of seventy disciples was sent out in pairs, only Mark says that the twelve were sent out two by two.

If Jesus sent out the twelve in pairs, it is quite possible that the pair grouping in Matthew reflects knowledge of this fact. It may even replicate the actual pairings that Jesus set up, but the more important point is that it fits with the "two by two" pairing in the commissioning.[4] The fact that Jesus sent out the twelve two by two, found only in Mark, thus provides a reasonable explanation of the paired names in Matthew and (in some texts) in Luke.

Mark's list of the twelve (Mark 3.16–19) follows almost the same order and contains all the same names as Matthew's, but it is not, in any text family, grouped into pairs, because Mark puts "ands" between *all* the names. Thus Matthew's grouping into pairs is not copied from Mark, and mere carelessness in copying from Mark would not explain the paired *pattern* in Matthew. One slight order difference in Mark compared to Matthew is interesting in itself: Mark lists Peter, James, and John first and then doubles back to include Andrew, Peter's brother. From there on the list is identical to Matthew's except that the order of Matthew and Thomas is reversed and the phrase "the tax collector" added to Matthew's name.[5] The grouping of Peter, James, and John in Mark fits with the fact that Peter, James, and John are frequently treated in the Gospels as a special inner group who were with Jesus on special occasions—e.g., at the Transfiguration. Mark seems to have mentally grouped those three together but then seems to have gone back to pick up Peter's brother Andrew, completing that set of four before going on and listing all the others.

The fact that Mark does not list the disciples clearly in pairs gives us the ideal undesigned coincidence structure in which the explanation is not found in the same book as the question—the question here being why *Matthew* lists the disciples in pairs, and the answer being found only in Mark. The answer is that Jesus sent out the twelve two by two. Moreover, the unique structure in Matthew is found in a list that in other respects is very similar to the list in Mark, showing independence between the two even where (if one holds that Mark was the first Gospel) Matthew might otherwise be thought to be merely borrowing Mark's list.[6]

2. Herod and his servants

When Herod heard of Jesus and his miracles, the Gospels report that he was rather disconcerted and even worried that John the Baptist might have returned from death. Herod had had John the Baptist executed and may have had a guilty conscience about it.

> At that time Herod the tetrarch heard about the fame of Jesus, and he said to his servants, "This is John the Baptist. He has been raised from the dead; that is why these miraculous powers are at work in him." (Matthew 14.1–2)

Matthew's account of Herod's perplexity contains a unique detail—that Herod was musing about Jesus' identity *to his servants*. In other respects, these verses resemble Mark 6.16, but that verse does not state that Herod was speaking to his servants.[7] Why does Matthew specify that Herod spoke about this to his servants? Even more to the point, how could Matthew know, in the usual course of events, what Herod was saying to his servants?[8]

The answer is found in an otherwise unrelated passage in the Gospel of Luke.

> Soon afterward he went on through cities and villages, proclaiming and bringing the good news of the kingdom of God. And the twelve were with him, and also some women who had been healed of evil spirits and infirmities: Mary, called Magdalene, from whom seven demons had gone out, and Joanna, the wife of Chuza, Herod's household manager, and Susanna, and many others, who provided for them out of their means. (Luke 8.1–3)

This passage is not in any way *about* Herod or about his comments concerning Jesus. Luke is merely listing those who accompanied Jesus at this point in his ministry. Among these he mentions Joanna the wife of Chuza, Herod's household manager.[9]

In other words, Luke says that a follower of Jesus (or at any rate the husband of a devout follower of Jesus) was found among the important servants of Herod's household. It was therefore quite natural that information about Herod's doings and about his reaction to the stories of Jesus should come back to the community of Jesus' followers and make it into Matthew's Gospel. If Herod knew that one of his servants was connected to Jesus through his wife, it would also make sense that he would be discussing this matter with his servants and giving his own superstitious conclusions about Jesus' true identity.

The indirectness of this coincidence is particularly lovely. Only one part of the puzzle is found in each Gospel, and the connection cannot possibly be the result of design. It is beyond belief that Luke would have inserted this casual reference to Chuza in a list unconnected in any other way with Herod or with the beheading of John, in order to provide a convenient explanation for the detail about Herod's servants mentioned only in Matthew. This coincidence provides clear evidence of the independence of Matthew and Luke and confirms them both.

3. Woe to Bethsaida!

Both Matthew and Luke record that Jesus called down woe upon various cities and towns that had seen his works and had not believed on him. Here is Matthew's version:

> Then he began to denounce the cities where most of his mighty works had been done, because they did not repent. "Woe to you, Chorazin! Woe to you, Bethsaida! For if the mighty works done in you had been done in Tyre and Sidon, they would have repented long ago in sackcloth and ashes. But I tell you, it will be more bearable on the day of judgment for Tyre and Sidon than for you. And you, Capernaum, will you be exalted to heaven? You will be brought down to Hades. For if the mighty works done in you had been done in Sodom, it would have remained until this day. But I tell you that it will be more tolerable on the day of judgment for the land of Sodom than for you." (Matthew 11.20–24)

The wording in Luke 10.13–15 is very similar.

The allusion to Capernaum is easy to explain in terms of other passages in the Gospel of Matthew. Matthew 4.13ff says that Jesus actually settled in Capernaum and alludes to the prophecy that the people who dwell in darkness have seen a great light. Matthew 8.5ff relates that Jesus healed a centurion's son in Capernaum, and Matthew 8.14ff implies, if we assume that Peter's house was in Capernaum (which seems indicated by the context) that Jesus did many miracles in Capernaum. So it is not difficult to explain the reference to mighty works in Capernaum from within Matthew itself.

This is not true for Chorazin and Bethsaida. In fact, there is no reference to Chorazin anywhere else in the Bible except in these "woe" passages, and no reference to Bethsaida elsewhere in Matthew. Mark 8.22ff mentions a blind man healed outside of Bethsaida but says that Jesus took him outside the village to heal him and commanded him to go home afterwards without entering the village. This does not seem like a strong candidate for a mighty work done in Bethsaida that should have led them to repentance and belief in Jesus, since it is unclear what the inhabitants of the village would have known.

A much better candidate is found in Luke 9.10ff:

> On their return the apostles told him all that they had done. And he took them and withdrew apart to a town called Bethsaida. When the crowds learned it, they followed him, and he welcomed them and spoke to them of the kingdom of God and cured those who had need of healing. Now the day began to wear away, and the twelve came and said to him, "Send the crowd away to go into the surrounding villages and countryside to find lodging and get provisions, for we are here in a desolate place." But he said to them, "You give them something to eat." (Luke 9.10–13) [10]

The account of the feeding of the five thousand follows. Luke is therefore implying that Jesus did healing miracles amongst a large crowd of people and fed five thousand people in an uninhabited area near the town of Bethsaida.[11] Matthew also says that Jesus healed the sick on the same day as the feeding of the five thousand (Matt 9.14), but he never mentions that these events took place near Bethsaida.

Luke, therefore, explains Matthew by answering the question, "Why did Jesus say that mighty works were done at Bethsaida?" This detail concerning the location of the feeding of the five thousand is found only in Luke.

Both the woes and the statement that the miracles took place near Bethsaida are found in Luke, so this is not a case where each Gospel has exactly one side of the coincidence. The fact remains, however, that Luke's statement concerning the location of the feeding of the five thousand (and other miracles at the same time) confirms Matthew's account of the woes. Both fit with the hypothesis that Jesus really did mighty works near Bethsaida and later condemned Bethsaida for unbelief on this basis.

It might be suggested that perhaps Luke fictionally set the occurrence of these events near Bethsaida in order to explain the woes, which he includes in his own Gospel and could have gotten from Matthew if Matthew wrote before Luke.[12] But this would be an implausibly subtle attempt on Luke's part at self-confirmation, especially since the "woes" occur in a completely different passage in Luke. Even more pointedly, Luke says nothing about miracles at Chorazin at all, which disconfirms any such hypothesis. If Luke were setting miracles in locations merely in order to fit with the woes, without factual backing, he could have done as much for Chorazin as for Bethsaida.[13]

While the "woes" are not unique to Matthew, because they are also in Luke, this undesigned coincidence confirms Matthew's and Luke's independence *from Mark* at this point and their reliability on the matters they report independently of Mark.

4. Got a new tomb handy?

As I discussed in the previous chapter, the treatment of Joseph of Arimathea is slightly different in each Gospel. Each has its own emphasis, and several have unique details. The one remaining detail which I did not list there is at the core of another undesigned coincidence.

Both Luke and John record that Joseph of Arimathea buried Jesus in a tomb that had not previously been used. Luke 23.52 says that Joseph took down Jesus' body, "wrapped it in a linen shroud and laid him in a tomb cut in stone, where no one had ever yet been laid." John gives more details at this point and agrees with Luke that the tomb had never been used:

> Now in the place where he was crucified there was a garden, and in the garden a new tomb in which no one had yet been laid. So because of the Jewish day of Preparation, since the tomb was close at hand, they laid Jesus there. (John 19.41–42)

John implies that the tomb was selected because it was nearby. But surely this cannot be the whole story. Joseph would presumably not be allowed the use of someone else's previously unused tomb *merely* because it happened to be conveniently located! How did Joseph of Arimathea come to have access to a new tomb that had never been used before?[14]

One may surmise that the tomb might have belonged to Joseph or perhaps to Nicodemus (based on John's statement that Nicodemus was also involved in the burial). Or one can conjecture more broadly that it must have belonged to *some* follower of Jesus. Only Matthew clearly answers the question:

> When it was evening, there came a rich man from Arimathea, named Joseph, who also was a disciple of Jesus. He went to Pilate

and asked for the body of Jesus. Then Pilate ordered it to be given to him. And Joseph took the body and wrapped it in a clean linen shroud and laid it in his own new tomb, which he had cut in the rock. And he rolled a great stone to the entrance of the tomb and went away. (Matt 27.57–60)

I noted in the previous chapter that only Matthew mentions that Joseph of Arimathea was rich. Matthew is also the only writer to mention the related point that Joseph laid Jesus in his *own* tomb. This uniqueness in Matthew is especially noteworthy since, in several respects, Matthew's wording and details about the burial are quite similar to Mark's. For example, both mention the linen sheet in which Joseph wrapped Jesus, Mark 15.46 says that the tomb was "cut out of the rock," both say that Joseph rolled a stone across the entrance, and both mention the two Marys who saw where Jesus was laid. This makes it all the more remarkable that Matthew's dropped-in details, indicating independence of Mark in the very place where *dependence* might seem most obvious, can be corroborated. For Mark does *not* say (as Luke and John do) either that the tomb was new or that no one had ever been buried there before, and he does *not* say, as Matthew does, that it was Joseph's own tomb. Matthew therefore could not have been getting those details from Mark.

The background of this incident has a surprisingly modern ring to it. In our own day it is not uncommon for foresighted people with sufficient disposable income to purchase a burial plot for themselves and even to pre-pay some or all of their funeral expenses. Joseph had apparently done the first-century Jewish equivalent of pre-paying for his burial by having his own tomb-cave cut in rock near Jerusalem. When he took charge of Jesus' body, this tomb was available for the burial, and he doubtless had this plan in mind when he decided to step forward and ask for the body from Pilate.

Here Matthew explains another Synoptic Gospel (Luke) as well as John. Luke and John leave the reader to conjecture that the tomb *may* have been Joseph's own. But that is not their emphasis, and they show multiple signs of independence from Matthew at just this place in the narrative. Their wording about the new tomb is different; although Matthew says that the tomb was new, he does not use the phrase "in which no one had yet been laid" or any similar phrase, while Luke and John do. As I noted in the previous chapter, Luke and John each record specific different things from Matthew. Luke strongly emphasizes Joseph of Arimathea's goodness, and if Luke were following Matthew's account of the burial, one might have thought that he would bring up the fact that it was Joseph's own tomb as further reason to praise him. Luke says that Joseph was a member of the council (which Matthew does not say), that he had not consented to the council's condemnation of Jesus' (which Matthew does not say), and that he was waiting for the kingdom (which Matthew does not say). (Some, though not all, of these Lukan points are found in Mark, but Mark says nothing about the tomb's newness or about who owned it.) Luke is sufficiently independent from Matthew in this passage that there is little reason to think that he is simply drawing from Matthew's word "new" the conclusion that no one had previously been laid in the tomb. Similarly, John mentions Nicodemus, Joseph's previously secret discipleship, the nearness of the tomb to the place of crucifixion, the fact that the tomb was in a garden, and the quantity of spices used in the burial, none of which are found in Matthew or in any of the other Synoptic Gospels. Yet John agrees with Luke on the claim that no one had ever used the tomb before, while Matthew alone explains how it came about that Joseph had access to a never-used tomb.

Conclusion

Though there are only four undesigned coincidences in this chapter, that is partly an artifact of organization. Sometimes an undesigned coincidence can be placed in more than one category, as when Matthew's mention of the fact that Joseph of Arimathea actually owned the new tomb explains both Luke and John.

As Table 1, Table 2, and Table 3 show, all of the chapters thus far contain coincidences that uniquely confirm at least one Synoptic Gospel. Sometimes the unique material is in Mark, but each chapter also contains coincidences that show the independence of the other Synoptic Gospels (Matthew and/or Luke) from Mark and that confirm their reliability in material that they did not get from Mark. *Every single coincidence* discussed in this chapter supports Matthean independence from Mark (see Table 3, endnote 6 to this chapter, and discussion of individual coincidences) and confirms Matthew's material, even when the material in Matthew is also found in Luke.

For Luke, earlier chapters showed independent material confirmed by dovetailing with John (see Table 1 and Table 2). In this chapter, the coincidence concerning Herod's servants involves, on the one side, information unique to Matthew (that Herod was talking with his servants about Jesus) and, on the other side, information unique to Luke (that the wife of Herod's household manager was among Jesus' followers).

All of this means, as I pointed out in the introduction, that the theory of Markan priority does not provide any grounds whatsoever for dismissing material unique to other Gospels. To emphasize the fact that the argument from undesigned coincidences swings free of one's solution to the Synoptic question, I have been careful not to use a single undesigned coincidence that could be plausibly explained by mere incomplete copying or elaboration of Mark on the part of Matthew or Luke.[15]

Thus far all of the coincidences I have discussed have taken the question and answer form—a question or puzzle raised in one (or more) Gospels and explained by a detail in another Gospel. Chapter IV will be a bit different, for not all of the coincidences discussed there will follow this question-answer pattern. Yet they are so valuable that it is impossible to leave them out of this study.

Table 3: The Synoptic Gospels Explain Each Other

Coincidence	Matthew	Mark	Luke	John
†Matt 1. The paired disciples	10.2–4	**6.7**	6.14–15[1]	
†Matt, L 2. Herod and his servants	14.1–2		**8.3**	
†Matt, L*3. Woe to Bethsaida!	11.21		10.13; **9.10**	
†Matt 4. Got a new tomb handy?	**27.57–60**		23.52	19.41–42

† Indicates a coincidence that uniquely confirms one or more of the Synoptic Gospels.

* Indicates a coincidence connected with a miracle.

Matt indicates a coincidence that shows Matthean independence from Mark and that supports Matthew's reliability in matters on which he is independent from Mark.

L indicates a coincidence that shows Lukan independence from both Mark and Matthew and that supports Luke's reliability in matters on which he is independent.

Bold font indicates a passage that provides an explanation. Plain font indicates a passage that raises a question.

---

[1]Whether Luke is regarded as participating in this undesigned coincidence depends upon one's choice of text family.

IV

Still More Undesigned Coincidences in the Gospels

Introduction

The undesigned coincidences in this chapter do not fall into any single, neat category. Here are some examples of what makes them differ from the coincidences in Chapters I–III:

1) The coincidence may not involve an *explanatory* relationship between passages.
2) The coincidence may involve a Gospel and some other book of the New Testament rather than another Gospel.
3) The coincidence may require one to piece together an explanation partly from John and partly from a Synoptic Gospel.
4) The coincidence may use two passages from the same Gospel.

I worded my definition of an undesigned coincidence carefully in the introduction so that it could include these cases as well as the more classic type:

An undesigned coincidence is a notable connection between two or more accounts or texts that doesn't seem to have planned by the person or people giving the accounts. Despite their apparent independence, the items fit together like pieces of a puzzle.

This can happen when both passages are in the same book if the coincidence nonetheless appears not to be the result of deliberate contrivance on the part of the author. It can also happen when all the passages point indirectly to some fact standing behind them, as happens with the death of Joseph. There the "fitting together" does not arise from the fact that one passage explains another but rather from the fact that they fit together to support some hypothesis that explains them all. The same is true of coincidence #4 in this chapter. John states that Jesus came to Bethany six days before the Passover but gives no detailed chronology after that showing the six days; the daily chronology in Mark's account of Passion Week fits with and supports John.

While the coincidences in this chapter do not follow the familiar pattern of those in the earlier chapters, they are among the most interesting in the Gospels.

1. Where's Joseph?

Joseph, the husband of Mary, is an interesting and sympathetic character. He appears only in Matthew and Luke, and there only in early chapters connected with Jesus' conception, birth, and early childhood. These passages are among the most tempting for the skeptic to attribute to legend or elaboration. They include the miraculous conception of Jesus, dreams and visions on the part of Joseph, Mary, and the priest Zechariah, and the miraculous conception of John the Baptist. Not to mention the wise men, the star, the shepherds, and the angels. Moreover, the birth narratives in Luke are unique to Luke, and those in Matthew are unique to Matthew. Matthew's unique stories about Joseph include the flight to Egypt and the return from Egypt, both prompted by

divinely sent dreams. If ever there were a fertile field for specula-
tion that the Gospels contain fictional elaboration, the material
surrounding Joseph would seem to be it.

Yet here is a curious fact about the treatment of Joseph in the
Gospels: All four Gospels, including Matthew and Luke, are
consistent in that Joseph disappears from their pages after Jesus'
childhood.[1] The last we see of him is during the trip to Jerusalem
when Jesus is twelve years old in Luke 2. Joseph never appears
in person in any incidents whatsoever in the canonical Gospels
once Jesus' ministry has begun. Whatever temptation there may
have been to say what happened to Joseph or to tell more about
him, the Gospels don't do so. None of them do. He simply drops
out of sight.

But there is more. It is not simply that Joseph does not appear
after Jesus' ministry begins. Joseph is *conspicuously absent* even
when Jesus' family is *conspicuously present*. The passages in which
Joseph would have been expected to show up but is absent occur
in all four Gospels and in the first chapter of Acts. One such incident is described in all three of the Synoptic Gospels (though
Mark's account is longer than the others), another in Matthew
and Mark, and two unique incidents in John (three if one counts
the marriage at Cana).

It is difficult to avoid the conclusion that Joseph died some
time between Jesus' childhood and the beginning of his ministry. Moreover, it appears that the Gospel writers knew this. Their
accounts of incidents involving Jesus' family seem to presuppose
Joseph's death and are mutually confirming in that they all point
in that same direction. But they do not mention that Joseph was
dead. Neither Acts nor any Gospel bothers to stop and explain
what happened to Joseph or why he isn't showing up in more stories. Rather, they simply tell about the doings of Jesus' family *as*

if Joseph is already dead, in the manner of those who knew about the incidents and about who was and was not present; for them, it seems, Joseph's death was a shared background fact.

Here are the incidents:

1) Mark says that Jesus' family attempted to put a stop to his ministry, apparently fairly early on:[2]

> Then he went home, and the crowd gathered again, so that they could not even eat. And when his family heard it, they went out to seize him, for they were saying, "He is out of his mind."…And his mother and his brothers came, and standing outside they sent to him and called him. And a crowd was sitting around him, and they said to him, "Your mother and your brothers are outside, seeking you." And he answered them, "Who are my mother and my brothers?" And looking about at those who sat around him, he said, "Here are my mother and my brothers! For whoever does the will of God, he is my brother and sister and mother." (Mark 3.20–21; 31–35)

Matthew's and Luke's accounts of (apparently) the same incident do not include the statement that his family went out to seize him but do include their arrival and attempt to talk to Jesus, together with Jesus' answer (Matt 12.46–50; Luke 8.19–21).

This movement to confront Jesus is a joint, family movement. In modern parlance, Jesus' family has decided to "stage an intervention." What, precisely, prompted this decision is unclear. Luke 4 says that on one occasion when Jesus was in his home town fairly early in his ministry he so angered the people that they attempted to kill him (Luke 4.29–30). Mark 3.20 may mean that this intervention by his family occurred on the next occasion after that when he came to the region of Nazareth, gathering multitudes around him.[3] For my purpose the striking point is that it is Jesus' *brothers*, not his father, who are the male representatives of the family in this incident.[4] It is difficult to believe that Joseph would not have been involved if this decision by Jesus' own people to confront him had taken place while Joseph was alive (and both mentally and physically competent).

2) Matthew and Mark both recount that the people in Jesus' home region, so far from taking pride in a local boy who has grown up and become famous, are offended at his putting on such airs when he is merely a member of a family they know well:

> He went away from there and came to his hometown, and his disciples followed him. And on the Sabbath he began to teach in the synagogue, and many who heard him were astonished, saying, "Where did this man get these things? What is the wisdom given to him? How are such mighty works done by his hands? Is not this the carpenter, the son of Mary and brother of James and Joses and Judas and Simon? And are not his sisters here with us?" And they took offense at him. And Jesus said to them, "A prophet is not without honor, except in his hometown and among his relatives and in his own household." And he could do no mighty work there, except that he laid his hands on a few sick people and healed them. And he marveled because of their unbelief. (Mark 6.1–6)

The similar passage in Matthew 13.54–58 has the crowd saying, "Is not this the carpenter's son?" instead of "Is not this the carpenter?" but in either case Joseph is absent from the members of Jesus' family who are spoken of as present and alive at the time. Again, while the passage does not *say* that Joseph is dead, it is strongly consonant with that assumption.

3) John's account of the wedding at Cana emphasizes the role of Jesus' mother and also mentions that Jesus and his disciples were invited to the wedding, but it never mentions Joseph. I am

not breaking the wedding at Cana out as a separate incident, despite the prominence of Mary in the story, since no attempt is made in the account of the wedding at Cana to list or refer to Jesus' family as such. The wedding certainly fits with the pattern I am noting, but rather than leaning on it as a separate incident, I note here that it leads directly into John 2.12, which appears to tell of a journey Jesus took with his family shortly thereafter:

> After this he went down to Capernaum, with his mother and his brothers and his disciples, and they stayed there for a few days. (John 2.12)

Here, as in the other passages, is the unforced designation of Jesus' family as "his mother and his brothers" without any mention of his father.

A natural interpretation of John 2 is that the wedding at Cana involved friends of Jesus' family and that Jesus met his mother and other family members there and traveled from there with them to Capernaum. Either the tension recorded in Mark and the other Synoptics had not yet arisen or had been patched up—most probably the former. The absence of Joseph from this family group going to Capernaum is well explained by the hypothesis that he was already dead.

If John knew of these as real events within his own experience, it is quite plausible that he would record them in just this way, mentioning Jesus' "mother and brothers" as those present on the trip to Capernaum while not bothering to say explicitly that Joseph had already died. Indeed, if Joseph died prior to the beginning of Jesus' ministry, it might not even have occurred to the disciples to mention the reason for his absence when mentioning Jesus' family, since they might never have known Joseph personally and would not have associated him with Jesus' ministry at all.

4) One of the strongest indications that Joseph was dead at least by the time of Jesus' crucifixion is the statement that Jesus committed Mary to the charge of the beloved disciple at the cross and that she went to live in his house:

> [S]tanding by the cross of Jesus were his mother and his mother's sister, Mary the wife of Clopas, and Mary Magdalene. When Jesus saw his mother and the disciple whom he loved standing nearby, he said to his mother, "Woman, behold, your son!" Then he said to the disciple, "Behold, your mother!" And from that hour the disciple took her to his own home. (John 19.25–27)

It is extremely unlikely that this event would have occurred if Joseph were still alive. The account of it therefore further supports the conclusion that Joseph was already dead by this time. Yet again, John never mentions Joseph's death. The Gospel writer gives the strong impression that he *is* the beloved disciple (see, e.g., John 19.35), yet he never attempts to justify or explain his taking charge of Mary by reference to Joseph's death. (See coincidence #7 in this chapter for more on the commitment of Mary to the beloved disciple.)

5) The Book of Acts contains one allusion to Jesus' family in a group. Jesus' brother James is prominent in Acts, but Acts 1 contains the only reference to Jesus' family all together:

> Then they returned to Jerusalem from the mount called Olivet, which is near Jerusalem, a Sabbath day's journey away. And when they had entered, they went up to the upper room, where they were staying, Peter and John and James and Andrew, Philip and Thomas, Bartholomew and Matthew, James the son of Alphaeus and Simon the Zealot and Judas the son of James. All these with one accord were devoting themselves to prayer, together with the women and Mary the mother of Jesus, and his brothers. (Acts 1.12–14)

Here is a similar expression to those in the Gospels—"together with … Mary the mother of Jesus and his brothers."

The one person who does *not* appear to have been in the upper room as part of Jesus' family is Joseph his foster father. By this time it might almost seem that the point is old hat: Joseph is nowhere to be found, even when the rest of Jesus' family is listed. I emphasize it here because it is a distinct incident, found only in Acts, and because it is yet another data point, casually worded as are the others, supporting the earlier death of Joseph.

There are a few verses outside of the infancy and childhood narratives that mention that Jesus was, or was regarded as, the son of Joseph. These are Luke 3.23, Luke 4.22, John 1.45, and John 6.42. Of these, three are merely remarking that Jesus was considered to be Joseph's son and cannot be taken at all to imply that Joseph was alive at the time. The only *possible* exception is in John 6.41–42.

> So the Jews grumbled about him, because he said, "I am the bread that came down from heaven." They said, "Is not this Jesus, the son of Joseph, whose father and mother we know? How does he now say, 'I have come down from heaven'?"

One might take this to mean that Joseph is alive and that they know Joseph personally at that time. But a more plausible interpretation in context is that, since they believe that they know who Jesus' biological parents are, it is absurd for him to claim to have come down from heaven.[5] This verse cannot be regarded as an exception to the unanimous implication of the Gospels that Joseph simply was not around by the time of Jesus' ministry.

The unanimity of the Gospels on this point would be virtually impossible to contrive. By the time John was written the other Gospels were in place, with their subtle implications of Joseph's relatively early death. Yet, precisely because those implications (e.g., in Mark) are so subtle, if the second and third Gospel writers had *wanted* to include further stories about Joseph later in Jesus' life, they could have done so without actually contradicting anything already written. So could John, if he had desired to do so and were not trying to represent the facts truthfully. And if John chose to manufacture stories in which Joseph was notably absent for the purpose of agreeing with the unstated implications of earlier Gospels, why did he not draw attention to Joseph's death?

The simplest explanation of the disappearance of Joseph from the Gospel accounts is that Joseph actually did disappear and, moreover, that the Gospel writers left him out when mentioning Jesus' family because they were close to the facts and knew who was actually there when those events occurred.

Here a short digression is in order about the restraint of the Gospel writers. There are several areas in which, if the Gospel writers were not held back by considerations of truthfulness and the presence or absence of reliable information about real events, they would have been sorely tempted to invent. The further doings and eventual fate of Joseph fall into this category, as discussed above. The notorious absence of more information in the canonical Gospels about Jesus' infancy and childhood is another instance. Similarly, the author of Acts clearly knows of the importance of baptism in the early life of the church. The disciples are baptizing converts from the beginning of Acts. Yet nowhere in the Gospel of Luke is it ever mentioned that Jesus or his disciples baptized (in contrast with a baptizing ministry carried out by Jesus' disciples in John 4), nor does Luke contain a commission to baptize such as that found in Matthew 28.19. If the author of Luke, who was also the author of Acts, felt free to add incidents and to put words in Jesus' mouth, it would have been quite natural to add a reference to the importance of baptism on the part of Jesus' disciples.[6]

Perhaps most striking of all is the absence of any detailed account in any Gospel of Jesus' one-on-one, post-resurrection appearances to Peter and to his brother James. The former is mentioned in the briefest possible terms in a bit of dialogue but not described at all (Luke 24.34) and is mentioned in the Apostle Paul's creed in I Corinthians 15.5. The latter (the appearance to James) is mentioned only in I Corinthians 15.7. Yet Peter is obviously forgiven by the time we get to Acts (or even to John 21), and James the brother of Jesus is prominent in the early church in the book of Acts. We can only conjecture exactly how it came about that both James and Peter made it known that they had seen Jesus after his resurrection but that neither of them made an account of the private meeting available for publication. But withholding the details of such a private conversation is the sort of thing that happens all the time in real life. If the Gospel writers were trying truthfully to record only what they either knew directly or had reliable sources to tell them about, they would have very little to say about such meetings, exactly as we find. But if they felt free to invent dialogue and scenes in order to fill in where information was otherwise missing, why would they not have done so here? Their restraint points to the conclusion that they are truthful, reliable recorders.

2. Why ask Philip?

Here I return to the feeding of the five thousand, which has been a source for several coincidences in earlier chapters. One reason for the wealth of the coincidences surrounding the feeding of the five thousand is that it is included in all four Gospels; for both this item and the next I will discuss a delicate interlocking among several different accounts. This coincidence begins with the Gospel of John:

> Jesus went up on the mountain, and there he sat down with his disciples. Now the Passover, the feast of the Jews, was at hand. Lifting up his eyes, then, and seeing that a large crowd was coming toward him, Jesus said to Philip, "Where are we to buy bread, so that these people may eat?" (John 6.1–5)

Reading the story quickly, one might not stop to wonder about this, but the detail is worth questioning: Why Philip? Philip is not one of the *most* prominent disciples. Aside from the lists of the disciples and the passage in question, Philip comes up on only a few occasions, all of them in John. (These are John 1.43ff, at the first calling of several of the disciples, John 12.21ff, where some Greeks come and ask Philip to lead them to Jesus, and John 14.8ff, where Philip asks Jesus, "Show us the Father.") He is not one of the "inner three"—Peter, James, and John, who come up in story after story. He is not the treasurer of the group, who might have been thought to be concerned with doling out money for purchasing food. That was Judas Iscariot. There is, in fact, no particular reason apparent in John for Jesus' selection of Philip for this question.

It is possible that Philip was selected at random, and in fact it appears that other disciples were nearby when Jesus asked the question, for Andrew joins the discussion in verses 8–9, bringing forward the lad with the loaves and fish.

But a connection among three different passages provides a more satisfactory answer than Philip's being selected by chance for the question. In the previous chapter I discussed the claim in Luke that the feeding of the five thousand took place near the town of Bethsaida (Luke 9.10). There I argued that that claim dovetails with Jesus' condemnation of Bethsaida (found both in

Matthew and in Luke) for not repenting in the face of his mighty deeds. I pointed out that this is an especially apt connection given that the Gospels also say that Jesus performed healing miracles during the day leading up to the feeding of the five thousand.

Let us put together the statement that Jesus asked Philip where bread could be purchased with the claim that the whole event took place near Bethsaida and connect both of these with a completely different passage in the Gospel of John:

> The next day Jesus decided to go to Galilee. He found Philip and said to him, "Follow me." Now Philip was from Bethsaida, the city of Andrew and Peter. (John 1.43–44)

John, in a passage completely unrelated to the feeding of the five thousand, mentions in passing that Philip was from Bethsaida. (John also mentions this in John 12.21.) Luke says that the feeding of the five thousand took place near Bethsaida. John does not give the location at all, but John (alone) records that Jesus asked *Philip*, "Where are we to buy bread?" just before the feeding of the five thousand.[7]

To be clear, I am not saying that Jesus was seriously proposing buying bread for the multitude! John, in fact, expressly says (v 6) that he was testing Philip, knowing himself that he planned to feed the people miraculously. That is very much the way in which Jesus interacted with his disciples. He would often say cryptic things or ask them questions merely to draw out their responses as part of his own teaching. One can even picture Jesus asking the question in a slightly teasing manner. The fact that Philip was from that vicinity makes the question (and the joke) more pointed. If Philip is from the nearby town, Jesus is in essence saying, "Philip, you're from around here. Where can we get bread for all these people?"[8]

This coincidence is a case where a Synoptic Gospel by itself does not explain John. Rather, a question is raised by John's account; it is answered only by putting together a statement in Luke with an entirely different and otherwise unrelated passage in John—a complex and interesting coincidence and one which makes any hypothesis of design on the part of John extremely unlikely. If John made up the detail that Jesus asked Philip, intending it to fit together with the location of the miracle, it is highly improbable that he would have left out of this account of the feeding either a reminder of Philip's home town *or* a mention of the location of the feeding, leaving the reader to find *both* of these for himself in other places, one of them in an entirely different Gospel! The same is true if John had happened upon a version of the story similar to Luke's, mentioning the location as Bethsaida. If the mention of Bethsaida was in some way influencing John's account, he would have been much more likely to mention the *town* than to invent a question to *Philip*, all the more so if Philip's connection to Bethsaida, mentioned in unrelated passages, was his own invention anyway.

Moreover, as I pointed out in Chapter II concerning John's detail that the Passover was near at hand, John has not made *any attempt whatsoever* to harmonize his account of the feeding of the five thousand with the accounts in the Synoptic Gospels. On the contrary, he has left rather striking loose ends. For example, he does not mention that Jesus taught or healed the people all day (as the Synoptics all say), so that the reader might get the impression that Jesus fed them almost immediately upon seeing them. We can therefore take it that, when John's account of this event does fit together in casual detail with the Synoptic Gospels (as it does again and again), it is *not* a result of design at all. This makes these agreements valuable indeed.

3. The *men* sat down[9]

The miracle of the feeding of the five thousand gets its name from the fact that all four Gospels record that number. Matthew's account emphasizes that the number refers specifically to males. "And those who ate were about five thousand men, besides women and children." (Matt 14.21) The word here for men is *andres*, meaning men as opposed to women. The statement that about five thousand *andres* were fed also occurs in Mark 6.44, Luke 9.14, and John 6.10, though these Gospels don't add "besides women and children."

Two of the Gospels give some idea of how this number was calculated. Mark 6.39–40 says, "Then he commanded them all to sit down in groups on the green grass. So they sat down in groups, by hundreds and by fifties." Similarly, Luke 9.14–15 says, "And he said to his disciples, 'Have them sit down in groups of about fifty each.' And they did so, and had them all sit down." No doubt having the crowd sorted into groups made it easier to distribute food to them. It also made it possible to get some idea of how many there were.

Notice that Mark and Luke could be taken to mean that Jesus had *all* the people sit down. Yet one would have thought that if all the people—men, women, and children—sat down in groups of approximately fifty to a hundred, the Gospels would not give their count exclusively in terms of the number of males fed, especially not as emphatically as Matthew does. So the claim in Luke and Mark that the people sat down in approximately equal groups provides only part of the explanation for the Gospels' agreement on an approximate count of five thousand *men*.

John makes no mention of the groupings, but his account does add a crucial piece to the puzzle.

Jesus said, "Have the people sit down." Now there was much grass in the place. So the men sat down, about five thousand in number. Jesus then took the loaves, and when he had given thanks, he distributed them to those who were seated. So also the fish, as much as they wanted. (John 6.10–11)

John says that Jesus said, "Have the people sit down." The word here is *anthropos*, meaning people or human beings. But who actually sat down? John says, "So the men sat down, about five thousand in number." Here the word is *andres*, a point that is clear in modern translations.

Putting this point from John together with the accounts in the other Gospels makes the scene fairly clear. Jesus wants an orderly distribution of the food. He tells the disciples to have the people sit down in groups (as Mark and Luke say), but it is the men who actually sit down (as John says). Presumably the food was distributed to the men and from them to the women and children. This explains how the men, specifically, could be approximately counted, leaving the number of women and children up in the air, as Matthew clearly indicates.

This is an intricate coincidence and a mentally satisfying one, depending as it does on subtle indications in various texts. Beyond this, it is true to human nature. It is extremely difficult to imagine getting a milling crowd of such a size, including children, who were no doubt running about and playing, all to sit down on the grass at the same time. It would be all the more difficult given that the crowds had been there all day as Jesus went among them healing and teaching, perhaps not even teaching all of them at the same time. We should not imagine the scene as akin to a concert or lecture but as more like a crowded fair. It is impressive enough that, in a world without sound systems or megaphones, the disciples were able to get even the men seated in groups of about fifty to a hundred. Not attempting to seat the children, and leaving the women free to look after them, would be only common sense in the culture and context.

Blunt, apropos of the many coincidences connected with the feeding of the five thousand, comments drily,

> Here again, then, I maintain, we have strong indications of veracity in the case of a miracle itself; and I leave it to others, who may have ingenuity and inclination for the task, to weed out the falsehood of the miracle from the manifest reality of the circumstances which attend it, and to separate fiction from fact, which is in the very closest combination with it.[10]

4. Six days before the Passover

John says that Jesus arrived in Bethany (near to Jerusalem) on his last visit to Jerusalem six days before the Passover. "Six days before the Passover, Jesus therefore came to Bethany, where Lazarus was, whom Jesus had raised from the dead. So they gave a dinner for him there." (John 12.1–2a) John says that what we now call the triumphal entry occurred the next morning.

> The next day the large crowd that had come to the feast heard that Jesus was coming to Jerusalem. So they took branches of palm trees and went out to meet him, crying out, "Hosanna! Blessed is he who comes in the name of the Lord, even the King of Israel!" (John 12.12–13)

In the following chapters in John, these six days are not spelled out. The rest of John 12 is taken up with the triumphal entry and with some of Jesus' sayings to the people in Jerusalem. Chapter 13 fast-forwards to the night of the Last Supper itself, beginning with the foot-washing. Several chapters of discourses from Jesus to his disciples follow, and Chapter 17 is his long prayer to the Father for believers, all of this apparently placed at the time of the Last Supper. In Chapter 18, they go to the

Garden of Gethsemane, where Jesus is arrested, and the passion and crucifixion follow.

It is a remarkable fact that, by making one minor assumption to kick off the sequence, we can actually find in the Gospel of Mark the "six days before the Passover" to which John refers, though Mark does not say that Jesus arrived at Bethany six days before the Passover.[11] Mark 11 contains that Gospel's account of the triumphal entry. The chapter begins with Jesus approaching Jerusalem:

> Now when they drew near to Jerusalem, to Bethphage and Bethany, at the Mount of Olives, Jesus sent two of his disciples and said to them, "Go into the village in front of you, and immediately as you enter it you will find a colt tied, on which no one has ever sat. Untie it and bring it." (Mark 11.1–2)

I concede that this gives at first sight the impression that Jesus sent the disciples to get the colt when he *first* approached Bethany. To lay out this coincidence it is necessary to take as a working hypothesis that Jesus actually first came to Bethany the day before, possibly toward evening, and that this verse is merely alluding to the fact that Bethany and Bethphage were close to Jerusalem and marked the approach to Jerusalem and the approximate location from which Jesus sent his disciples to get the colt. As some independent support for this assumption, Matthew mentions *only* Bethphage at the same point in his narrative—Matthew 21.1. This is all the more plausible given that there is quite a bit of action before Mark says (v 11) that it was late in the evening. There is the fetching of the donkey. There is the triumphal entry itself, which could not have been very fast with the cheering crowds gathered around. Mark also says that Jesus entered the Temple and "looked all around" (v 11). Altogether, though it is not impossible that these events could have taken place later in the day of his first coming to Bethany, depending on what time he first arrived at Bethany, the placement of the beginning of the sequence in the morning after he had slept at Bethany (as John does) makes more sense, though not stated clearly in Mark.

This working hypothesis is in turn supported by the coincidence with John that follows. For Mark carefully lists the evenings and mornings of Passion Week right up to a point which he labels as two days before the Passover. Assume, then, for the sake of the argument, that Jesus arrived at Bethany six days before Passover in an afternoon or evening and that he sent the disciples to find the donkey the next morning.

In verse 11 Mark says, of the day of the triumphal ride into Jerusalem, "And he entered Jerusalem and went into the temple. And when he had looked around at everything, as it was already late, he went out to Bethany with the twelve." This would therefore be the evening, *five days* before the Passover. Verse 12 is still following a careful sequence: "On the following day, when they came from Bethany, he was hungry." (This is the lead-in to the cursing of the fig tree.) In Mark this is followed by the cleansing of the Temple, and then Mark closes off the day explicitly in verse 19 saying, "And when evening came, they went out of the city." This would therefore, on the line of argument I am pursuing, be *four days* before the Passover.

Mark 11.20 begins, "And as they passed by in the morning…" This would be when they were coming back into the city by the same way on the next day, *three days* before the Passover. (This is when they see that the fig tree has withered.) Mark 13.1–4 closes off that day:

And as he came out of the temple, one of his disciples said to him, "Look, Teacher, what wonderful stones and what wonderful buildings!" And Jesus said to him, "Do you see these great buildings? There will not be left here one stone upon another that will not be thrown down. And as he sat on the Mount of Olives opposite the temple, Peter and James and John and Andrew asked him privately, "Tell us, when will these things be, and what will be the sign when all these things are about to be accomplished?"

It is a reasonable inference that Jesus was leaving the temple at the end of that day in the city and returning to Bethany, as he had done before, which is further confirmed by the fact that the private conversation with his disciples takes place on the Mount of Olives, which lay between the city and Bethany. This conversation and a discourse from Jesus on things to come take up the rest of Chapter 13.

Mark 14 begins with what can plausibly be taken to be the following day:

It was now two days before the Passover and the Feast of Unleavened Bread. And the chief priests and the scribes were seeking how to arrest him by stealth and kill him, for they said, "Not during the feast, lest there be an uproar from the people."

There is no reference to Jesus' going into Jerusalem on this day. Mark instead describes a supper on that day in Bethany and, in verses 10–11, Judas's trip into Jerusalem to meet with the chief priests and offer to betray Jesus. By the count I have been making from Mark 11ff, this would indeed be *two days* before the Passover.

I began, above, with *John's* statement that Jesus came to Bethany six days before the Passover. By making just one initial assumption, following John, that this was a reference to the afternoon or evening prior to the triumphal entry, I have counted forward using *Mark's* daily log of Jesus' activities, beginning with the triumphal entry. By this means I have come, just at the right moment, to a point where *Mark* states that it was now two days before the Passover. The agreement between the two Gospels is quite tight.[12]

This is all the more remarkable given that John himself gives no such daily log of Jesus' actions and that, in fact, there are well-known ways in which John's account of the passion is independent from and, some even argue, in conflict with Mark's. There is, to give one example, the rather famous claim that John "says" that Jesus was crucified before the first Passover meal because of John 18.28. I do not take this to be a real contradiction between John and Mark, as the argument seems to me decisive that the meal the leaders would have been prevented from eating by ritual unclean-ness (from entering Pilate's hall) was the *chagigah* in the middle of the day on Friday.[13] Therefore, John is not saying that Jesus was crucified on a different day from the day in the Synoptics, but nei-ther is he making any special attempt to coordinate with Mark.

In this coincidence concerning the six days, John's and Mark's chronologies of Passion Week agree in a subtle and fascinating way. Yet John's approach in other respects makes it quite clear that this was not the result of design.

A related point concerns the discussions in Chapters I and II of the intricate and detailed ways in which John's account of the trial scene before Pilate interlocks with Luke's. These coincidences, #7 and #8 in Chapter I and #5 in Chapter II, disconfirm the theory that John was deliberately altering things in his passion narrative. He is telling what happened as he believed and knew it to be, not changing events for theological or other reasons; this truthfulness causes his narrative and that of the Synoptics to fit together. It would be extremely strange for John to "place" the crucifixion on a day when it didn't really happen by a statement in John 18.28, which comes *just* at the point where the Jewish leaders bring Jesus to Pilate, but for him to be confirmed by undesigned coincidences as an astonishingly reliable source for what Jesus and Pilate said to one another and what Pilate said to the Jewish leaders. There is no reason to conjecture John's non-factual invention in the middle of his prosaic accuracy concerning that very scene.

The argument from undesigned coincidences tells us what sort of authors these are, sometimes in the very places where biblical criticism has tried to give us a different and, I contend, misguided portrait.

5. Inside information

The story of Jesus' arrest in John contains a slightly surprising detail.

> Then Simon Peter, having a sword, drew it and struck the high priest's servant and cut off his right ear. (The servant's name was Malchus.) (John 18.10)

The sudden insertion of the name of the servant is unexpected. He is a relatively minor character in the story, and it is odd that the Gospel writer should mention his name. It is still stranger that the Gospel writer would *know* his name. A group including servants of the high priest comes with Judas to arrest Jesus in the night. These are hardly likely to be friends of the disciples. How does this name come to be in the text at all? A reader with a skeptical bent of mind might even conjecture that the parenthetical name was added by the Gospel writer as a bit of invented detail to give an air of truth to the whole story.

Later in the same chapter of John comes another bit of detail related to this same servant.

One of the servants of the high priest, a relative of the man whose ear Peter had cut off, asked, "Did I not see you in the garden with him?" Peter again denied it, and at once a rooster crowed. (John 18.26–27)

This detail, like the previous one, is mentioned in passing. John says, casually, that one of those who questioned Peter was a relative of the servant whose ear Peter had cut off. There is nothing particularly implausible about the scenario. Several relatives might well all work for the high priest and be sent on the same mission to arrest Jesus, and if one's relative were the victim of Peter's sword, one would be quite likely to remember Peter's face seen in the torchlight in the garden. But how does the Gospel writer know these things about the makeup of the high priest's household? It seems that Peter himself might not even know the name of the man whose ear he cut off, much less who his kinsman was among the other servants.

The question is answered quite indirectly by another sentence in the same chapter.

Simon Peter followed Jesus, and so did another disciple. Since that disciple was known to the high priest, he entered with Jesus into the courtyard of the high priest, but Peter stood outside at the door. So the other disciple, who was known to the high priest, went out and spoke to the servant girl who kept watch at the door, and brought Peter in. (John 18.15–16)[14]

The relevant statement, of course, is that the other disciple was "known to the high priest." The text does not say how this came about; this point, too, is mentioned in passing. But this does explain how that disciple could know the name of the servant whose ear Peter had cut off and which other servant was his relative. John says that somehow or other this "other disciple" had an "in" with the high priest's household, including sufficient influence to admit himself and his friend to the high priest's courtyard. If he was familiar with the household, he could well have opportunity to know the servants' names and relationships.

The connection here is quite indirect, despite the fact that the three passages all occur in the same Gospel. In no way does the Gospel draw attention to the fact that the assertion that the other disciple was known to the high priest explains the author's access to the information about Malchus and his relative. Other indications are equally indirect. John 20.2 connects the "other disciple" with the "disciple whom Jesus loved," and John 19.26 and 35 implicitly connect the disciple whom Jesus loved with the author of the Gospel by saying that he was at the cross and that he bears witness to what he has seen. If the author of the Gospel was himself the "other disciple" who knew the high priest's household, this goes even further to explain the presence in John of the information about Malchus. But these are additional hints picked up from separate passages.

It is highly improbable that the author of the fourth Gospel included fictional details about the arrest in the garden and the baiting of Peter in the courtyard, alluded in an indirect fashion in other passages to equally fictional details intended to explain his access to this information, but never connected the dots for the reader. In the words of the 19th-century lawyer Edmund Bennett, "Forgers do not rest content with such roundabout confirmations."[15]

6. Who was Rufus?

Most Christians are familiar with the part of the crucifixion story in which Simon of Cyrene is forced by the Roman soldiers to carry Jesus' cross on the way to Golgotha. The incident emphasizes Jesus' exhaustion and weakness as well as the conditions of life under Roman rule. It can hardly have been pleasant to be Simon, who presumably would have preferred to mind his own business and who seems to have been grabbed at random and coerced to participate in the brutal scene.

All three Synoptic Gospels mention Simon of Cyrene; Mark's Gospel contains a unique detail.

> And when they had mocked him, they stripped him of the purple cloak and put his own clothes on him. And they led him out to crucify him. And they compelled a passerby, Simon of Cyrene, who was coming in from the country, the father of Alexander and Rufus, to carry his cross. (Mark 15.20–21)

If one reads this carefully, the question immediately springs to mind, "Who are Rufus and Alexander, and why are they mentioned here?"

Richard Bauckham argues that Mark's reference to Rufus and Alexander presupposes that these people were known to Mark's audience.[16] I consider this conclusion defensible since these names come up in Mark's Gospel "out of the blue" without further explanation and are attached to a person (Simon) who has no other role to play in the Gospel. This is not merely a matter of *leaving out* some particular, which might be merely the natural way in which witnesses talk without filling in explanatory details. It is a matter of *including* the names of people who have no role otherwise in the narrative, as if these names were meaningful in some special way. A valuable point in Bauckham's discussion is that the phrase "of Cyrene" would presumably have been sufficient to distinguish this Simon from others, so that is not a likely explanation for Mark's using the lengthier reference to Simon's sons.

Bauckham's points are well-taken, but here I want to note the coincidence between this passage and one of the greetings at the end of Paul's epistle to the Romans. "Greet Rufus, chosen in the Lord; also his mother, who has been a mother to me as well." (Rom 16.13)[17]

By itself, this might just be a coincidence of names. Why think that the "Rufus" of Romans 16 is the same as the "Rufus" of Mark 15? It's important to keep in mind that multiple, unconnected people could have the same name in Biblical times as in our own. Bauckham points out two pertinent facts that point in opposite directions on this question.[18] On the one hand, Paul's reference to his close connection with Rufus's mother as being in some sense (presumably metaphoric or spiritual) his own mother indicates that Rufus had gone to Rome from the eastern side of the Mediterranean (where Jerusalem was), since Paul had never been in Rome at the time that he wrote this epistle. While this would by no means necessitate the conclusion that the two are the same Rufus, it would slightly confirm it. On the other hand, Bauckham raises the caution that "Rufus" was not an uncommon name, being treated by the Jews as a Latin equivalent of "Reuben," so the Rufus of Romans 16 could be a different person.

The greeting from Paul to a Christian Rufus in Rome is worth considering in this context chiefly because of a longstanding patristic tradition that Mark's Gospel was originally written in Rome with inhabitants of Rome as its first audience.[19] With that fact in mind, we have three points of evidence coming together—the "out of nowhere" reference to Rufus and Alexander in Mark, as though perhaps they are known to the audience of the Gospel, the reference in Romans to a Rufus who was a Christian in Rome, and the tradition that Mark's Gospel was written in Rome. In this way the reference to Rufus in Romans confirms, via a plausible conjecture, the unique reference to Rufus in Mark as the son of Simon of Cyrene and thereby confirms the historical reliability of Mark.

7. "Woman, behold your son!"

I have already discussed in #1 in this chapter the statement in John that from the cross Jesus committed his mother to the care of the beloved disciple (John 19.26–27). In that section the incident formed part of the overall pattern supporting the conclusion that Joseph had died, probably prior to Jesus' ministry and certainly prior to Jesus' crucifixion. But there is another question that arises from that passage. We know from many verses (which were also discussed in section #1) that Jesus had brothers. Why did Jesus go out of his way to commit Mary to the beloved disciple if she had other living sons to care for her?[20] This decision is especially surprising in the context of a society in which close kinship was important. Even the consideration (by itself) that the other disciples were not personally present at the cross would not require so pointed an act by Jesus as declaring Mary to be the "mother" of the beloved disciple and him to be her new "son."

The Gospel of John itself provides the answer, though in an entirely different context. In John 7, the Feast of Booths is at hand, and Jesus' brothers taunt him to go up to the feast and perform miracles to attract attention:

> Now the Jews' Feast of Booths was at hand. So his brothers said to him, "Leave here and go to Judea, that your disciples also may see the works you are doing. For no one works in secret if he seeks to be known openly. If you do these things, show yourself to the world." For not even his brothers believed in him. (John 7.2–5)

This incident, though never connected by the Gospel writer to the commitment of Mary to the beloved disciple, answers the question quite well: Jesus knew that Mary would want someone to care for her, at least during her time of mourning, who had not made fun of his ministry and who had loved him and been faithful to him. Though there is ample evidence that some or all of Jesus' brothers later converted to the new Christian movement,[21] it was during and after the trauma of the crucifixion that Mary was lacking a sympathetic son to be with her.[22]

This coincidence, like #5 in this chapter, involves passages within the same Gospel, though John's assertion that Jesus' brothers did not believe on him is consonant with the picture in Mark 3.20ff of the "family intervention" and with Jesus' wry remark in Mark 6.4 that a prophet is without honor in his own household and among his own relatives. Despite the fact that both sides of this coincidence—both the question and the answer to it—are found in John, the coincidence has force. It is worth remembering at all times that such subtle indications of verisimilitude are of little value to the forger, and I quote again the wise words of J.S. Howson:

> An intentional and contrived coincidence must be of such a character as to *strike* the reader. Otherwise it fails of its purpose. If it was kept latent for the intelligent … critics of a later age to find out, it has not attained the end for which it was meant at the time of its contrivance.[23]

The best explanation of these passages in John is that Jesus' brothers really had been scornful of his ministry as recorded in John 7 and that, therefore, Jesus during his crucifixion wanted to give Mary a different "son" as recorded in John 19. The Gospel author, who may have been the beloved disciple himself, knew about both incidents and recorded them as they happened, as a truthful witness would do, without feeling any need to explain the connection between them.

8. The net did not break

The last coincidence in Chapter I of this book concerns an appearance of Jesus in John 21 to his disciples after his resurrection. Obviously, that coincidence concerns a miracle, since the conversation in which it is embedded could not have taken place at any time before Jesus' resurrection. But another miracle is recorded in the same passage: The disciples haul in a great draught of fish after casting their net on the other side of the boat at Jesus' command (John 21.4–12).

This miracle bears a notable resemblance to a story told in Luke 5.4–11.[24] There, too, the disciples have fished all night and have caught nothing. There, too, Jesus gives them a command to do something they would not otherwise have done. In Luke the command is to launch out into the deep during the daytime after an unsuccessful night and try again. In John the command is to cast the net onto the other side of the boat. In both stories Peter is central. In Luke it is Peter's boat that goes out again at Jesus' command after Peter has expressed skepticism and has made it clear that he is obeying only to please Jesus (Luke 5.5). In John, Peter invites the other disciples to come fishing with him (John 21.3), it is Peter who throws himself into the sea to go as quickly as possible to Jesus after another disciple recognizes Jesus (v 7), and it is Peter who draws the net up onto the shore (v 11). Both stories are followed by a memorable exchange between Jesus and Peter. In Luke, Peter falls at Jesus' feet and begs Jesus to depart from him, a sinful man (Luke 5.8). Jesus reassures him that from now on he will be a "fisher of men" (Luke 5.10). In John the catch of fish is followed by Jesus' probing Peter, asking if he loves him and enjoining him to feed his sheep. Both fish miracles are connected with following Jesus. Luke says that after the miracle of the fish the disciples left all and followed him

(Luke 5.11). In John, Jesus pointedly commands Peter, "Follow me" (John 21.19–22).

Do all of these parallels mean that John merely made up the miracle of the fish after Jesus' resurrection, copying it from Luke? Not at all. To begin with, my list of parallels in the previous paragraph was deliberately cherry-picked to emphasize similarities. One could just as easily emphasize differences. In Luke, the boat is at the shore when Jesus starts to give orders. In John, the disciples are out on the water when Jesus shows up. In Luke, Peter expresses reluctance. In John, there is no record of any argument when Jesus says to cast the net on the other side. In Luke, the fish are dragged into the boats (Luke 5.7). In John, the fish are towed to land and pulled up onto the shore (John 21.8, 11). In Luke, there is no meal of fish after the catch; in John, there is. And so forth. One can often produce an appearance of astonishing similarity merely by selecting details to give that impression.[25]

John's account, moreover, is full of unique, vivid detail. John lists the seven disciples who went on the fishing expedition, giving names to all but two of them (v 2). John says that Peter had to put on a garment before flinging himself into the water because he was "stripped for work" (v 7). The boat came in dragging the fish in the net because they were only about a hundred yards from shore (v 8). When they came to land they saw a fire of coals with bread and fish (v 9). Peter dragged the fish ashore in response to a command by Jesus to bring some of the fish they had caught (v 10). There were 153 fish (v 11).[26]

Here I want to focus on one detail emphasized in John 21.11: "And although there were so many [fish], the net was not torn." This point is striking because John does not include the earlier miracle of the fish, recorded in Luke, anywhere in his own Gospel. One might read John's account by itself and think that he is merely mentioning the fact that the net did not break despite the size of the haul. Taken by itself, this might be only another circumstantial detail such as those I listed in the previous paragraph. But, if one considers the hypothesis that these miracles actually occurred, another reason for John's mentioning this point comes to mind: John remembered that there had been an earlier, similar, miracle, and he remembered that that time the net *did* break:

> And Simon answered, "Master, we toiled all night and took nothing! But at your word I will let down the nets." And when they had done this, they enclosed a large number of fish, and their nets were breaking. They signaled to their partners in the other boat to come and help them. And they came and filled both the boats, so that they began to sink. (Luke 5.5–7)

In the miracle reported in John 21, there was only one boat, but there were no such mishaps. "Although there were so many [fish], the net was not torn." Nor did any boat begin to sink.

These details do not fit an hypothesis that John is exaggerating the earlier miracle and thus producing a made-up miracle in his own Gospel. If anything, the fact that the catch of fish in Luke not only broke the nets but also began to sink two boats might mean that the number of fish in Luke is *greater* than the number in John 21. But given that John 21 also says that they could not haul the catch into the boat because of the quantity of fish (v 6), it is difficult to tell which number is supposed to be greater. This is exactly what we would expect if the events *actually took place.* One account isn't copied, magnified, or manipulated from the other. One isn't meant to look like a greater or lesser miracle than the other. Rather, they are just different—two accounts of two different events that vary in random details as two different, but in some respects similar, events might vary.

And John, remembering that earlier catch and mentally noting the contrast, mentions, "The net was not torn."

Conclusion

This chapter illustrates the variation in strength within the scope of the argument from undesigned coincidences. The inference that Joseph was dead before Jesus' ministry began and that the Gospel writers knew that is supported by many different passages in the Gospels and one in Acts. The refusal of the Gospel writers to introduce later stories about Joseph when they could have done so (since no Gospel actually *says* that he was dead) is also evidence for their historicity and truthfulness. It is difficult to deny that Joseph died fairly early in Jesus' life and that the Gospels' reportage reflects this fact in multiple ways. In contrast, the force of the argument that the Rufus of Mark 15 is the Rufus of Romans 16 is more suggestive than knock-down.

This same variation in strength, combined with the toughness that comes from a cumulative case and from a variety of types of evidence, has been visible throughout this first section of the book. If the argument that the feeding of the five thousand took place at Bethsaida from the "woes" of Matthew combined with Luke 9.10 seems less than decisive by itself, it is worth remembering that this same point is supported by Jesus' question to Philip about where to buy bread and the intricate connection with the independent attestation in John that Philip was from Bethsaida. And so on, through the other points about the feeding of the five thousand.

The argument of Part I includes places where the Synoptic Gospels, though earlier, explain John, where John explains the Synoptics, and where the Synoptics explain each other. This final chapter has included a coincidence involving all four Gospels and

Acts (#1), a coincidence where Luke and two separate passages in John are intertwined (#2), one where Luke and Mark, Matthew, and John all come together to explain the count of men fed (#3), a surprisingly precise connection in the chronology of Passion Week between Mark and John (#4), two coincidences between or among casual details within John (#5 and #7), a connection between Mark and one of the Pauline Epistles (#6), and a tacit contrast in John between a miracle he describes and a similar miracle in Luke (#8). The reader need not give the same evaluation that I do to every one of the arguments in Part I or of the sub-arguments that support them in order to see that the cumulative case from undesigned coincidences for the reliability of the Gospels is forceful and resilient.

The big picture is this: *This is what truth looks like.* This is what memoirs from witnesses look like. This is what it looks like when people who are trying to be truthful and who possess reliable memories of things that really happened have those memories put down in writing. This is evidence for the Gospels hidden in plain view.

Table 4: Other Undesigned Coincidences

Coincidence	Matthew	Mark	Luke	John	Other
J 1. Where's Joseph?	12.46–50; 13.54–58	3.20–21, 31–35; 6.1–6	8.19–21	2.12; 19.25–27	Acts 1.12–14
†*JL 2. Why ask Philip?			**9.10**	**1.43–44**; 6.5	
*J 3. The *men* sat down	14.21	6.39–40	9.14–15	6.10–11	
†J 4. Six days before Passover		11.11–12, 20; 13.1–4;14.1		12.1–2, 12–13	
J 5. Inside information				18.10, **15–16**, 26–27	
† 6. Who was Rufus?		15.20–21			**Romans 16.13**
J 7. "Woman, behold your son!"				19.25–26; **7.2–5**	
†*JL 8. The net did not break			5.4–11	21.3–11	

† Indicates a coincidence that uniquely confirms one or more of the Synoptic Gospels.

* Indicates a coincidence connected with a miracle.

J indicates a coincidence that involves material unique to John.

L indicates a coincidence that shows Lukan independence from both Mark and Matthew and that supports Luke's reliability in matters on which he is independent.

Bold font indicates a passage that provides an explanation. Plain font indicates a passage that raises a question, unless all passages for a coincidence are listed in plain font. In that case, the coincidence does not follow the question-explanation form.

PART TWO

Hidden in Plain View
in Acts and
the Pauline Epistles

INTRODUCTION

Why is Acts Important?

The book of Acts is a gold mine of evidence for the truth of Christianity that is not always fully appreciated. The external evidence that supports its historical reliability is particularly striking. "For Acts," Roman historian A. N. Sherwin-White writes, "the confirmation of historicity is overwhelming. . . . [A]ny attempt to reject its basic historicity even in matters of detail must now appear absurd. Roman historians have long taken it for granted."[1] Though I will be focusing here on the internal evidence for the reliability of Acts, I urge readers to investigate the external evidence as well.[2] Acts displays even more incidental connections to external history than the Gospels do, and it is easy to see the reason for the increase. The events of the Gospels all take place within a relatively small portion of space and time, a few years in first-century Palestine. It is remarkable how much historical confirmation there is for the Gospels nonetheless, but in Acts the limitation to a narrow locality is removed, and the time period covered is also significantly longer. Acts, through its accounts of the travels of Paul, is a bridge between the almost entirely Jewish world of the Gospels and the larger Roman world. Thus there are many incidental confirmations of Acts from sources such as geography and non-Christian history.[3]

Acts is important not only because it is so well-supported but also because of its value to the argument for Christianity. The significance of Acts in Christian apologetics is so great that even a strategy intended to get around the need to argue that the Gospels are historically reliable cannot avoid assuming that *Acts* is historically reliable. If one wishes to argue, for example, that the short creed given by Paul in I Corinthians 15, beginning at verse 3, has a very early origin, earlier even than the writing of the Gospels, on the grounds that it was likely taught to Paul shortly after his conversion, one must decide approximately when Paul was converted. But it is almost impossible to get a fix on the date of the conversion of Paul without using the book of Acts as an historical source.

Similarly, if one wants to argue, without assuming that the Gospels tell us what the disciples attested to, that the eleven disciples were transformed by their belief that Jesus rose from the dead, it is difficult to get any clear idea of what this transformation looked like without using the early chapters of Acts. Acts is the only first-century source we have that claims to include speeches given by the apostles themselves during the very first days of the founding of Christianity—the sermons of Peter in Acts 2–4 and the response of Peter and John to the Jewish leaders in Acts 4.19–20. If these are accurate records of the substance of what was said, they show that the apostles testified from the beginning to Jesus' physical resurrection and claimed to be eyewitnesses to this fact. Moreover, Chapters 1–12 of Acts, including the threats from the Sanhedrin, the stoning of Stephen, the persecution by Saul of Tarsus, and the execution of James the son of Zebedee, make it clear that from the earliest preaching at Pentecost the disciples faced the danger of death and proclaimed their message boldly nonetheless. There was no question of their starting a movement initially hoping to get something out of it other than severe danger and alienation from their own people. There is no other historical source that makes this fact as patent as does the book of Acts.

So it turns out that, even if one wants to try to do without the Gospels as reliable sources concerning original apostolic testimony and teaching (a strategy I do not recommend at all), one cannot easily do without Acts. But then an interesting point emerges: Acts was certainly written by the same person who wrote the Gospel of Luke. If one can argue convincingly that Acts is reliable and was written by someone close to the events (e.g., a companion of the Apostle Paul), who would have had a chance to interview those claiming to be eyewitnesses of the resurrected Jesus, there is no longer any reason to grant critical doubts on these points regarding the Gospel of Luke. A successful defense of Acts therefore allows us to reason backwards to the reliability of Luke.

Acts itself contains additional information about Jesus' post-resurrection appearances in Acts 1, which asserts that Jesus showed himself to the disciples over a period of forty days by "many proofs" and recounts a conversation between Jesus and the disciples not given in any of the Gospels. The same chapter contains the most detailed first-century account of Jesus' ascension.[4] Support for the conclusion that Acts was written by someone close up to the facts is support for the conclusion that Acts 1 represents actual apostolic testimony.

Acts is therefore important both because it *can be* supported independently of the Gospels and because, when it *is* supported independently of the Gospels, it gives us crucial evidence, both directly and indirectly, that the resurrection of Jesus occurred.

In the next two chapters I will examine evidence from undesigned coincidences between Acts and the Pauline Epistles.

A difference between Acts and the Gospels is that the coincidences I will examine for Acts virtually never concern different direct accounts of the same event in different documents, though this type of undesigned coincidence came up often in my discussion of the Gospels. (The one exception for Acts is Paul's escape from Damascus.) Most often, the undesigned coincidences between Acts and the epistles are of some other kind. For example, a comparison between the epistles and Acts makes it possible to hypothesize when in the course of the events in Acts Paul wrote a certain epistle, though Acts never once states that Paul wrote to any church. The details of Paul's companions, his actions, and his travels at a time period described in Acts mesh beautifully with what is stated or implied in the epistles. Or a reference in an epistle to what the recipients know about fits with a passage in Acts that shows *why* they would have known about that event in the life of Paul. Paul is rather fond of phrases like "You know" or "you yourselves know," followed by a reference to some fact about his own life or companions, and these can be excellent places to look for undesigned coincidences. The indirectness of these coincidences is especially lovely. It would not only be difficult to contrive such casual correspondences but also would not be the type of thing that a deceiver would even think to do.

Moreover, as in the Gospels, the fact that difficulties and even alleged contradictions remain between the narrative in Acts and the epistles shows that the author of Acts, if he had access to the epistles at all (which he may not have had), was not attempting even a simple and obvious harmonization of his work with the epistles, much less a subtle and almost unnoticeable harmonization.

A point about the numbering of the coincidences in these chapters on Acts is in order: There is a certain amount of arbitrariness in the way that I have grouped and hence numbered the coincidences. What I mean by this is that several of the numbered points I discuss between Acts and the epistles contain sub-points and multiple data points, which means that one could number them in a different way and come up with a larger total coincidence count. For example, in the discussion of Paul's funding in Corinth in Chapter V, I discuss more than one connection between the epistles and Acts—both the more general point about Paul's working with his hands at a trade (alluded to repeatedly in the epistles and named as tent-making in Acts) and a more detailed point concerning what appears to be a change of ministry model in Corinth after the arrival of Paul's associates. Similarly, the discussion of Apollos in Chapter V notes three different data points connecting Apollos as described in Acts with direct or indirect allusions in I Corinthians, yet these are grouped together as a single numbered coincidence. There are several other sections in these chapters that bring together multiple connections between the epistles and Acts. This is worth keeping in mind when trying to gauge the strength of the argument from undesigned coincidences. "How many coincidences are there?" is not an easy question to answer in a cut-and-dried way and hence may not give us the best handle on the force of the case.

I have divided the discussion in Part II into two parts. Chapter V describes coincidences between Acts and the universally acknowledged Pauline Epistles; Chapter VI discusses coincidences between Acts and the other Pauline Epistles. This division is not intended to cast doubt upon the authorship of the second set of epistles, and my calling the second group "other Pauline Epistles" hopefully makes that clear. Nor do I mean to suggest that Christian apologists and scholars should be confined to arguments from what is acknowledged by all or even most contemporary New Testament scholars. (My general conclusion to this book will make that amply clear.) The evidence is what it is, and much of what I am arguing throughout this book, such as my defense of the reliability and memoir status of all four Gospels, is scarcely representative of fashionable New Testament scholarship. I am making this division in Part II both for convenience and for the sake of the reader who wants to know what can be said for Acts when arguing from epistles whose Pauline origin is acknowledged even by non-conservative New Testament scholars.[5] What I call here "universally acknowledged Pauline Epistles" are all within the set that critical New Testament scholar Bart Ehrman calls "undisputed Pauline Epistles." Again, this is not at all because I believe that Ehrman's opinion on the question of Pauline authorship is to be deferred to; the division between the epistles in Chapters V and VI is an organizational device that some readers may find useful.

William Paley, whose *Horae Paulinae* supplied the core of most of the coincidences I will discuss in the next two chapters, uses the coincidences to support both the Pauline origin of the epistles and the veracity of Acts. This is historically and philosophically correct. The existence of a coincidence between Acts and an epistle is an item of data that can point in more than one direction; this puzzle-like fitting between documents gives us reason to believe both that the epistle was written by Paul and that Acts is an historically reliable memoir of the Apostle Paul. My interest here is chiefly in the latter point: The trustworthiness of Acts is evident from an intricate web of connections hidden in plain view.[6]

V

Coincidences Between Acts and the Universally Acknowledged Pauline Epistles

1. "I returned again to Damascus"

This first coincidence between Acts and the epistles involves two separate accounts of events early in the story of Paul. Acts states clearly that Paul's conversion took place on the way to Damascus and that Paul continued on to Damascus after being blinded by his experience:

> Now as he went on his way, he approached Damascus, and suddenly a light from heaven shone around him. And falling to the ground he heard a voice saying to him, "Saul, Saul, why are you persecuting me?" And he said, "Who are you, Lord?" And he said, "I am Jesus, whom you are persecuting. But rise and enter the city, and you will be told what you are to do." The men who were traveling with him stood speechless, hearing the voice but seeing no one. Saul rose from the ground, and although his eyes were opened, he saw nothing. So they led him by the hand and brought him into Damascus. (Acts 9.3–8)

That Acts is accurate in locating Paul's conversion near Damascus and his immediate residence afterwards in Damascus is confirmed in a casual and indirect way by Paul's account in Galatians:

For I would have you know, brothers, that the gospel that was preached by me is not man's gospel. For I did not receive it from any man, nor was I taught it, but I received it through a revelation of Jesus Christ. For you have heard of my former life in Judaism, how I persecuted the church of God violently and tried to destroy it. And I was advancing in Judaism beyond many of my own age among my people, so extremely zealous was I for the traditions of my fathers. But when he who had set me apart before I was born, and who called me by his grace, was pleased to reveal his Son to me, in order that I might preach him among the Gentiles, I did not immediately consult with anyone; nor did I go up to Jerusalem to those who were apostles before me, but I went away into Arabia, and returned again to Damascus. Then after three years I went up to Jerusalem to visit Cephas and remained with him fifteen days. (Gal 1.11–18)

Notice that in this passage Paul never mentions Damascus until *after* the trip into Arabia. One can infer that he had been in Damascus immediately after his conversion only by the statement that, after going into Arabia, he "returned again to Damascus."[1]

It might seem that this is a small matter, but if Acts were ahistorical, written much later, or written by someone who had no reliable access to the story of Paul's conversion, why should the author of Acts place it on the way to Damascus and state that Paul went on to that city afterwards? Why Damascus, of all the possible cities where the conversion story might be placed? Damascus does not even feature prominently in the rest of the book of Acts.

One might conjecture that the author of Acts had access to Galatians and mined Galatians for details to put into his own version of the story and make it sound believable, even if he never knew Paul, were writing later, or were writing a partly fictional history. But here we come up against a point that rules out that hypothesis: The book of Galatians, especially this very passage, has been famously used to argue that the account of Paul's early movements in Galatians *contradicts* the account given in Acts 9. In particular, it is pointed out that Acts 9 never mentions the trip to Arabia, and it is alleged that Acts 9 makes it sound like Paul remained in Damascus the entire time until he was forced to escape over the wall (see the next coincidence). Also, though Paul implies in Galatians that he left Damascus and went to Jerusalem after three years, the notes of time in Acts do not (it is claimed) seem to indicate such a long time period.

The point is not that these and other alleged contradictions between Acts and Galatians are unresolvable or even all that difficult. The author of Acts states that Paul was forced to leave Damascus by a plot against him after "many days" (Acts 9.23), a time indicator that could easily include three years involving a trip to Arabia and a return to Damascus which the author of Acts did not know about or chose not to mention.[2] However, if the author of Acts were *working from* the text of Galatians and attempting to make his own work correspond to Galatians, he would almost certainly not have *inserted* Damascus into his narrative on the basis of Paul's passing remark while *leaving out* any reference to Paul's trip to Arabia or to the passing of three years.[3] Why would the author of Acts have inserted a subtle correspondence with Galatians while leaving out more obvious points that require harmonization? Such an hypothesis requires an author of Acts who is both carefully devious and surprisingly bumbling at the same time.

The casual correspondence concerning Damascus is evidence that the author of Acts knew about Paul independently of the Epistle to the Galatians.

2. Paul's escape from Damascus

Both the book of Acts and one of the Pauline Epistles tell about Paul's escape from Damascus early in his ministry. But they do so in different terms. Acts says,

> When many days had passed, the Jews plotted to kill him, but their plot became known to Saul. They were watching the gates day and night in order to kill him, but his disciples took him by night and let him down through an opening in the wall, lowering him in a basket. (Acts 9.23–25)

In II Corinthians, Paul tells the same story like this:

> At Damascus, the governor under King Aretas was guarding the city of Damascus in order to seize me, but I was let down in a basket through a window in the wall and escaped his hands. (II Cor 11.32–33)

In this coincidence, the two accounts agree on *core facts* while giving notably different *surrounding details*. Both agree that Paul was in danger in Damascus after his conversion and had to be smuggled out of the city by being let down in a basket from the wall. The account in II Corinthians to that extent corroborates the information in Acts.[4]

But was the account in Acts copied from II Corinthians? As with Galatians in the previous coincidence, it seems quite clear that the answer is a resounding, "No." For if the author of Acts were getting his information from II Corinthians and writing his story in that way, why would he have failed to mention the role of the governor (the Greek word in II Corinthians is *ethnarch*) and instead inserted a plot by the Jews, which Paul does not mention? Even if he were being creative and had no great interest in accuracy, one would not expect him to get creative in such a strange way while basing his account on II Corinthians.

As in the previous case, it is not that the accounts are actually in conflict. The *ethnarch* may well have agreed to the Jews' plan in order to make them happy. It may even have been his job to deal specially with Jewish issues.[5] The attempted capture may have been carried out by the forces of the *ethnarch* at the instigation of Jewish enemies of Paul, or the *ethnarch* may have given Paul's Jewish enemies his permission to try to apprehend Paul themselves. In that sense, we can readily regard the accounts as supplementing each other. The point is that the account in Acts looks quite independent of that in II Corinthians. However the author of Acts learned about these events, he picked up a different set of details. So the fact that Acts agrees with II Corinthians supports the conclusion that the author of Acts had his own means of knowing about the facts he relates.

Paley's comment is apt:

> The account in the Epistle of St. Paul's escape from Damascus, though agreeing in the main fact with the account of the same transaction in the Acts, is related with such difference of circumstance, as renders it utterly improbable that one should be derived from the other. ... [I]f we be satisfied, in general, ... that the one was not known to the writer of the other, or not consulted by him; then the accordances which may be pointed out between them, will admit of no solution so probable, as the attributing of them to truth and reality as to their common foundation.[6]

3. Paul of the tribe of Benjamin

In Philippians 3.5–6, Paul gives a list of details about himself which Paley sets aside as being too plainly stated in Acts to participate in undesigned coincidences. Paley is particularly concerned that these facts would have been easy for a forger to collect from

Acts if he were attempting to fake a letter to the Philippians from Paul.[7] Paul says of himself in Philippians,

> If anyone else thinks he has reason for confidence in the flesh, I have more: circumcised on the eighth day, of the people of Israel, of the tribe of Benjamin, a Hebrew of Hebrews; as to the law, a Pharisee; as to zeal, a persecutor of the church; as to righteousness under the law, blameless. (Phil 3.4b–6)

But there is one detail here which fits with Acts in that indirect manner so dear to Paley's own heart. Both in these verses and in Romans 11.1 Paul asserts that he is of the tribe of Benjamin. That can be put together with the following facts: Paul's name prior to his conversion was Saul (Acts 9, throughout). At some point he came to be called Paul (Acts 13.9). The chapters of Acts describing his conversion and the time period thereafter use "Saul" until 13.9, which states that he was also called Paul, and Acts uses "Paul" consistently thereafter. In I Samuel 9.1, we learn that Saul, the first king of Israel, was of the tribe of Benjamin.

While it is by no means a knock-down argument, it is not at all implausible that Paul (formerly Saul) was originally named for the first king of Israel and that his parents were especially likely to do so because Saul was the most famous member of their tribe in Israel's history.[8]

Someone might object that Saul's later negative history—the fact that the Lord eventually rejected him and chose David to replace him as king, his jealousy and long pursuit of David—would make it unlikely that anyone would name a child after him. But there are several responses to this. First, the very fact that Paul was named Saul makes it plausible that he was named after the first king of Israel (or named after someone who was named after the first king) even aside from the knowledge of his tribe. Apparently any intuition we might have that Saul was such a "bad guy" in the Israelite mind that no one would name a child after him is sociologically incorrect. Second, the Old Testament is much less consistently negative about Saul than one might think from memories only of Bible stories about his trying to pin David to the wall with a spear and chasing him about the wilderness. The initial descriptions of Saul in I Samuel 9 emphasize his handsomeness and his great height (9.2) and God's special revelation to Samuel that he has chosen Saul to be king in order to defeat the Philistines (9.16). God stresses to Samuel that the chosen king is from the tribe of Benjamin, which Saul himself describes with humility as the least of the tribes (9.21). When Saul eventually kills himself after defeat by the Philistines (I Sam 31.4) and an Amalekite falsely claims responsibility for his death and brings David his crown and armlet, David is furiously angry. He executes the self-claimed killer and mourns for Saul (II Sam 2.1–27). David's poetic lament for Saul and Jonathan glorifies Saul as a great warrior, likening him to an eagle or a lion (II Sam 1.23). It is not surprising that later descendants of the tribe of Benjamin, proud of their own lineage, would name a son "Saul."

The fact that Paul's former name was Saul is so much a matter of common biblical knowledge that anyone familiar with the New Testament scarcely thinks of it as the kind of thing that can be, or needs to be, confirmed. It is easy to forget that Acts is our *only* primary source for this piece of information. Yet Acts never mentions that Saul/Paul was of the tribe of Benjamin. On the other side, Paul never mentions in any of the epistles, including Philippians and Romans, that his former name was Saul. This is a classic, simple, and subtle undesigned coincidence in which the two items of information from separate sources fit together extremely well, while the absence of any allusion to Paul's tribe in

Acts (which would have been easy enough to insert) disconfirms any idea that the author of Acts was inventing Paul's earlier name on the basis of the brief mentions of his tribe in the epistles.[9]

4. "Shamefully treated at Philippi"
In I Thessalonians 2.2, Paul says,

> But though we had already suffered and been shamefully treated at Philippi, as you know, we had boldness in our God to declare to you the gospel of God in the midst of much conflict.

Here Paul alludes to a time when he was mistreated at Philippi, an incident that, he says, the Thessalonians knew about. What was the incident in Philippi, and how did the Thessalonians know about it?[10]

Paul does allude in his epistles to events in his life that are not recounted anywhere in Acts. It is another sign that the book of Acts was not based on the epistles that the author of Acts does not attempt to tell even more (and more exciting) adventures. II Corinthians 11.24–25 lists more beatings and shipwrecks than are found anywhere in Acts, and the shipwreck Paul discusses there does not appear to be the one described in Acts 27. So by no means should we expect to find in Acts a parallel for all the particular adventures to which Paul happens to allude in the epistles. But if we *do* find a strong candidate for such an event, and if its placement and context in Acts happen to agree in specific ways with what Paul says in an epistle, this is further evidence of the accuracy of Acts.

Acts 16 (which I will not quote at length) tells how Paul and Silas were beaten and thrown into prison in Philippi at the instigation of some annoyed slave owners whose prophetic slave girl they had exorcised. This beating without trial was unlawful (Paul later told the officials of Philippi) because he and Silas were

Roman citizens. Evidently in this incident Paul did not have a chance to head off the beating by making his citizenship known, as he did later in Acts 22. Then comes the well-known story of the earthquake at midnight in which their chains fell off, followed by the conversion of the Philippian jailor. The next morning, Paul asserted his Roman citizenship, wrung an apology from the worried city elders, and went on his way.

> But when it was day, the magistrates sent the police, saying, "Let those men go." And the jailer reported these words to Paul, saying, "The magistrates have sent to let you go. Therefore come out now and go in peace." But Paul said to them, "They have beaten us publicly, uncondemned, men who are Roman citizens, and have thrown us into prison; and do they now throw us out secretly? No! Let them come themselves and take us out." The police reported these words to the magistrates, and they were afraid when they heard that they were Roman citizens. So they came and apologized to them. And they took them out and asked them to leave the city. (Acts 16.35–39)

As I will discuss later in this chapter, Paul's itinerary in this particular journey through the cities of Macedonia and Greece is laid out in some detail in Acts. Both Philippi and Thessalonica were in the province of Macedonia. Map 1, which represents a portion of what is usually known as Paul's second missionary journey, shows the location of these cities (see page 187). Acts implies at the beginning of Chapter 17 that Paul came to Thessalonica not long after the incidents in Philippi.

> Now when they had passed through Amphipolis and Apollonia, they came to Thessalonica, where there was a synagogue of the Jews. And Paul went in, as was his custom, and on three Sabbath days he reasoned with them from the Scriptures, explaining and

proving that it was necessary for the Christ to suffer and to rise from the dead, and saying, "This Jesus, whom I proclaim to you, is the Christ." And some of them were persuaded and joined Paul and Silas, as did a great many of the devout Greeks and not a few of the leading women. (Acts 17.1–4)

This passage fits perfectly with Paul's brief statements in I Thessalonians. In Acts it says that Paul came to Thessalonica on the same missionary journey after his mistreatment in Philippi. Paul knew his rights as a Roman citizen and had been outraged that he had been flogged and imprisoned without trial by the authorities at Philippi. From the phrase "had been treated shamefully at Philippi, as you know" and from the passage in Acts, one can picture Paul telling the story, still full of indignation, to the new converts he made at Thessalonica.

Trouble arose for Paul in Thessalonica as well, which explains Paul's further statement to the Thessalonians that he preached among them "in the midst of much conflict."

But the Jews were jealous, and taking some wicked men of the rabble, they formed a mob, set the city in an uproar, and attacked the house of Jason, seeking to bring them out to the crowd. And when they could not find them, they dragged Jason and some of the brothers before the city authorities, shouting, "These men who have turned the world upside down have come here also, and Jason has received them, and they are all acting against the decrees of Caesar, saying that there is another king, Jesus." And the people and the city authorities were disturbed when they heard these things. And when they had taken money as security from Jason and the rest, they let them go. (Acts 17.5–8)

I will have more to say later about this riot in Thessalonica, which fits with other comments in I Thessalonians.

As with the coincidences between Acts and both Galatians and II Corinthians, so it is here: There is strong evidence that the correspondences are not a result of dependence by the author of Acts on I Thessalonians. From Acts one would most naturally infer that Paul's converts at Thessalonica were all Jews or at least Gentile God-fearers. Acts mentions only Paul's preaching in the synagogue and lists Jews and "devout Greeks" as his converts. There is no mention of Gentiles who were formerly idolaters as being among the converts, unless one takes the "leading women" in this sense. Yet I Thessalonians 1.9 says that the Thessalonians "turned to God from idols to serve the living and true God." If the author of Acts were taking his cues from I Thessalonians and inserting the story of Paul's and Silas's flogging at Philippi and their subsequent travel to Thessalonica in an attempt to make a connection between his book and I Thessalonians, it is highly likely that he would have made it clear that idol-worshipers were also converted at Thessalonica.

Similarly, in I Thessalonians 1.9–10, Paul says that the Thessalonians are his witnesses that he worked night and day to support himself and lived in a holy and blameless way among them, taking no money from them. (I will discuss later the fascinating subject of Paul's funding during this period of his ministry.) One might well infer from this statement that Paul was with them for some time. Yet the only time indication in Acts is the reference to Paul's reasoning in the synagogue on three Sabbaths. To be sure, Acts does not say how long after this it was that the riot occurred and that Paul was forced to leave, so there is no actual contradiction between Acts and I Thessalonians. But if the author of Acts were *basing* his account of Paul's journeys on the epistles, he would in all probability have made a clearer reference to Paul's staying in Thessalonica for a long enough time for them to know and witness his hard work and honesty in money matters.[11]

The correspondences between Acts and I Thessalonians, which confirm Acts, are the result of knowledge independent of Paul's epistles.

5. How did the Philippians know Timothy?

When Paul writes to the Philippians, he says,

> I hope in the Lord Jesus to send Timothy to you soon, so that I too may be cheered by news of you. For I have no one like him, who will be genuinely concerned for your welfare. For they all seek their own interests, not those of Jesus Christ. But you know Timothy's proven worth, how as a son with a father he has served with me in the gospel. (Phil 2.19–22)

From this passage one can infer that the Philippians knew Timothy and had seen him in action as Paul's assistant.

The connection between this passage in Philippians and the book of Acts is particularly subtle and beautiful. At the beginning of Acts 16 (vv 1–3) Paul first begins to travel with Timothy, who is a Christian from the vicinity of Lystra and Iconium. There is no further explicit mention of Timothy in this chapter after the beginning of the journey. (Verses 10 and following contain one of the famous "we" passages in which the author of Acts explicitly indicates that he was with Paul.) The chapter describes Paul's travels in some detail, taking him across Asia Minor to Troas. From there he sails to Macedonia (see Map 1). When Paul reaches Philippi, the narrative describes Paul's missionary efforts in some detail, along with his persecutions, discussed in the previous section. Acts 17 tells how Paul left Philippi, how he came to Thessalonica, how a riot arose there, and how Paul was forced to leave that city.

Then comes this:

The brothers immediately sent Paul and Silas away by night to Berea, and when they arrived they went into the Jewish synagogue. Now these Jews were more noble than those in Thessalonica; they received the word with all eagerness, examining the Scriptures daily to see if these things were so. Many of them therefore believed, with not a few Greek women of high standing as well as men. But when the Jews from Thessalonica learned that the word of God was proclaimed by Paul at Berea also, they came there too, agitating and stirring up the crowds. Then the brothers immediately sent Paul off on his way to the sea, but *Silas and Timothy remained there*. Those who conducted Paul brought him as far as Athens, and after receiving a command for Silas and Timothy to come to him as soon as possible, they departed. (Acts 17.10–15, emphasis added)

Here, then, is Timothy with Paul at Berea after all the travels from the region in Asia Minor where Paul first picked him up.[12] Though Silas is the most prominent of Paul's companions on this journey, Acts implies that Paul had more companions than Silas—the author himself, for one. Acts 16.1 gives the impression that Paul intended to travel with Timothy for an extended period. It certainly looks like Timothy went with Paul all along, though unmentioned for some time in Acts, through the various cities, until Timothy was eventually left behind temporarily with Silas when the Christians hustled Paul out of Berea for his safety. But if that is true, it follows that Timothy was with Paul during his missionary work in Philippi.

This, then, explains how the Philippians knew Timothy's proven worth and how they had seen Timothy labor with Paul as a son with a father. But see how indirect the connection is! Acts never states that Timothy was with Paul at Philippi. One must *infer* it from other statements about Timothy in Acts—from the point where Timothy was taken along by Paul on his missionary travels in Acts 16 and from the later statement that Silas and Timothy were left behind at Berea. It would be absurd to suppose that the author of Acts deliberately inserted these references to Timothy in order to imply, roundabout, that Timothy was in Philippi and thereby connect Acts with the epistle. In the unlikely event that the author wished to give his book verisimilitude by connecting it with that verse in Philippians, he would have inserted an explicit reference to Timothy's devoted work with Paul *in Philippi.* As it stands, the connection serves as yet another piece of evidence that, as the "we" passage itself implies, the author of Acts was closely acquainted with the Apostle Paul and knew his companions and his movements at this time.

Paley puts the point well.

> [W]hat I wish to be observed is, that in comparing, upon this subject, the Epistle with the history, we do not find a recital in one place of what is related in another; but that we find, what is much more to be relied upon, an oblique allusion to an implied fact.[13]

6. Who caused the trouble in Thessalonica?

Paul tells the Thessalonians,

> For you, brothers, became imitators of the churches of God in Christ Jesus that are in Judea. For you suffered the same things from your own countrymen as they did from the Jews... (I Thess 2.14)

I have already noted the interesting fact that Paul appears in I Thessalonians to be writing to a largely Gentile audience, converted from paganism, despite the fact that in Acts the emphasis is upon converts in Thessalonica from among the Jews and God-fearers.

Here Paul implies that the Thessalonians are in danger of persecution from their "own countrymen" rather than from the Jews.

Then he continues in a short rant against his Jewish persecutors:

> ...who killed both the Lord Jesus and the prophets, and drove
> us out, and displease God and oppose all mankind by hindering
> us from speaking to the Gentiles that they might be saved...
> (I Thess 2.15–16)

Here Paul implies that it was a Jewish group that drove him out of Thessalonica, and he specifically accuses them of hindering him from speaking to the Gentiles. In this compressed account, he assigns a role in the troubles in Thessalonica both to the Gentiles and to the Jews, implying that the Thessalonians are in danger from their fellow Gentiles but that in some way a group of Jews has also been involved.

F.F. Bruce points out that this anger against the Jews is uncharacteristic of Paul, either as portrayed in Acts or in the epistles.[14] Paul was at pains to urge that he loved his own nation and did not wish to accuse them and that he prayed constantly for their salvation (e.g., Rom 10.1ff, Acts 28.19). Bruce concludes that this unusually bitter digression in I Thessalonians requires a circumstantial explanation concerning some *particular* group of Jews who have done something that has especially enraged Paul. This explanation, as Bruce says, is precisely what we find in the full account in Acts.

Paul, of course, did not need to explain everything to the Thessalonians. They knew the circumstances well enough, but Acts fills in corresponding details. Acts 17, quoted in #4, says that the Jews agitated the crowds, presumably the Gentile crowds, in Thessalonica by spreading a rumor that Paul was teaching sedition against Caesar. According to Acts, the mob dragged some Christians before the (Gentile) city authorities, who demanded a peace bond from Jason and the other Christians. Immediately thereafter, Paul left the city.

All of this makes perfect sense in terms of the politics of the time. Outside of the distinctively Jewish territories of the Roman Empire, it was more difficult for Jewish agitators to persecute Paul or Gentile Christians *directly*. They thus had to attempt to stir up the larger Gentile populace of a city. Acts 17 states that they did this in Thessalonica and then followed Paul to Berea and used this same tactic there. So in Thessalonica the Christians suffered from "their own countrymen" rather than (directly) from the Jews, but Paul also had grounds for indignation against Jewish persecutors who in effect "drove him out" of that city and other cities because they did not want him to share his message with the Gentiles. (See also Acts 13.50, 15.2–6, 15.19, and 18.12–17.) It seems to be this incessant hounding that so angered Paul and occasioned his strong language in I Thessalonians. These persecutors were not content with stopping his preaching to the Jews but pursued him from city to city and tried to prevent him from speaking to the Gentiles as well.

The complexity of the Thessalonian situation and of the persecution faced by Paul and the Thessalonians, hinted at by Paul's comments in the epistle, is thus well-explained by Acts. At the same time, the considerations already discussed make it clear that the story of Paul's work in Thessalonica as given in Acts is independent from the epistle of I Thessalonians.[15]

7. Paul's funding in Corinth[16]

It is one of the distinctive personality traits of the Apostle Paul, a trait that emerges repeatedly in the epistles and occasionally in Acts, that he is touchy about money. He frequently says things designed to refute any suspicion that he is in the ministry for what he can get out of it. In both I Thessalonians 2.9 and II Thessalonians 3.8 Paul emphasizes that he worked night and day so as not to be a financial burden on the Thessalonians when he was with them. In I Corinthians 4.12 Paul emphasizes that up to the time of writing he is working with his own hands to support himself.[17] In II Corinthians 7.2 he stresses that he has never exploited the Corinthians financially.

One of Paul's passionate protestations concerning money occurs II Corinthians:

> Or did I commit a sin in humbling myself so that you might be exalted, because I preached God's gospel to you free of charge? I robbed other churches by accepting support from them in order to serve you. And when I was with you and was in need, I did not burden anyone, for the brothers who came from Macedonia supplied my need. So I refrained and will refrain from burdening you in any way. (II Cor 11.7–9)

From this one infers that some money was delivered to Paul from Macedonia while he was working in Corinth.

This point also comes up when Paul praises the Philippians, harking back to his first association with them:

> And you Philippians yourselves know that in the beginning of the gospel, when I left Macedonia, no church entered into partnership with me in giving and receiving, except you only. Even in Thessalonica you sent me help for my needs once and again. (Phil 4.15–16)

Both Philippi and Thessalonica are in the province of Macedonia (see Map 1), but Corinth is, of course, in Greece. Its region was called Achaia at that time. When Paul traveled from Philippi to Thessalonica and eventually to Corinth (precisely the journey recorded in Acts 16–18), he would have been leaving Macedonia by way of Thessalonica. We can therefore reasonably infer from Philippians as well as from II Corinthians that, during the journey recounted in these chapters in Acts, Paul received money from Macedonia after leaving that province.[18]

The description of Paul's first work in Corinth given in Acts fits well with these passages in one direct way and in one even more subtle and fascinating way. First of all, Acts tells how Paul worked with his hands.

> After this Paul left Athens and went to Corinth. And he found a Jew named Aquila, a native of Pontus, recently come from Italy with his wife Priscilla, because Claudius had commanded all the Jews to leave Rome. And he went to see them, and because he was of the same trade he stayed with them and worked, for they were tentmakers by trade. (Acts 18.1–3)

This is significant in itself, since the epistles imply repeatedly that Paul worked at some physical trade but never specify what it was.[19]

As the passage continues, a more detailed connection to the epistles emerges. I will quote the next two verses of Acts 18 in three different translations—first in the King James Version, then in the ESV, and finally in the NASB:

> And he reasoned in the synagogue every sabbath, and persuaded the Jews and the Greeks. And when Silas and Timotheus were come from Macedonia, Paul was pressed in the spirit, and testified to the Jews that Jesus was Christ. (Acts 18.4–5, KJV)

> And he reasoned in the synagogue every Sabbath, and tried to persuade Jews and Greeks. When Silas and Timothy arrived from Macedonia, Paul was occupied with the word, testifying to the Jews that the Christ was Jesus. (Acts 18.4–5, ESV)

> And he was reasoning in the synagogue every Sabbath and trying to persuade Jews and Greeks. But when Silas and Timothy came down from Macedonia, Paul began devoting himself completely to the word, solemnly testifying to the Jews that Jesus was the Christ. (Acts 18.4–5, NASB)

The King James translation is derived from a different text family from the other two translations. The difference is that the word "spirit" occurs in the text family from which the KJV is derived but the word "word" occurs in the same place in the text family from which the more modern translations are derived. This substitution occurs in the sentence concerning Paul's being "pressed" or "occupied"—was he pressed or occupied in *spirit* or in/with the *word*?

There are also different choices that can be made in translating the words that are the same in all text families. The verb that describes Paul's state of mind ("pressed," "occupied," "devoted") after Silas and Timothy arrived (*syneicheto*) can mean different things. It might mean "pressed," "crowded," (Luke 8.45) or "held" (Luke 22.63) and sometimes has a medical meaning, as when one is taken or oppressed by a sickness (Acts 28.8). *The Pulpit Commentary* (in loc.) points out that this verb as used here should perhaps be considered to indicate something going on continuously.[20] The NASB translation seems, in the light of all these considerations, quite literal.

What these verses convey is that Paul became *particularly* dedicated to preaching after the arrival of Silas and Timothy from Macedonia. Why should this be? It is difficult to imagine a person more continuously dedicated at all times to preaching than the Apostle Paul! Why should the arrival of Timothy and Silas make any difference?

If, however, one takes these verses together with the earlier verses about Paul's tentmaking craft, a clearer picture emerges:

Prior to the arrival of Silas and Timothy, Paul works during the week at tentmaking and dedicates himself to preaching only on the Sabbath, when manual labor is forbidden to him as a Jew. After Silas and Timothy arrive, he is suddenly able to devote himself to preaching all the time and no longer has to work at his trade. What this suggests is that Silas and Timothy *brought money to Paul from Macedonia.*

This is exactly what Paul says in II Corinthians—that money came to him in Corinth from Macedonia with some Christian brothers. And, since Philippi was in Macedonia, this also fits with Paul's praise of the Philippians for having sent him money after he left Macedonia. This money may well have come originally from Philippi and may have been sent after him with Timothy and Silas.[21]

This wonderfully indirect confirmation of Acts would have been more difficult for William Paley to see because both the Greek text family that has "word" instead of "spirit" and other translations of verse 5 were unavailable to him. The coincidence is particularly clear from the NASB.

As we shall see later, this is not the only situation in which a financial transaction is taking place during some time period but is left out in Acts. The author of Acts may not even have known that Timothy and Silas brought money to Paul. The delicacy of the confirmation is its greatest strength. Acts does not state that money came from Macedonia with Paul's co-workers, yet the hypothesis that it did both explains Acts and coincides perfectly with the epistles.

8. The character and activities of Apollos

We should not expect that Acts would mention all the fellow-workers Paul discusses in his epistles. To the contrary, the fact that Acts leaves out some of those Paul mentions is further evidence of the independence of Acts from the epistles. The most striking of these omissions is Titus, who figures importantly in II Corinthians but never once comes up in Acts.[22]

But as I will show in this chapter and the next, when Acts does mention the same people mentioned in the epistles, the minute yet unforced correspondences between what Acts tells and what emerges from the epistles is an important confirmation of the accuracy of Acts and of the association of the author of Acts with Paul. Such is the case with Apollos.

In the First Epistle to the Corinthians Paul repeatedly mentions someone named Apollos, stressing his and Apollos's agreement as servants of Christ and insisting that the Christians should not break up into factions centered on, among others, himself and Apollos.

> For it has been reported to me by Chloe's people that there is quarreling among you, my brothers. What I mean is that each one of you says, "I follow Paul," or "I follow Apollos," or "I follow Cephas," or "I follow Christ." Is Christ divided? Was Paul crucified for you? Or were you baptized in the name of Paul? (I Cor 1.11–13)

> For when one says, "I follow Paul," and another, "I follow Apollos," are you not being merely human? What then is Apollos? What is Paul? Servants through whom you believed, as the Lord assigned to each. I planted, Apollos watered, but God gave the growth. So neither he who plants nor he who waters is anything, but only God who gives the growth. (I Cor 3.3–7)

The sentence, "I planted, Apollos watered, but God gave the growth" shows Paul's ability to make a proverb. The sentence also implies, as a fact already known to the Corinthians, that Paul worked in Corinth *first* and that Apollos came later and "watered" what Paul had "planted."

This is exactly what Acts implies. Paul's initial ministry in Corinth occurs early in Acts 18. Afterwards, Paul travels to Ephesus, leaves Priscilla and Aquila there, and goes on further journeys of his own. It is while Paul is elsewhere, at the end of Acts 18, that Apollos comes to Ephesus and receives instruction in the new Christian doctrines:

> Now a Jew named Apollos, a native of Alexandria, came to Ephesus. He was an eloquent man, competent in the Scriptures. He had been instructed in the way of the Lord. And being fervent in spirit, he spoke and taught accurately the things concerning Jesus, though he knew only the baptism of John. He began to speak boldly in the synagogue, but when Priscilla and Aquila heard him, they took him aside and explained to him the way of God more accurately. And when he wished to cross to Achaia, the brothers encouraged him and wrote to the disciples to welcome him. When he arrived, he greatly helped those who through grace had believed, for he powerfully refuted the Jews in public, showing by the Scriptures that the Christ was Jesus. And it happened that while Apollos was at Corinth, Paul passed through the inland country and came to Ephesus. (Acts 18.24–19.1a)

This passage indicates that Apollos, having been convinced that Jesus was the Messiah, eventually decided to go to Corinth and that he had a popular and fruitful ministry there. This, of course, was *after* Paul's initial work in that city, just as I Corinthians says—Paul planted, and Apollos watered. Acts does not belabor the point. It simply tells a story in which, as it happens, Apollos ends up working at Corinth after Paul's initial church-planting work. It would be highly implausible to conjecture that the author of Acts *made up* this string of comings and goings for Apollos and Paul in order to fit his narrative with the unstated implication of Paul's proverbial comment in the epistle. Rather, the author of Acts knew these facts about Apollos and Paul independently; they fit together with what Paul says in the epistle because both are founded on truth. This type of connection is what one would expect if the epistle and the history are both accurate records of the same people's activities at the same period.[23]

But there is more. Repeatedly in I Corinthians Paul makes defensive-sounding statements about his own lack of worldly eloquence, making something like a theological virtue out of it. One of these passages even occurs in the context of his concern over their factionalism:

> I thank God that I baptized none of you except Crispus and Gaius, so that no one may say that you were baptized in my name. (I did baptize also the household of Stephanas. Beyond that, I do not know whether I baptized anyone else.) For Christ did not send me to baptize but to preach the gospel, and not with words of eloquent wisdom, lest the cross of Christ be emptied of its power. (I Cor 1.14–17)

> And I, when I came to you, brothers, did not come proclaiming to you the testimony of God with lofty speech or wisdom. For I decided to know nothing among you except Jesus Christ and him crucified. And I was with you in weakness and in fear and much trembling, and my speech and my message were not in plausible words of wisdom, but in demonstration of the Spirit and of power, so that your faith might not rest in the wisdom of men but in the power of God. (I Cor 2.1–5)

It is not much of a stretch to infer that, in the factional strife in the Corinthian church, those who criticized Paul were focusing on the fact that he was neither impressive in person nor eloquent, in contrast to their preferred speaker, Apollos. These comments of Paul's fit with the account in Acts of Apollos as "an eloquent man" whose gifts were especially appreciated in Corinth.[24]

One more point in Paul's epistles to the Corinthians confirms the account of Apollos in Acts. In II Corinthians Paul is even more frustrated by the feeling that his ministry has been disparaged, and he emphasizes his authority with the believers at Corinth based on the fact that they are his own converts:

> Are we beginning to commend ourselves again? Or do we need, as some do, letters of recommendation to you, or from you? You yourselves are our letter of recommendation, written on our hearts, to be known and read by all. And you show that you are a letter from Christ delivered by us, written not with ink but with the Spirit of the living God, not on tablets of stone but on tablets of human hearts. (II Cor 3.1–3)

This comment dovetails with the statement in Acts that, when Apollos first went *to Corinth*, he was sent with letters of recommendation from the believers at Ephesus. It is possible that Paul does not have Apollos personally in mind when writing this in II Corinthians. In that case, the verse fits with Acts by alluding to letters of recommendation as a practice in the early church. But there is also plausibility to the suggestion that some in the Corinthian church were still comparing Paul with Apollos and that Paul, though not wishing to attack Apollos, nonetheless in his frustration alludes to the fact that he, unlike "some," does not need such letters to commend himself.

9. "If Timothy comes…"

For the next three coincidences I will discuss, maps will be especially important; Map 2 is designed to help with the current number (see page 188). I begin with the fact that, in I Corinthians, Paul speaks as if he has already sent Timothy to the church at Corinth prior to writing the epistle:

> That is why I sent you Timothy, my beloved and faithful child in the Lord, to remind you of my ways in Christ, as I teach them everywhere in every church. (I Cor 4.17, ESV)

> Now if Timothy comes, see that he is with you without cause to be afraid, for he is doing the Lord's work, as I also am. (I Cor 16.10, NASB)

I have given the NASB translation of the second verse rather than the ESV (which I am usually using), because the Greek translated "if Timothy comes" in the NASB (and similarly in the King James Version) is translated as "when Timothy comes" in the ESV. For various reasons, the translation "if" seems to be the better one, though this coincidence does not depend heavily upon it.[25] In either event, the clear implication is that Timothy is on his way but that Paul does not expect Timothy to arrive until *after the letter*. Therefore, he can give instructions to the Corinthians *in the letter* about how they are to treat Timothy.

This gives a rather specific indication about the writing of I Corinthians. It seems to have been written after Paul had sent Timothy on a journey that he thought would or might take him eventually to Corinth. But Paul expected his letter to get to Corinth before Timothy did. Further evidence from the epistle shows that Paul probably wrote it from Ephesus:

> I will visit you after passing through Macedonia, for I intend to pass through Macedonia, and perhaps I will stay with you or even spend the winter, so that you may help me on my journey, wherever I go. For I do not want to see you now just in passing. I hope to spend some time with you, if the Lord permits. But I will

stay in Ephesus until Pentecost, for a wide door for effective work has opened to me, and there are many adversaries. (I Cor 16.5–9)

In a particularly lovely connection, it is possible to pinpoint, with the help of a little geography, a moment in the narrative in Acts that would make all these conditions come together.

Now after these events Paul resolved in the Spirit to pass through Macedonia and Achaia and go to Jerusalem, saying, "After I have been there, I must also see Rome." And having sent into Macedonia two of his helpers, Timothy and Erastus, he himself stayed in Asia for a while. (Acts 19.21–22)

This passage provides an apt point for the writing of I Corinthians for many reasons. First, Paul's own proposed itinerary corresponds in the two passages. In I Corinthians, Paul intends to come to Corinth from Ephesus by way of Macedonia. In other words, he intends, after Pentecost, to take the overland route from Ephesus to Corinth. In Acts, Paul has the same intended journey in mind—to pass through Macedonia and eventually on south to Achaia, of which Corinth was a principal city.

Second, at just this point in Acts Paul sends Timothy and Erastus ahead of him into Macedonia. Acts does not say that Paul told Timothy to pass on to Achaia (Greece) after going through Macedonia. The author of Acts may well not have known all of Paul's plans for Timothy. And any lack of certainty about Timothy's eventual itinerary would fit with the slight uncertainty in Paul's phrase in I Corinthians, "If Timothy comes…" Timothy's approximate route from Ephesus to Corinth, overland through Macedonia, is marked on Map 2.

Timothy, then, would have eventually traveled to Corinth in a somewhat roundabout fashion. But there is a direct sea route from

Ephesus to Corinth by which Paul could have sent his epistle.[26] Howson also notes the external point that Ephesus and Corinth were both major centers of trade and that, with a good wind, a letter could travel from Ephesus to Corinth fairly quickly.[27] In fact, it is presumably because of the existence of this shorter sea route that Paul emphasizes in I Corinthians 16.5 that he plans to go to Corinth only *after* going through Macedonia rather than going directly from Ephesus (by sea). Otherwise they might have expected him to arrive sooner. But he almost certainly sent his letter by the fastest way.

This was typical of Paul's concern for his converts. He wrote to them incessantly, sometimes repeatedly (I and II Thessalonians appear to have been written close together), and was sometimes in anguish until he heard back from them. II Corinthians (2.12,13, 7.5–8) shows this pattern in particular concerning the Corinthians. Paul tells there how anxious he was until he met with Titus who brought him word of how they were responding to the earlier letter—that is, the letter we know as I Corinthians. It is therefore extremely plausible, based on the epistles alone, that Paul sent I Corinthians from Ephesus to Corinth by the fastest route possible.[28] This beautifully brings together the implications of both the epistle and Acts, providing strong reason to believe that Paul wrote I Corinthians from Ephesus after making these plans and sending Timothy ahead, at about Acts 19.22 when he "stayed in Asia for a while."[29]

Another clue makes Acts 19.22 a highly plausible point for the writing of I Corinthians. Acts 20.1–3 states that Paul, after traveling through Macedonia (a journey about which I will have more to say in the next section) came to Greece and stayed there for three months. This three-month period fits well with Paul's suggestion in I Corinthians 16.6 that he may spend the next winter in Corinth when he comes.[30]

These connections between Acts and the Corinthian epistles are simultaneously so precise and so subtle that they provide especially exciting confirmation of the reliability of Acts. It appears that the author of Acts had accurate information not only about Paul's actions and those of his companions but even sometimes about his plans for future travel. Yet he does not seem to have known all of the reasons for Paul's actions or everything that was on his mind, just as could well be the case with a companion.[31]

The next two coincidences concern the same period of Paul's life and show the same level of minute accuracy on the part of the author of Acts; they also further support my conclusions here about the time at which I Corinthians was written.

10. The collection for the church at Jerusalem

I have argued in the previous section that Paul wrote I Corinthians around the time of Acts 19.22 and that our ability to place it there by clues in the Pauline Epistles is evidence for the reliability of Acts. Even more evidence for the detailed accuracy of Acts comes from further clues in Romans, I Corinthians, and II Corinthians about a collection Paul was taking up for the Christians in Jerusalem.[32] Each of these epistles can be placed in Acts with precision by way of these clues, and the epistles make it clear that Paul's mind was much occupied with the collection. Yet, astonishingly, Acts *never mentions* that Paul was taking up a collection at this point in his journeys and alludes only once to the fact that Paul brought alms to Jerusalem.

In Romans, Paul describes a collection of money that he has recently gathered and his intention to take it to Jerusalem.

> At present, however, I am going to Jerusalem bringing aid to the saints. For Macedonia and Achaia have been pleased to make some contribution for the poor among the saints at Jeru-

salem. For they were pleased to do it, and indeed they owe it to them. For if the Gentiles have come to share in their spiritual blessings, they ought also to be of service to them in material blessings. (Rom 15.25–27)

Romans, then, was written at a time when Paul had recently finished gathering a collection from Macedonia and Achaia and was planning to go to Jerusalem to deliver the money.

Backing up in time, II Corinthians appears to have been written at a time when Paul was in Macedonia, had collected money there, and was planning to come to Corinth (in Achaia) from there, expecting (or at least hoping) that the Corinthians would have their portion of the collection ready.

> We want you to know, brothers, about the grace of God that has been given among the churches of Macedonia, for in a severe test of affliction, their abundance of joy and their extreme poverty have overflowed in a wealth of generosity on their part. For they gave according to their means, as I can testify, and beyond their means, of their own accord, begging us earnestly for the favor of taking part in the relief of the saints… (II Cor 8.1–4)

Paul, a canny fundraiser, first brags to the Corinthians about the Macedonians and then tells them that he has been bragging to the Macedonians about them, that he plans to bring some Macedonians with him when he comes to Corinth, and that he wouldn't want the Corinthians to be embarrassed by not being ready with their offering:

> Now it is superfluous for me to write to you about the ministry for the saints, for I know your readiness, of which I boast about you to the people of Macedonia, saying that Achaia has been ready since last year. And your zeal has stirred up most of them. But I am sending the brothers so that our boasting about you may not

prove empty in this matter, so that you may be ready, as I said you would be. Otherwise, if some Macedonians come with me and find that you are not ready, we would be humiliated—to say nothing of you—for being so confident. So I thought it necessary to urge the brothers to go on ahead to you and arrange in advance for the gift you have promised, so that it may be ready as a willing gift, not as an exaction. (II Cor 9.1–5)

II Corinthians also indicates that Paul had traveled to Macedonia from Asia Minor, just as one would expect given that he started from Ephesus.

When I came to Troas to preach the gospel of Christ, even though a door was opened for me in the Lord, my spirit was not at rest because I did not find my brother Titus there. So I took leave of them and went on to Macedonia. (II Cor 2.12–13)

Troas is directly along the overland route from Ephesus to Macedonia.

Backing up yet again in time, I have argued in the previous section that I Corinthians was apparently written shortly *before* Paul traveled to Macedonia. He expresses in I Corinthians his intention (I Cor 16.5ff) to go to Macedonia and to come into Achaia (to Corinth) from there. Paul is also thinking about the collection in I Corinthians 16, where he gives specific instructions to the church at Corinth about getting the collection ready so that there will be no hasty gathering up when he arrives.

Now concerning the collection for the saints: as I directed the churches of Galatia, so you also are to do. On the first day of every week, each of you is to put something aside and store it up, as he may prosper, so that there will be no collecting when I come. And when I arrive, I will send those whom you accredit by letter to carry your gift to Jerusalem. If it seems advisable that I should go also, they will accompany me. (I Cor 16.1–4)[33]

At the time of writing I Corinthians Paul does not yet know whether the churches will want him to be responsible for escorting the money to Jerusalem. This point has been settled by the time that he writes Romans.

Acts agrees perfectly with this entire order of travel, without mentioning fund-raising as a purpose of the journey. As already noted, in Acts 19.22 Paul sketches out an intended itinerary for himself—traveling from Ephesus overland to Macedonia, from there into Achaia, and from there to Jerusalem. In fact, Acts 19.22 says that at that time he also intends to go on to Rome, which is confirmed in Romans as well (Rom 15.22, 28). (As it turned out in the end, his journey to Rome from Jerusalem was made as a prisoner, which was presumably not what he was hoping for.)

Not only Paul's intentions but also his actions coincide in Acts and the epistles, for Acts 20.1 says that Paul left Ephesus (after the riot), traveled north and west to and through Macedonia (a point which coincides with his passing through Troas as noted in II Corinthians 2.12), eventually came down into Greece, stayed in Greece for three months, and was planning to leave for Syria (see Map 3, page 189).

> After the uproar ceased, Paul sent for the disciples, and after encouraging them, he said farewell and departed for Macedonia. When he had gone through those regions and had given them much encouragement, he came to Greece. There he spent three months, and when a plot was made against him by the Jews as he was about to set sail for Syria, he decided to return through Macedonia. (Acts 20.1–3)

Syria was the name of the Roman province where Jerusalem was located. So Paul was intending to sail from Greece, the location of Corinth, to Syria and travel to Jerusalem, which fits perfectly with his carrying the alms from the regions he had just visited to the Christians at Jerusalem.

As I have already argued, Paul wrote I Corinthians toward the end of his stay in Ephesus, around Acts 19.22. At that time he was urging the Corinthians to get the collection ready. But now we can say more. Paul apparently wrote II Corinthians during his time in Macedonia—hence, at approximately Acts 20.1–2. And the writing of Romans fits perfectly at the end of the three months in Greece mentioned in Acts 20.3 (probably the winter Paul spent with the Corinthians), when Paul was preparing to take the collected money to Jerusalem. All of these placements in Acts are supported by clues relating to the collection taking place during this time, which Acts does not mention.

Acts says that, due to a plot against him, Paul had to go to Jerusalem by going back overland, and Acts 20–21 goes over that route in detail. Eventually, according to Acts, Paul did arrive in Jerusalem in Acts 21.17ff and there met with the church leaders. The Jews in Jerusalem were opposed to Paul, and a riot against him in the Temple led to his being taken into protective custody by the Roman soldiers, which turned into imprisonment (Acts 21.27ff). This imprisonment sets off the story that occupies the rest of Acts—Paul's imprisonment in Caesarea, his appeal to Caesar, and his eventual journey to Rome as a prisoner. In Acts 24 Paul is a prisoner in Caesarea making his defense before the governor Felix, and there we find the one and only, highly indirect, allusion in Acts to the collection for Jerusalem:

> Now after several years I came to bring alms to my nation and to present offerings. (Acts 24.17)

Paul, a master of rhetorical care, refrains from stating that the members of his nation to whom he was bringing alms were Jewish *Christians*. This comment by Paul in Acts creates a garden-variety undesigned coincidence between the epistles and Acts, confirming the accuracy of the record of Paul's speech in Acts 24. But the coincidence there is only one part of the whole story; in the larger picture, a host of geographical and other correspondences concerning the collection confirm Paul's travels as described over several chapters of Acts.

The connections between these portions of Acts and the epistles are so minute that there can be little doubt about at least the approximate relations between the events described in Acts and those alluded to in the epistles. Yet they are so indirect that there can be no question of their being the result of design on the part of the author of Acts. This is strong confirmation that the author of Acts knew a great deal about what Paul was doing during this time period but that, as is the normal way with truthful witnesses, he and Paul had different emphases and interests in what they wrote. Paley's comment about the placement of Romans in Acts is applicable to the argument as a whole.

> Here, therefore, ... fetched from three different writings, we
> have obtained the several circumstances...which the Epistle to
> the Romans brings together, namely, a contribution in Achaia for
> the Christians at Jerusalem; a contribution in Macedonia for the
> same; and an approaching journey of St. Paul to Jerusalem. We
> have these circumstances—each by some hint in the passage...
> or by the date of the writing in which the passage occurs—fixed
> to a particular time; and we have that time turning out, upon ex-
> amination, to be in all the *same*; namely, towards the close of St.
> Paul's second visit to the peninsula of Greece. This is an instance
> of conformity beyond the possibility ... of random writing to pro-

duce. I also assert, that it is in the highest degree improbable that it should have been the effect of contrivance and design.[34]

11. "All the way around to Illyricum"

Paul gives the Romans a geographical summary of his missionary work up to the time of his writing the epistle:

> For I will not venture to speak of anything except what Christ has accomplished through me to bring the Gentiles to obedience—by word and deed, by the power of signs and wonders, by the power of the Spirit of God—so that from Jerusalem and all the way around to Illyricum I have fulfilled the ministry of the gospel of Christ; (Rom 15.18–19)

Everyone knows where Jerusalem is, but where was Illyricum? As Map 3 shows, Illyricum was a province to the northwest of Macedonia. Its southern portion was approximately where northern Albania is today. Just a few verses later, Paul tells the Romans that he hopes to visit Rome and eventually to go to Spain, which was yet further west than either Illyricum or Rome. It seems that in this passage Paul is giving both an eastern and a northwestern reference point (Jerusalem and Illyricum) indicating approximately the geographical sweep of his ministry thus far, followed immediately by his hopes to travel farther west still, to Rome and Spain.

I have already gone over independent evidence that the writing of Romans occurred around the time of Acts 20.3 while Paul was staying in Greece. Here is a fascinating additional geographical point: During that same journey in Acts, just before the point where I have placed the writing of Romans, there would indeed have been an opportunity for Paul to have traveled as far northwest as Illyricum, but in his earlier journey to Macedonia recorded in Acts, there appears to be no such opportunity.[35]

Acts 20.2 describes this second journey of Paul through Macedonia in general terms. "When he had gone through those regions and had given them much encouragement, he came to Greece." The Greek, literally, for "given them much encouragement" is something like "...having exhorted them with much talk..." (The Holman version translation is, "...when he had passed through those areas and exhorted them at length, he came to Greece.") Given the wording concerning Paul's travel and the emphasis on his "much talk," it is entirely possible that Paul traveled around in Macedonia during this time and got as far as its northwestern border with Illyricum, which would allow him to list Illyricum as the farthest western limit of his ministry thus far in the letter he wrote shortly after to the Romans. I have indicated the uncertainty and possible wideness of Paul's travel through Macedonia on this journey in Map 3.

In contrast, when Paul went through Macedonia on the second missionary journey in Acts 16.9–17.15, no such general expressions occur. Paul's travel in those chapters is charted quite precisely along the *eastern* edge of Macedonia, with the cities named one by one. (See Map 1.) On that journey, according to Acts, Paul left for Macedonia from Troas (Acts 16.11) and landed at Samothrace. From there on the next day they went to Neapolis, then to Philippi (where the events discussed in #4 took place). Thence Paul traveled to Amphipolis and Apollonia and on to Thessalonica (17.1–2). Forced to leave Thessalonica by the uprising discussed in #6, they went to Berea (Acts 17.10). Hustled out of Berea when further trouble arose, Paul was escorted firmly down to Athens by believers concerned for his safety (17.15). It seems quite clear that the author of Acts has left no room for a visit "all the way around to Illyricum" in his account of *that* journey through Macedonia.

How perfect, then, to find that there *is* space for wider travel in the journey recorded briefly in Acts 20.2, just before the writing of Romans. This is often called "Paul's third missionary journey," and Bible maps sometimes show it as following precisely the same course through Macedonia as Paul's second missionary journey. But in fact Acts 20.2 does not say that he followed that same course along the eastern edge of Macedonia. It is understandable that map-makers should not attempt to indicate this uncertainty, and no doubt Paul did visit the churches in Macedonia that he had founded previously and gave them, among others, much exhortation. But while he was "going through those regions," Paul with his tireless missionary zeal might well have ventured further in Macedonia than before, going "all the way around to Illyricum"—that is, at least as far as the border on the northwest between Macedonia and Illyricum.

Yet nothing could be more indirect than this confirmation of Acts. Acts makes no mention whatsoever of Illyricum in Acts 20. It is so implausible as not to deserve serious consideration that the author of Acts would have listed Paul's itinerary so tightly in an *earlier* journey in Chapters 16–17 and left it vague on this *second* journey through Macedonia in Chapter 20 *just because* he wanted to leave room in the Chapter 20 for Paul to travel "all the way around to Illyricum" as mentioned in Romans. If the author of Acts were contriving a journey to fit with this passing geographical indication in Romans, he would state openly that Paul traveled as far northwest as Illyricum on his second trip through Macedonia. Any hypothesis of clever contrivance is rendered all the more wildly implausible (if possible) by the fact that the dating of Romans to the early verses of Acts 20 is an inference from *other* indirect evidence.

12. Priscilla and Aquila and the greetings in
I Corinthians and Romans

Having laid the groundwork in the previous sections for locating the epistles of I Corinthians, II Corinthians, and Romans in relation to the events in the book of Acts, I can now more easily present a fascinating set of coincidences concerning Paul's fellow workers Priscilla and Aquila, mentioned multiple times in both Acts and the Pauline Epistles.

According to Acts, Paul first meets Priscilla and Aquila in Corinth in Acts 18. They have traveled there after being expelled from Rome by the emperor Claudius, who ordered all Jews to leave Rome. Paul works with them at tent-making, a craft I have discussed above in the section on Paul's funding in Corinth. They travel on with Paul, eventually arriving in Ephesus, where they stay for an unspecified time while Paul goes on further travels. While in Ephesus without Paul, Priscilla and Aquila meet Apollos and teach him the full truth of Christianity at the end of Acts 18, after which he travels to Corinth. This is the last mention of them in Acts. Paul eventually returns to Ephesus and has a ministry there for several years in Acts 19.

Paul mentions Aquila and Priscilla three times in the greetings of his letters, but one of these occurs in II Timothy, which appears to have been written after the end of Acts and is not relevant to the coincidences I am discussing here.[36] In I Corinthians, Paul sends greetings *from* Aquila and Priscilla to the church at Corinth.

> The churches of Asia send you greetings. Aquila and Prisca, together with the church in their house, send you hearty greetings in the Lord. (I Cor 16.19)

The obvious inference is that they were with Paul at the time that he was writing the letter; as I have already argued, at the time he was apparently in Ephesus (I Cor 16.8) and had just sent Timothy ahead to Macedonia, as mentioned in Acts 19.21. Hence, I infer that Priscilla and Aquila were in Ephesus at the time. One could infer from I Corinthians alone that they were with Paul in Ephesus.

By the time that Paul writes Romans, however, he believes that they are in Rome, for he sends greetings *to* them at the end of that epistle.

> Greet Prisca and Aquila, my fellow workers in Christ Jesus, who risked their necks for my life, to whom not only I give thanks but all the churches of the Gentiles give thanks as well. Greet also the church in their house. (Romans 16.3–5a)

The explicit reference in Romans 15.25–27 to the completion of the collection for the Christians in Jerusalem, which was in process during the writing of I Corinthians, makes it undeniable that Romans was written after I Corinthians. Paul's wording in Romans 15.25, as I have discussed repeatedly above, gives the strong impression that he is just about to embark on a journey to take the collected money to Jerusalem: "At present, however, I am going to Jerusalem bringing aid to the saints."

So we can infer from Romans and its relation to I Corinthians that, some time between the writing of I Corinthians and the completion of the collection for the Christians in Jerusalem (and the completion of the letter to the Romans), Priscilla and Aquila left Ephesus and traveled to Rome. One can also gather that there had been enough time for Paul either to have heard of their arrival in Rome or to surmise that they had arrived and were hosting a house church in Rome as they had done in Ephesus.

To put together these inferences from the epistles with the account in Acts and see how they confirm Acts, we can begin with a wider picture and then move to more detailed matters of time.

First, Acts connects Aquila and Priscilla with Corinth, Rome, and Ephesus in ways that are confirmed in broad outline by the greetings in the epistles. Paul first meets them in Corinth and works with them there, according to Acts. One can presume that they were involved to some degree in his founding of the church there. Later they instruct Apollos, who is then sent to Corinth and is useful to the Christians there. It is entirely plausible that they would have wanted to send greetings to the church at Corinth if they were with Paul when he was writing to that church.[37] Acts says that they had previously lived in Rome, so it is not implausible that they would have returned there when the edict against the Jews in Rome was lifted.[38] They may even have left behind property in Rome to which they could return. This fits in general terms with the greeting *to* them in the book of Romans. As for Ephesus, the book of Acts places them there at the end of Chapter 18, and it is from there later in Chapter 19 that, it seems, Paul wrote the Epistle to the Corinthians in which he conveys their greetings. So Acts does not introduce them into the story too late for them to be referred to in the greetings in I Corinthians, and it places them in Ephesus at approximately the right time.

So far, then, we have several coincidences already between the epistles and the account in Acts concerning Aquila and Priscilla. But there is something even subtler and more detailed to notice when one takes into account the *precise* placement of I Corinthians and Romans in relation to Acts. For there must be time in Acts between the probable writing of I Corinthians and the probable writing of Romans for Aquila and Priscilla to leave Ephesus and return to Rome, so that Paul can send greetings *from* them in I Corinthians but *to* them in Romans. On these points, as well, the notes of time in Acts fit with the epistles, even though Acts never mentions Priscilla and Aquila in Chapters 19 and 20.

If Paul wrote I Corinthians during the time when he stayed in Asia Minor after sending Timothy and Erastus to Macedonia (Acts 19.21–22), there is no difficulty about his having Priscilla and Aquila with him. A simple assumption is that they stayed in Ephesus all along throughout Paul's three-year (or so) ministry there recounted in Chapter 19. But what about after that? It seems that I Corinthians was written, broadly speaking, between the end of a winter (possibly AD 56) and Pentecost. This time of year can be gathered from several hints. There is the fact that the feast of the Passover and the days of Unleavened Bread appear to have been on Paul's mind at that time, as shown by his metaphors in I Corinthians 5.6–8. More specifically, there is his stated intention to begin traveling soon, which might well mean that winter had recently ended, and his reference to possibly spending "the winter" with the Corinthians. Such a phrase would normally indicate that one is writing *after* a winter has passed and thinking of the *next* winter (I Cor 16.6–7). And there is his explicit statement, already noted, that he intends to stay in Ephesus *until Pentecost* (I Cor 16.8), the next major Jewish feast after the feast of Unleavened Bread. Acts does not say how long Paul stayed in Ephesus between the time of sending Timothy and Erastus ahead and the riot that precipitated his leaving, so we don't know if he was able to keep to his intention of staying until Pentecost or not. In any event, the time during which he stayed in Ephesus, mentioned in Acts 19.22, seems to have been no more than two or three months at most, and possibly less. After the dramatic scene of the riot, Paul leaves Ephesus, goes overland through Macedonia, and spends some unspecified time in those regions (Acts 20.2), after which he travels south into Greece (Achaia), most probably to Corinth, and spends three months there (Acts 20.3). After that three-month period, he intends to sail on his journey to Jerusalem (planned as far back as Acts 19.21), but as it happens he has to go back the long way through Greece and Macedonia, rather than sailing east directly, because of a plot against him (Acts 20.3). By the time we reach Acts 20, verse 4, he has reached Philippi in Macedonia, and it is the days of Unleavened Bread again. "Again," I say, if indeed I Corinthians was written about the time of Unleavened Bread in the previous year. The best placement for the completion of Romans is *precisely* at the end of Acts 20.3, when Paul is about to leave for Jerusalem.[39] Putting all of this together yields something on the order of eleven months between the writing of I Corinthians and the completion of Romans, when he sends a greeting to Aquila and Priscilla in Rome.

This would be more than enough time for them to have returned to Rome from Ephesus, especially if they left shortly after Paul finished writing I Corinthians. Colin Hemer puts yet another whole year into Paul's journeys through Macedonia before he comes down to Corinth in Acts 20.3.[40] I am inclined to think that Hemer is mistaken on this point (see note 30), but if he is right, then there was all the more time for Aquila and Priscilla to return to Rome and even to send Paul explicit word of their safe arrival and news of a church meeting in their household.

Notice how easy it would have been for a fictionalizing, or even partially fictionalizing, author of Acts to have made a mistake on these matters. If he were treating Priscilla and Aquila as characters to be moved about at will, if he were making them do things, name-dropping, having run across them in an epistle, he could easily have slipped up. Suppose, for example, that the author of Acts, having (say) Romans in hand, had made Priscilla and Aquila return to Rome and set up a ministry there some time early in Acts 19. Then they would not have been with Paul in Ephesus at the apparent time of his writing I Corinthians. Or suppose that he had I Corinthians in hand instead and noted their presence with Paul there, then had them, as devoted fellow workers, stay with Paul and accompany him on his unspecified travels in Acts 20.1–3, ending up with him in Achaia in Acts 20.3. That would have been a mistake as well, for in that case Paul could not have sent greetings *to them in Rome* when he wrote to that city just at that time. Similarly, if the author of Acts had had Paul leave for Jerusalem immediately after his residence in Ephesus rather than traveling around for a time, there would not have been time for Aquila and Priscilla to have traveled back to Rome before the Epistle to the Romans was written.

Speaking of the mention of Priscilla and Aquila in the book of Romans, Paley says,

> Now what this quotation leads us to observe is, the danger of scattering names and circumstances in writings like the present, how implicated they often are with dates and places, and that *nothing but truth can preserve consistency* (emphasis added).[41]

Paley seems to have in mind the idea that a forger writing Romans could easily have erred if he borrowed the names of Priscilla and Aquila from Acts, but his point is just as shrewd when applied to Acts. An author of Acts who was merely "scattering names and circumstances" could have stumbled over any one of several tripwires—those pesky dates and places. As it is, we have consistency in a case where, as Paley says, only truth will preserve it.

The independence of Acts from the epistles should be evident in the very indirectness of the connections. Acts does not even attempt to place Aquila and Priscilla explicitly with Paul at the time of the writing of I Corinthians. Indeed, the author of Acts does not show any awareness that Paul wrote to the Corinthians at all. But Acts leaves the possibility open that they were with

Paul at the time that we can infer the letter was written. And the same for Romans. But there is more: I have already pointed out that Acts never alludes to the collection, so much on Paul's mind when he was writing I and II Corinthians and Romans. Nor does it make any reference to Paul's anxiety for the church at Corinth, so evident in the epistles. More still: Romans expressly refers to some way in which Aquila and Priscilla risked their lives for Paul, using the vivid phrase "risked their necks," yet the book of Acts describes no such incident. One can only conjecture what it might have been.[42] If one imagines the author of Acts as someone without significant independent knowledge of the events, partially inventing a biography of Paul by using the epistles, it is not to be believed that he would have dropped Aquila and Priscilla into his own book on the basis of Romans without inventing some clear, dramatic incident in which they risked their necks for Paul.

Priscilla and Aquila are at the core of an interconnected web of coincidences between Paul's epistles and Acts, remarkable both in its intricacy and its evident lack of contrivance. Its perfection is no accident. It is the effect of truth.

13. "You yourselves know..."[43]

This is not the first instance, and it will not be the last, where Paul's explicit reference to what someone else knows forms the core of an undesigned coincidence. Such statements by Paul are useful in a special way, because it may happen that one doesn't have any more information in that passage or even in that book about how it came about that the people in question knew what Paul says they knew. For example, Paul tells the Thessalonians that they know that he was shamefully treated at Philippi (#4, above), but naturally he doesn't bother to tell *them* how they know this. If they know it, presumably they remember how they came to know it. Thus this comment by Paul provides excellent confirmation of Acts when one finds there that Paul would indeed have come to Thessalonica figuratively and perhaps literally smarting from his ill-treatment in Philippi. In the same way, he says to the Philippians that they know Timothy's character well (#5, above), but he doesn't need to tell them explicitly that they know this because Timothy was with him when he first came to Philippi and started a church there. We can however, infer this from Acts, and the connection confirms the account in Acts of Paul's travels at that time.

Something similar happens in the coincidence I am discussing now, though the statement "You know…" from Paul that kicks off this coincidence comes up in a speech in Acts. Astonishingly, one can infer the accuracy of the record in Acts of *that* speech to *that* audience by way of a quite separate comment by Paul in an epistle that was not even written to the same audience.

As Paul is journeying to Jerusalem for the last time recorded in Acts, he meets at Miletus with the elders of the church at Ephesus. There follows a moving farewell speech (Acts 20.18–35) in which Paul expresses his belief that he will never see them again (a point on which he may in fact have been wrong), and everyone ends up in tears.

I must briefly digress here in order to mention that this entire speech is so strongly Pauline in tone and spirit that it all by itself debunks the notion that "the Paul of Acts" is different from "the Paul of the epistles." The speech breathes the personality of the author of the epistles, including both his genuine love and warm-heartedness and what one might less charitably be inclined to call his emotional manipulativeness and self-dramatization. The same Paul who brings the elders of Miletus to tears with his references to his own trials and tears (Acts 20.19) and his prediction of never seeing them again (Acts 20.25, 36–38) is the Paul who attempts, probably successfully, to induce Philemon to free the slave Onesimus by telling him that he "owes him his own life" (Philem vv 17–19). He is the same Paul who says so much about his own trials and distresses in I Corinthians and reminds his readers that he is their spiritual father (I Cor 4.8–14). The same Paul who launches, at this intimate moment of farewell to his dear friends, into a spirited defense of his own blamelessness in financial matters (Acts 20.33–35) is the Paul who harps on this theme repeatedly in the epistles (see #7, above) and who is almost painfully defensive about his apostleship in II Corinthians 11–12. The same Paul who urges the Corinthians to be imitators of himself (I Cor 4.16), who says that the "care of all the churches" comes upon him daily (II Cor 11.28), and who earnestly uses his apostolic authority, his love, and the sheer force of his personality to dissuade the Galatians from yielding to the demand of circumcision (Gal 4.16–20) is the Apostle Paul who tells the elders in Acts 20.29–32 that after his departure they will be assailed by false teachers and should resist, remembering how he himself "admonished them with tears" during his ministry. These connections are akin to undesigned coincidences between the epistles and Acts, though they do not confirm specific events, companions, or other details. I mention them in part to show that the scope of evidence internal to the New Testament goes beyond undesigned coincidences as I have been discussing them in this book.[44]

A specific coincidence of detail arises from Paul's self-defense concerning finances:

> "I coveted no one's silver or gold or apparel. You yourselves know
> that these hands ministered to my necessities and to those who
> were with me. In all things I have shown you that by working

hard in this way we must help the weak and remember the words
of the Lord Jesus, how he himself said, 'It is more blessed to give
than to receive.'" (Acts 20.33–35)

Paul is therefore implying that while he was in Ephesus with
these very men he worked with his hands to support himself.
Acts says (Chapter 18, see #7) that Paul worked as a tentmaker in
Corinth, but it does not mention this at Ephesus. In this speech in
Acts Paul *implies* that he did work to support himself and his co-
workers when he was in Ephesus, but the narrative in Acts never
says this in Chapter 19, which describes the period in Ephesus to
which the speech alludes.

This detail about Paul's working with his hands in Ephesus
can, as it happens, be confirmed by way of a verse in I Corinthians. As I have frequently noted, Paul comes very near to saying
in so many words that he is writing from Ephesus in I Corinthians 16.8 when he says that he will now remain in Ephesus until
Pentecost. What Paul goes on to say supports the comment in
Acts to the elders of Ephesus:

> To the present hour we hunger and thirst, we are poorly dressed
> and buffeted and homeless, and we labor, working with our own
> hands. (I Cor 4.11–12)

In other words, he is working with his own hands *at Ephesus*, as
the speech in Acts implies, since the epistle says that he is working with his own hands "to the present hour."

But see how indirect all of this is. As noted before, Acts never
even mentions that Paul wrote any epistle to anyone. It would
be incredibly roundabout for the author of Acts to confirm his
history's accuracy by putting this comment into a speech that he
invented and attributed to Paul to the elders of Ephesus, *not* men-

tioning that Paul worked with his hands at Ephesus in the narrative, *not* mentioning that Paul wrote an epistle to Corinth from Ephesus, and simply hoping that someone might notice that Paul implies indirectly, in I Corinthians, that he was working with his hands when he in Ephesus. It would be incredible in the precise sense of "not to be believed." The correct explanation is that Paul really was working with his hands in Ephesus, that he mentioned it in the letter to the Corinthians, that he made the speech recorded in Acts 20 in which he mentioned it to the elders of Ephesus, and that the author of Acts had access to what Paul said to them.

Conclusion

The minute correspondences I have discussed here between Acts and the Pauline Epistles make a strong case that Acts was written by someone who knew the Apostle Paul personally. The author appears to have had intimate, accurate knowledge, independent of the epistles, of both Paul's general history and his detailed movements, even sometimes of his intentions. Moreover, the author of Acts was careful and precise, what we would call a detail person. In the next chapter, I will discuss several coincidences between the other Pauline Epistles and the book of Acts that paint the same picture.

Table 5: Coincidences Between Acts and the Universally Acknowledged Pauline Epistles

Coincidence	Acts	Rom	I Cor	II Cor	Gal	Phil	I Thess
1. "I returned again to Damascus"	9.3–8				1.17		
2. Paul's escape from Damascus	9.23–25			11.32–33			
3. Paul of the tribe of Benjamin	13.9 (I Sam 9.1)					3.4–6	
4. "Shamefully treated at Philippi"	16.16–39,17.1						2.2
5. How did the Philippians know Timothy?	16.1–3, 17.14					2.19–22	
6. Who caused the trouble in Thessalonica?	17.1–5,13						2.14–16
7. Paul's funding in Corinth	18.1–5			11.8–9		4.15–16	
8. The character and activities of Apollos	18.24–19.1		1.11–13, 1.17, 2.1–5, 3.3–7	3.1–3			
9. "If Timothy comes"	19.21–22, 20.3		4.17, 16.5–10				
10. The collection for the church at Jerusalem	19.21–22, 20.1–3, 24.17	15.25–27	16.1–6	2.12–13, 8.1–4, 9.1–5			
11. "All the way around to Illyricum"	16.9–17.15, 20.2	15.18–19					
12. Aquila and Priscilla and the greetings in I Corinthians and Romans	18.2, 24–28, 19.21–22, 20.1–4	15.25–27, 16.3–5	16.8, 19				
13. "You yourselves know…"	20.33–35		4.11–12, 16.8				

Map 1: A Portion of Paul's Second Missionary Journey

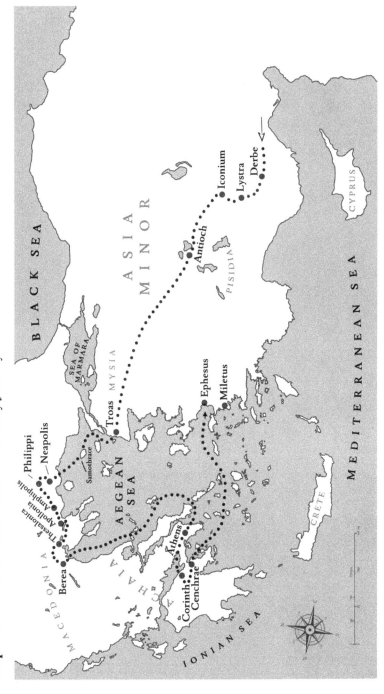

Map 2: Two Routes to Corinth

Map 3: A Portion of Paul's Third Missionary Journey

VI

Coincidences Between Acts and the Other Pauline Epistles

Introduction

In this chapter, I will discuss coincidences between Acts, on the one hand, and Ephesians, Colossians, and I and II Timothy, on the other. The last chapter had thirteen coincidences, while this one has only seven, but there are a number of reasons why this is unsurprising. First, it is highly plausible that I and II Timothy (and Titus, for that matter) were written later than the period of time covered by Acts. The extreme difficulty in finding any place within the time period covered by Acts that fits the details mentioned in the Pastoral Epistles is well-known and has even been used as one argument that they were not written by the Apostle Paul at all. That is the wrong conclusion to draw, since the narrative of Acts ends during a time when Paul was imprisoned in Rome, not at the end of his life. Paul, an unstoppable force when it came to letter-writing, would certainly have continued writing letters as long as he could possibly do so, and it is not at all improbable that we have letters by him from a period after the end of Acts.

Paul appears to have written Colossians during the Roman imprisonment that begins at the end of Acts. He expressly says that those to whom he writes have never met him personally (Col 2.1), which means that his letter to them, unlike those to the Corinthians, Philippians, and Thessalonians, will not contain allusions to a previous time with them or to their firsthand knowledge of his sufferings and work.

Concerning Ephesians, the situation is rather curious. I find Paley's reasoning convincing that the words "at Ephesus" do not represent the main destination of the letter (and may not even have been in the original manuscript) and that this epistle is the letter sent to Laodicea mentioned in Colossians 4.16.[1] The conclusion arises in part from the absence of personal notes in the letter, which is rather unusual for Paul, but that is not all the internal evidence. Paley notes that Paul speaks of having *heard of* his recipients' faith (Eph 1.15), which is nearly identical to what he says to the Colossians in Colossians 1.3. Since Paul says expressly that he has never met the Colossians, that similarity is an argument that the recipients of the letter "to the Ephesians" were also not personally known to him. Paul also says that he is "assuming" that the recipients had "heard of the stewardship of God's grace that was given to [him] for [them]," which is an odd locution if he had ministered to them personally. He also says (Eph 3.3–4) that they can learn more about his teaching of the mystery of Christ when they read a different letter that he has written. This does not sound like a letter from Paul to those who had listened to his preaching over a period of years, as the Ephesians had done according to Acts 19.

More evidence comes from the sharp contrast with Paul's way of writing to others. He says that he thanks God whenever he *remembers* the Philippians (Phil 1.3), that he continually *remembers* the faith and love of the Thessalonians (I Thess 1.3), and that he *remembers* Timothy all the time in his prayers (II Tim 1.3). He says that Timothy has *followed* his teaching and conduct (II Tim 3.10), not that Timothy has heard of his doctrine or can read about it in another letter. The overwhelming similarities in content and wording between Ephesians and Colossians are also pertinent, as they make it nearly impossible to deny that the two epistles were written by the same person at about the same time. Combined with the explicit statement in Colossians 4.16 that Paul was writing a letter at about the same time to Laodicea, these similarities further support the inference that what we have designated as the epistle "to the Ephesians" was a circular letter that went to Laodicea (among other places) rather than a letter to the church of Ephesus to whom Paul was so well known. I will continue to refer to the epistle as "Ephesians" for convenience. Since the letter was in all probability intended to circulate among the churches of the region, the Ephesians would very likely have read it, but I have doubts that they were the primary audience intended by Paul. If Paul knew that the readers would be mostly people who did not know him, this would reduce the number of personal references and greetings that might link the epistle to Acts.

Finally, the most probable time of Paul's writing Ephesians and Colossians, based on the internal evidence of those epistles, is during his imprisonment in Rome described briefly (and perhaps only partially) at the end of Acts. It is not surprising that there should be relatively fewer points of contact between Acts and any letters written during that imprisonment than between Acts and letters written during Paul's prior journeys.

All of these factors combine to reduce the number of undesigned coincidences between these epistles and Acts, and as it happens I have not found any coincidences between Acts and II Thessalonians or Titus that I wished to include. (The book of Philemon contributes to #6 in this chapter.) Paley discusses coincidences for II Thessalonians and Titus, but many of them relate to their interconnections with each other and with other epistles rather than with Acts. That is a fascinating study in itself and is evidence for Pauline authorship, but it is only indirectly relevant to my goal of pointing out how the epistles confirm Acts.[2]

I am therefore pleased to present, despite all of this, seven undesigned coincidences between Acts and Ephesians, Colossians, and I and II Timothy. I believe that the reader will find them as interesting and valuable as those discussed in the previous chapter. As before, the order in which I present them is based approximately upon the order of the passages in Acts that they support.

1. The roster of widows

Before Paul ever shows up in Acts, the narrative describes some of the problems that confronted the new Christian movement. One of these emerges even before the disciples realize clearly that they are supposed to take the gospel to the Gentiles.

> Now in these days when the disciples were increasing in number, a complaint by the Hellenists arose against the Hebrews because their widows were being neglected in the daily distribution. And the twelve summoned the full number of the disciples and said, "It is not right that we should give up preaching the word of God to serve tables. Therefore, brothers, pick out from among you seven men of good repute, full of the Spirit and of wisdom, whom we will appoint to this duty. But we will devote ourselves to prayer and to the ministry of the word." (Acts 6.1–4)

While it is impossible to date this period of the church precisely, it is before the stoning of Stephen in Acts 7, of which Colin Hemer says that it is "suitable to the … troubled last years of Pilate," which would put it prior to AD 36.[3] It is certainly supposed to be prior to the death of Herod Agrippa in AD 44, told in Acts 12. And of course these events are supposed to have occurred prior to Paul's conversion in Acts 9.

If the author of Acts were indeed a close companion of Paul, he might well have had opportunity to learn from Christians in Jerusalem about these events concerning the widows and the appointment of men to administrate the alms for them. It is interesting to note that there was at this time a "daily distribution" of food to the widows. The whole description indicates that the matter was organized and that there were widows who expected to receive each day what they needed.

Fast forward to the time period of I Timothy, approximately three decades later. There Paul gives a list of criteria for widows to be "enrolled" for receiving assistance:

> Let a widow be enrolled if she is not less than sixty years of age, having been the wife of one husband, and having a reputation for good works: if she has brought up children, has shown hospitality, has washed the feet of the saints, has cared for the afflicted, and has devoted herself to every good work. (I Tim 5.9–10)

The emphasis here appears to be on restricting the list of enrolled widows to those who are worthy; the NASB translation captures this emphasis slightly better than the ESV. "A widow is to be put on the list only if she is not less than sixty years of age, having been the wife of one husband," etc.[4]

Paul's way of writing strongly implies that this listing of widows was a well-established practice and that he needs only to give some specific instructions to Timothy about how to carry it out in his own jurisdiction. This is exactly what we would expect to find if the enlistment of widows for aid had been carried out for a long time. As is always the case with such practical matters of charity, continual adjustment of the nitty-gritty details is required on a prudential basis, and these details vary from one venue to another. But there is no question that Timothy knows all about "the list." Paley's comment is apt:

> Now this is the way in which a man writes, who is conscious that he is writing to persons already acquainted with the subject of his letter; and who, he knows, will readily apprehend and apply what he says by virtue of their being so acquainted: but it is not the way in which a man writes upon any other occasion.[5]

Of course, it would be possible for such a practice to be local rather than general among the Christians—e.g., to have been developed only in Ephesus, where Timothy was apparently then working (I Tim 1.3), and known to Paul and Timothy. These verses in I Timothy do not necessarily imply that the use of a roster of needy widows to whom the church renders assistance goes all the way back to a much earlier period in the church.

Nonetheless, the confirmation is there. James refers to looking after orphans and widows (James 1.27), but in I Timothy there is no mention of orphans, and the age of the widows Paul specifies would not lead one to expect that they would have dependent children, especially in a culture that expected early independence from the young. Indeed, Paul implies (I Tim 5.3–4, 16) that if there are surviving children or grandchildren, it is *their* responsibility rather than the church's to care for a widow. So James is referring to a different service to the needy from that which Paul is describing in I Timothy, while Paul's description bears a clear resemblance to what we find in Acts 6. Both in I Timothy and in Acts, the service is for widows, specifically, rather than for needy people in general or for other categories of those in need, and in both places the help is administered in a

formal and organized fashion. A justified inference on the basis
of these texts is that the church's practice from its earliest days in
enrolling believing widows continued to be a feature of Christianity and was spread with the gospel to other locations, including Ephesus. Paul's knowledge of the practice (and, implicitly,
Timothy's) coincides well with the account of its origins in Acts
and indirectly confirms that account.

2. Mark, the kinsman of Barnabas

The book of Acts does not tend to emphasize fallings-out or tensions within the early church, but Acts does mention an argument
between Barnabas and Paul concerning John Mark:

> And after some days Paul said to Barnabas, "Let us return and
> visit the brothers in every city where we proclaimed the word of
> the Lord, and see how they are." Now Barnabas wanted to take
> with them John called Mark. But Paul thought best not to take
> with them one who had withdrawn from them in Pamphylia and
> had not gone with them to the work. And there arose a sharp
> disagreement, so that they separated from each other. Barnabas
> took Mark with him and sailed away to Cyprus, but Paul chose
> Silas and departed, having been commended by the brothers
> to the grace of the Lord. (Acts 15.36–40)

This account of the disagreement is certainly true to human nature. The reason for Barnabas's advocacy of John Mark as a travel
companion might have been as simple as his feeling that Paul was
too harsh and that John Mark would be helpful on the upcoming
journey. In fact, Paul himself later asked Timothy to bring Mark
with him, in all probability the same Mark, because he found him
useful in the ministry (I Tim 4.11). One could argue that Mark's
usefulness is part of the explanation for the falling-out between

Barnabas and Paul. Paul himself later realized what Barnabas had known all along and had presumably argued for—that Mark was a valuable worker not to be permanently discarded over one incident in which he dropped out of a missionary trip.

The account of the disagreement in Acts also fits with the character of the Apostle Paul as it emerges in the epistles. Paul was an exacting ministry boss. Zeal was the salient feature of his own character, and he demanded complete commitment from those who worked with him. He ceaselessly sent away and summoned back Timothy, Titus, Erastus, Tychicus, and others all around the rim of the Mediterranean Sea and expected that they would consider it a privilege to be so used for Christ. He was also inclined to regard any lack of full loyalty to himself and his ministry as a failure of loyalty to Jesus Christ (see II Tim 4.10,16). That such a person would be unwilling to have John Mark on another journey after he turned back from a previous one is only too plausible.

Barnabas, as portrayed elsewhere in Acts, is quite different in personality. He took a risk on Paul himself and brought him to the other disciples in Jerusalem after his conversion when everyone else was afraid to welcome their former persecutor (Acts 9.26–27). That his evaluation of the wisdom of bringing Mark on a second journey would differ from Paul's is no great surprise.

The story in Acts of the disagreement between Paul and Barnabas therefore has multiple lines of support, including epistles that give a sense of Paul's character and Mark's later usefulness. But a phrase in Colossians provides a specific piece of information that fills out the picture even more.

> Aristarchus my fellow prisoner greets you, and Mark the cousin of Barnabas (concerning whom you have received instructions—if he comes to you, welcome him), and Jesus who is called Justus. (Col 4.10–11)

Most modern translations use the word "cousin" for the relationship between Mark and Barnabas, though some older translations say "sister's son." Either way, Paul is clearly saying that Mark is Barnabas's kinsman.

This provides an excellent explanation both for the initial choice of Mark to go with Paul and Barnabas in Acts 13 and for Barnabas's strong advocacy in Acts 15.[6] Barnabas would be especially unlikely to yield to Paul's rejection of Mark given that Mark was his relative and, presumably, was chosen as their companion partly for that reason. But Acts says nothing about this familial relationship, and the author of Acts may not even have known about it.

Paul in the epistles, on the other side, says nothing at all about the earlier falling-out with Barnabas concerning Mark. By the time of the Epistle to the Colossians the entire conflict is long past and set aside; Paul's tone about Mark is completely positive.

The independence of the accounts is therefore clear. It would be absurd to suppose that the author of Acts *invented* a conflict between Barnabas and Paul which is not mentioned anywhere in the epistles, inspired by a reference to a family relationship between Barnabas and Mark in a completely positive passage in Colossians. All the more absurd since Acts doesn't even mention the relationship.

Paul *does*, as it happens, record a conflict with Barnabas in Galatians 2 over a different matter (eating with Gentiles), but this comes up nowhere in Acts—further evidence that the author of Acts was not borrowing information about Barnabas from the epistles. The best explanation of the coincidence concerning Mark's kinship with Barnabas is that the author of Acts wrote about the conflict because it actually happened and he knew about it. The family relationship, in turn, was part of the cause of Barnabas's loyalty to Mark. This is a classic undesigned coincidence, pointing to an elegant explanation of independent data.

3. Timothy's upbringing
Paul in II Timothy gives high praise to Timothy's religious upbringing.

> I am reminded of your sincere faith, a faith that dwelt first in your grandmother Lois and your mother Eunice and now, I am sure, dwells in you as well. (II Tim 1.5)

> But as for you, continue in what you have learned and have firmly believed, knowing from whom you learned it and how from childhood you have been acquainted with the sacred writings, which are able to make you wise for salvation through faith in Christ Jesus. (II Tim 3.14–15)

It is important to remember that the "sacred writings" would not refer to any part of what we call the New Testament. From these verses we can infer that Timothy grew up with a knowledge of the Jewish Scriptures and that one or both of his parents were Jewish. The first of these verses emphasizes his inheritance of sincere faith from his mother and grandmother but makes no mention of his father, which leads to the inference that perhaps his father died when he was young or was a Gentile. There is presumably some reason for the exclusion of Timothy's father from the affectionate, named list of those whose faith has been a model to Timothy.[7]

How do these inferences fit with what Acts relates?

> Paul came also to Derbe and to Lystra. A disciple was there, named Timothy, the son of a Jewish woman who was a believer, but his father was a Greek. He was well spoken of by the broth-

ers at Lystra and Iconium. Paul wanted Timothy to accompany him, and he took him and circumcised him because of the Jews who were in those places, for they all knew that his father was a Greek. (Acts 16.1–3)

What we could infer indirectly from the allusions in II Timothy to Timothy's upbringing is borne out in this passage. Timothy's father was a Gentile, resulting in his not having been circumcised in infancy, though his mother was both Jewish by ethnicity and a Christian believer. Acts does not explicitly say that Timothy's father was not a Christian believer, but that seems to be implied.

The coincidence is perfect but also indirect. In Acts, for example, there is no mention of Timothy's grandmother. As I have discussed above, it is unlikely in any case that Acts is borrowed in any way from II Timothy or that the author of Acts had access to II Timothy. If from nothing else, this is evident from the extreme difficulty, amounting in my opinion to impossibility, of fitting the time of writing of II Timothy into any portion of Acts, which of course leads to the inference that it was written later than Acts. But we can even argue for the independence of this specific information in Acts. If the account in Acts were based on II Timothy, it seems quite unlikely that the author would have refrained from mentioning the name of Timothy's mother or of his grandmother, mentioned so conveniently in the epistle.

The correspondence between II Timothy and Acts concerning Timothy's background has the ring of truth. Timothy's father was a Greek and his mother Jewish, he was raised from childhood in the knowledge of the Old Testament Scriptures, and both Paul and the author of Acts knew about him and described him accurately.

4. How did Timothy know of Paul's persecutions?

Here I come to another undesigned coincidence that arises from Paul's statement that someone knows about an aspect of his life, giving rise to the question, "How did he know that?"

Paul gives a list of ways in which Timothy has followed his career and his manner of life, intending this catalog to encourage Timothy to remain steadfast.

> You, however, have followed my teaching, my conduct, my aim in life, my faith, my patience, my love, my steadfastness, my persecutions and sufferings that happened to me at Antioch, at Iconium, and at Lystra—which persecutions I endured; yet from them all the Lord rescued me. (II Tim 3.10–11)

Paul had undergone so many persecutions in his missionary travels in so many different places that the specification of Antioch, Iconium, and Lystra in this verse should capture the attention. Why did he mention *those* persecutions as the ones that would be familiar to Timothy?[8]

To answer that question it is necessary to look at two different passages in Acts. One of these comes earlier in Acts than the passage about Timothy's father and mother; the other is the same Acts passage discussed in the previous coincidence. (The order of discussion of this coincidence and the last is therefore somewhat arbitrary.)

Acts explicitly recounts in what is usually known as Paul's first missionary journey the persecutions at Antioch, Iconium, and Lystra to which Paul alludes here in II Timothy.[9] At the end of Acts 13, Paul and Barnabas are driven out of Pisidian Antioch. In Acts 14.1, they come to Iconium and begin converting people through preaching in the synagogue. There is trouble immediately, and verse 5 says that "an attempt was made by both Gentiles and Jews, with their leaders, to mistreat and stone them," at which point they transfer operations to the country surrounding Lystra and Derbe (vv 6–7) and continue to preach. In verse 19 Jews come to Lystra from Antioch and Iconium, win over the crowds, stone Paul, and leave him for dead outside the city. With characteristic energy, Paul revives, re-enters the city, and leaves the next day for Derbe (v 20).[10]

These are indeed persecutions in Antioch, Iconium, and Lystra, coming close together in time, out of which Paul was delivered. They are almost certainly the persecutions to which Paul alludes in II Timothy. Paley notes that Paul lists the cities in II Timothy in the same order in which he came to them in Acts on this journey.[11]

But how was it that Timothy had followed those particular persecutions? Why does Paul emphasize them *to him*? I must stress that Timothy is not mentioned in Acts 13 and 14 at all, nor connected in those chapters in any way with those cities. But in Acts 16, on Paul's *next* visit to the region, the narrative says,

> Paul came also to Derbe and to Lystra. A disciple was there, named Timothy, the son of a Jewish woman who was a believer, but his father was a Greek. He was well spoken of by the brothers at Lystra and Iconium. (Acts 16.1–2)

So Timothy was living in one of these towns, and he was known and commended by the Christians in that region—Lystra, Derbe, and Iconium all being near one another. As Paley shrewdly points out, these verses say that Timothy was *already* a well-known disciple at this time.[12] He must therefore have accepted Christianity *previously*. A small but relevant further point is that I Timothy 1.2 may well imply that Timothy had been taught the Christian faith first by Paul. It is therefore probable that Timothy had become a believer in Jesus during Paul's previous visit to the region, which was precisely when Paul underwent the persecutions at Antioch, Iconium, and Lystra in Acts 13 and 14. Timothy may even have witnessed the stoning of Paul at Lystra and, as a new member of the Christian community, would surely have heard of it at the time that it occurred. These persecutions would have made a strong impression on his mind, especially if they coincided with the time of his own first acquaintance with Paul and his own conversion to Christianity.

Notice how indirect all of this is. One *infers* from II Timothy that Paul had some special reason to mention those persecutions to Timothy and to say that they were known to Timothy. One *notes* the point in Acts 13–14 where the narrative describes persecutions in those towns. One then *infers* from Acts 16 that Timothy was already a disciple from that region and had been converted during Paul's previous visit to the region, described in Acts 13–14, during which the persecutions took place. The minute convergence confirms the accuracy of the accounts in Acts while being clearly undesigned.

5. Paul's imprisonment for the Gentiles

In Ephesians, Paul is quite explicit about the cause of his imprisonment. It is not any general persecution against Christianity. Rather, he states that he is in prison specifically for the Gentiles. Paul begins one of his long and convoluted sentences like this:

> For this reason I, Paul, a prisoner for Christ Jesus on behalf of you Gentiles…(Eph 3.1)

It is easy to read past such an introductory phrase, especially if one is hurrying on to find the verb (so often elusive in Paul's sentences), but the wording of the introduction is worth pondering.

Paul is saying that he is a prisoner not just for Jesus Christ, but for Jesus Christ *on behalf of the Gentiles.*

He stresses in Colossians, almost certainly written at about the same time, that he is imprisoned on account of what he calls "the mystery of Christ."

> At the same time, pray also for us, that God may open to us a door for the word, to declare the mystery of Christ, on account of which I am in prison.... (Col 4.3)

This same phrase, "the mystery of Christ," occurs in Ephesians, where he spells out its content:

> When you read this, you can perceive my insight into the mystery of Christ, which was not made known to the sons of men in other generations as it has now been revealed to his holy apostles and prophets by the Spirit. This mystery is that the Gentiles are fellow heirs, members of the same body, and partakers of the promise in Christ Jesus through the gospel. (Eph 3.4–6)

These references to the "mystery" in Colossians and Ephesians, taken together, explain what Ephesians 3.1 says—namely, that Paul regarded himself as being in bondage specifically for his preaching that the Gentiles were to be included in the people of God.[13]

This point concerning the cause of Paul's imprisonment is amply borne out in Acts throughout the whole tenor and arc of Paul's ministry. Nothing in that history appears to be *based on* these implications in the epistles. Rather, the tensions concerning the Gentiles and Paul's ministry to them are part of the fabric of both the story in Acts and the teaching in the epistles (Galatians is a notable example), and the fact that Paul's imprisonment was a result of Jewish objections to his ministry to the Gentiles arises naturally and almost inevitably in the course of the story in Acts.

It would be tedious to relate the entire history of Jewish-Gentile relations in connection with the new Christian body in Acts, as it is one of the main themes of the book. Here are a few points concerning Paul, culminating with Paul's own statement *in Acts* that he was imprisoned because of his preaching to the Gentiles, which dovetails with the similar statement in Ephesians. Early in Paul's missionary ministry, he and Barnabas tell the Jews of Pisidian Antioch that they are turning to the Gentiles with the gospel (Acts 13.46–50), and it is immediately after this that they are driven out of Antioch. After this, the Jews who oppose Paul's ministry pursue him from one city to the next and try to prevent the Gentiles from listening to him. In Acts 15.1 some Jewish believers tell new Gentile converts that they must become Jewish proselytes and keep the law of Moses in order to be saved. Paul strongly opposes this, and he is eventually vindicated by the Jerusalem council (Acts 15.6–29), where the church leaders decide that the Gentile converts do not have to be circumcised and follow all the laws of Moses to be part of the church.

After several more years, when Paul is once again in Jerusalem, the issue of the Gentiles and Paul's teaching still has not gone away. The apostles are supportive of Paul's ministry, but they are having trouble with some Jews who believe in Jesus Christ but are "zealous for the law" and who have heard rumors that Paul's teaching is radical and contrary to the Jewish law. The leaders of the Jerusalem church suggest a placating maneuver.

On the following day Paul went in with us to James, and all the elders were present. After greeting them, he related one by one the things that God had done among the Gentiles through his ministry. And when they heard it, they glorified God. And they said to him, "You see, brother, how many thousands there are among the Jews of those who have believed. They are all zealous for the law, and they have been told about you that you teach all the Jews who are among the Gentiles to forsake Moses, telling them not to circumcise their children or walk according to our customs. What then is to be done? They will certainly hear that you have come. Do therefore what we tell you. We have four men who are under a vow; take these men and purify yourself along with them and pay their expenses, so that they may shave their heads. Thus all will know that there is nothing in what they have been told about you, but that you yourself also live in observance of the law. But as for the Gentiles who have believed, we have sent a letter with our judgment that they should abstain from what has been sacrificed to idols, and from blood, and from what has been strangled, and from sexual immorality." Then Paul took the men, and the next day he purified himself along with them and went into the temple, giving notice when the days of purification would be fulfilled and the offering presented for each one of them. (Acts 21.18–26)

The passage presents a rather surprising picture, especially in light of what is to follow in the narrative. *Many thousands* of allegedly Christian believers are nonetheless so "zealous for the law" that the apostolic leaders regard them as a serious cause for concern. The apprehensive sentences, "What then is to be done? They will certainly hear that you have come" are rather telling. While we cannot be sure that the leaders think that the believers who are "zealous for the law" will be violent, no clear distinction is made in Acts between the zealots who happen to believe in Jesus and those who riot and beat Paul later in the same chapter. And those whom the church leaders wish to placate are evidently hearing and accepting rumors spread by the persecutors who have hounded Paul, sometimes with violence, all along. The words of the church leaders give a snapshot of a church and synagogue with fluid boundaries between them.

Whatever Paul may have thought of the probability that the leaders' suggestion would calm the agitators, he went along with it. Things did not turn out well.

> When the seven days were almost completed, the Jews from Asia, seeing him in the temple, stirred up the whole crowd and laid hands on him, crying out, "Men of Israel, help! This is the man who is teaching everyone everywhere against the people and the law and this place. Moreover, he even brought Greeks into the temple and has defiled this holy place." For they had previously seen Trophimus the Ephesian with him in the city, and they supposed that Paul had brought him into the temple. Then all the city was stirred up, and the people ran together. They seized Paul and dragged him out of the temple, and at once the gates were shut. And as they were seeking to kill him, word came to the tribune of the cohort that all Jerusalem was in confusion. He at once took soldiers and centurions and ran down to them. And when they saw the tribune and the soldiers, they stopped beating Paul. (Acts 21.27–32)

The mob flares into violence based on the accusation that Paul has taught everywhere "against the law and this place" and that he has profaned the Temple by bringing a Gentile into it. The latter error, says the narrator, probably arose from Paul's open friendship with the Gentile Christian Trophimus. When Paul asks leave to speak to the crowd, they are momentarily quiet and listen but break out once more, yelling for his blood, when he says that Jesus sent him to the Gentiles:

> "And he [Jesus] said to me, 'Go, for I will send you far away to the Gentiles.'" Up to this word they [the Jewish crowd] listened to him. Then they raised their voices and said, "Away with such a fellow from the earth! For he should not be allowed to live." (Acts 22.21–22)

The narrative throughout Acts shows that Paul's ministry to the Gentiles was a continual cause of conflict with his fellow Jews. His faithfulness to this ministry resulted in his being nearly beaten to death by a mob in the Temple, a fate from which the Roman soldiers rescued him. Protective custody quickly turned into outright imprisonment by the Romans. The remainder of Acts tells of his being tried by the Roman authorities and kept in prison by them partly to please his Jewish opponents, his appeal to Caesar, and his journey to Rome after that appeal.

All of this dovetails very well with Paul's statement in the epistles that he is in prison "for you Gentiles" and his implication that he has been imprisoned for the "mystery" of the union of Jews and Gentiles in the church of Christ. Moreover, there is the following statement by Paul in Acts, in his defense before Agrippa:

> "And the Lord said, 'I am Jesus whom you are persecuting. But rise and stand upon your feet, for I have appeared to you for this purpose, to appoint you as a servant and witness to the things in which you have seen me and to those in which I will appear to you delivering you from your people and from the Gentiles—to whom I am sending you to open their eyes, so that they may turn from darkness to light and from the power of Satan to God, that they may receive forgiveness of sins and a place among those who are sanctified by faith in me.' Therefore, O King Agrippa, I was not disobedient to the heavenly vision, but declared first to those in Damascus, then in Jerusalem and throughout all the region of Judea, and also to the Gentiles, that they should repent and turn to God, performing deeds in keeping with their repentance. *For this reason the Jews seized me in the temple and tried to kill me.* To this day I have had the help that comes from God, and so I stand here testifying both to small and great, saying nothing but what the prophets and Moses said would come to pass: that the Christ must suf-

fer and that, by being the first to rise from the dead, he would proclaim light both to our people and to the Gentiles." (Acts 26.15–25, emphasis added)

Here Paul expressly says that the Jews seized him and tried to kill him because he obeyed Jesus' command to preach to the Gentiles, a point in full agreement with his speech to the mob and their reaction several chapters earlier.

What we have is an allusion by Paul in Ephesians and Colossians to the cause of his imprisonment, combined with the spelling out in Acts of the complex historical story that lies behind that allusion. Acts also indicates, in Paul's speech to Agrippa, that Paul himself regarded the Jews' anger at his mission to the Gentiles as the cause of his imprisonment, even though technically it was the Romans who had him in custody. Paul's own words in the epistles point to the fuller story in Acts and confirm the accuracy both of the narrative and of the speech attributed to him.

6. Aristarchus

Paul refers to Aristarchus twice in his epistles, once in Colossians and once in Philemon. Philemon, be it noted, is currently one of the "universally acknowledged Pauline Epistles." It happens that I did not use any undesigned coincidences from it in the previous chapter, chiefly because most of its coincidences confirm the Pauline authorship of Colossians rather than (directly) the reliability of Acts. Here, Colossians and Philemon work together to support Acts, so I have chosen to include the coincidence regarding Aristarchus in this chapter.[14]

In both of these references, Paul makes it clear that Aristarchus is with him during his imprisonment, presumably in Rome. Colossians 4.10 says, "Aristarchus my fellow prisoner greets you." Philemon says, "Epaphras, my fellow prisoner in Christ Jesus, sends greetings to you, and so do Mark, Aristarchus, Demas, and Luke, my fellow workers." (Philem vv 23–24)

There is ample reason to believe that Colossians and Philemon were written at approximately the same time. Paley summarizes much of this evidence,[15] which includes the correspondences in the names of those who were with Paul at the time, coincidences concerning Onesimus, references to Archippus in both epistles, and more.

The fact that Aristarchus was with Paul in Rome in turn confirms the second of two mentions of Aristarchus in Acts. The first mention is in Acts 19, where both Aristarchus and Gaius are in great danger from a mob in Ephesus. There they are said to be Paul's traveling companions and Macedonians (Acts 19.29). In Acts 27, when Paul has appealed to Caesar and is going to be taken to Rome, we find the second reference to Aristarchus.

> And when it was decided that we should sail for Italy, they delivered Paul and some other prisoners to a centurion of the Augustan Cohort named Julius. And embarking in a ship of Adramyttium, which was about to sail to the ports along the coast of Asia, we put to sea, accompanied by Aristarchus, a Macedonian from Thessalonica. (Acts 27.1–2)

Acts thus indicates that Aristarchus, who had previously been Paul's traveling companion, began the trip to Rome with Paul, and one could infer from Acts that he ended up at Rome with Paul. That fits very well with his joining in greetings in Paul's letters written from Rome. Those greetings in the epistles therefore indirectly confirm the mention in Acts of his accompanying Paul on the voyage to Rome. I note as well that this voyage is one of the "we" passages in Acts and that the implication that the author of Acts traveled to Rome with Paul therefore fits nicely with the fact that Paul sends greetings from Luke to the Colossians (Col 4.14) and to Philemon (v 24), though of course it does not provide decisive evidence that Luke, specifically, was the author of Acts.

Paley addresses the issue of independence between Colossians and Acts thus:

> [I]f you suppose the history to have been made out of the Epistle, why the journey of Aristarchus to Rome should be recorded, and not that of Marcus and Justus [who are both mentioned as sending greetings in Colossians], if the groundwork for the narrative was the appearance of Aristarchus' name in the Epistle, seems to be unaccountable.[16]

Paley's point is well-taken and can be expanded. Since Mark comes up earlier in Acts as the cause of strife between Barnabas and Paul, it would make sense from a purely literary point of view for the author of Acts to place him on the trip to Rome with Paul as a sign that the rift was healed and to give readers a further story about a character who has already been introduced. If Acts is historical, of course, there are many possible reasons for not mentioning Mark on the ship to Rome with Paul, the most obvious of which is that he may not have been on the ship at all. He may have come to Rome later during Paul's imprisonment. But if the author of Acts is *making things up*, and especially if he is doing so based upon Colossians, where Mark is mentioned in such a cordial way, why mention Aristarchus as a companion on the journey to Rome but not Mark?

There is more: Paul says that Demas and Epaphras send greetings in both Colossians and Philemon, and Epaphras receives much more fulsome praise in Colossians than Aristarchus. Aristarchus comes up only briefly in Colossians, but Paul devotes two full verses (Col 4.12–13) to saying how earnestly Epaphras is concerned for and prays for the churches at Colosse, Laodicea, and Hierapolis. Yet Acts mentions neither Demas nor Epaphras anywhere. If Acts were based upon Colossians and/or Philemon and if Aristarchus were introduced fictionally from those epistles, it is arbitrary at best that Aristarchus alone should have been chosen for mention on the journey to Rome.

Moreover, a derivative introduction of Aristarchus into Acts based on the epistles would make more sense in the final chapter of Acts. Were Acts based on the epistle at this point, it would have been more likely to include an explicit statement that he was Paul's companion at the very time of the imprisonment at the end of the book, not a mention of him as *embarking* with Paul on the ship to Italy back in Chapter 27. The mention of him in Acts leaves it to be inferred that he went all the way to Rome with Paul, and Acts does not state or even imply that he stayed with Paul in Rome for any significant time. The confirmation is far too subtle to be contrived.

7. An ambassador in a chain

For this last undesigned coincidence I must beg the reader's indulgence. In most translations of the New Testament this final coincidence is not hidden in plain view, and this is the only section in this book that depends crucially upon the Greek in a fashion that cannot be inferred from the English translation. Indeed, most translations, both ancient and modern, positively obscure a central piece of evidence for this coincidence. I owe the core to Paley, to whose historical and linguistic information I have added, and I include this item both because it is so interesting and because it falls within the category this chapter discusses—coincidences between Acts and the other Pauline Epistles. Paley calls it "a coincidence of that minute and less obvious kind, which, as hath been repeatedly observed, is of all others the most to be relied upon." [17]

In Ephesians 6.18–20, Paul requests the prayers of the Ephesians:

> To that end keep alert with all perseverance, making supplication for all the saints, and also for me, that words may be given to me in opening my mouth boldly to proclaim the mystery of the gospel, for which I am an ambassador in chains, that I may declare it boldly, as I ought to speak.

The ESV, which I am quoting here, has the phrase "an ambassador in chains." The King James has "an ambassador in bonds." The vast majority of translations, both old and new, have one or the other of these phrases. I have been able to find only three translations that give the Greek more literally—the Darby Bible, the Douay-Rheims, and Young's. Douay-Rheims and Young's have "an ambassador in a chain," and Darby has "an ambassador [bound] with a chain." In point of fact, as Paley notes, the Greek word is *halusei*, "chain," singular.[18]

One might reasonably ask what possible difference it could make whether the Greek word for "chain" is singular or plural. Nor am I arguing for wooden literalism in translation; I love the ring of the King James phrase "an ambassador in bonds." In this case, however, the verbal point is important to an undesigned coincidence.

If we turn now to Acts 28, we find Paul's imprisonment described in this way:

> And when we came into Rome, Paul was allowed to stay by himself, with the soldier who guarded him. (Acts 28.16)

I will explain below the historical significance of this reference to the soldier who guarded him. The narrative continues,

> After three days he called together the local leaders of the Jews, and when they had gathered, he said to them, "Brothers, though I had done nothing against our people or the customs of our fathers, yet I was delivered as a prisoner from Jerusalem into the hands of the Romans. When they had examined me, they wished to set me at liberty, because there was no reason for the death penalty in my case. But because the Jews objected, I was compelled to appeal to Caesar—though I had no charge to bring against my nation. For this reason, therefore, I have asked to see you and speak with you, since it is because of the hope of Israel that I am wearing this chain." (Acts 28.17–20)

The last word here, "chain," a chain to which Paul evidently gestures, is the same as the word in Ephesians—*halusin*, "chain," singular.[19] In both places, then, Paul describes his imprisonment similarly by saying that he is bound by a chain.

The reader might wonder whether this coincidence between the wording in the epistle and in Acts is just a manner of speaking with no special significance. Perhaps this was Paul's common way, or the most common way at the time, to speak of imprisonment. Does it refer to any particular mode of imprisonment? We already know that Ephesians appears to have been written from an imprisonment, and we already know that Acts describes an imprisonment in Rome at the end of the book. If Acts were partly fictionalized or unreliable, the author might well have had Paul use some expression or other to refer to his being a prisoner. Does this linguistic similarity between Ephesians 6 and Acts 28 provide any *additional* evidence for the accuracy of Acts beyond the reference to imprisonment?

As Paley points out, there are actually multiple ways of referring to being a prisoner, some of which are used elsewhere in Acts and some of which are used elsewhere in the epistles.[20] This particular word—this singular word for "chain"—is used by Paul in the epistles only twice (Eph 6.20, II Tim 1.16).

One of the other relevant terms comes up earlier in Acts. After Paul makes his defense before Agrippa in Caesarea (Acts 26), the following exchange occurs:

> And Agrippa said to Paul, "In a short time would you persuade me to be a Christian?" And Paul said, "Whether short or long, I would to God that not only you but also all who hear me this day might become such as I am—except for these chains." (Acts 26.28–29)

Here Paul uses a different Greek word altogether, and here it really is in the plural: *desmōn*, bonds or chains. So if the author of Acts were inventing these speeches by Paul, he chose for some unknown reason to put a *different* word into Paul's mouth in the speech to Agrippa, and it is an unexplained coincidence that both the word and the number are the same in Acts 28 and in Ephesians 6, one of only two places where Paul uses that word in the epistles.

I do not mean to imply that *desmoi*, bonds or chains, in the plural, always meant literally multiple bonds or chains. In fact, Paul uses the plural noun *desmōn* in Colossians 4.18 ("remember my chains") apparently with reference to the same imprisonment that he describes in Ephesians 6 using the singular "chain." Paul also uses the plural noun *desmoi* (in some form or other) for "bonds" or "imprisonment" in Philippians 1.7, 1.13–16, and Philemon verse 10. So the two methods of description (the singular *halusis* and the plural *desmoi*) are apparently compatible. Paley states that the noun *desmos* (and presumably its plural) could be used to describe "any…species of personal coercion."[21] Another generic terms that Paul uses for imprisonment is the verb *dedemai*—"have been bound"—used in Colossians 4.3.[22]

But, although other words could apparently be used widely for imprisonment or bondage, no passage comes to light that shows the singular noun, *halusis*, "a chain," used in a way that refers to the state of bondage generally as opposed to a *literal* method of binding the prisoner with a single chain. In other words, it appears that this noun in the singular really did refer to a particular form of shackling. That is also Paley's conclusion: "[B]ut ἅλυσις, in the single number, [was applicable] to none but this."

Moreover, based on other evidence, this method appears to have involved being bound with a chain to a soldier, according to Roman practice. In Acts 12.6–7 Peter is bound to *two* soldiers with *two* chains, and the plural, *haluseis*, is used. The Jewish historian Josephus records that Herod Agrippa was imprisoned for a time by the Emperor Tiberius and that, when a man saw Agrippa bound and wished to approach and speak to him, he had to ask permission from the soldier to whom he was bound (*Antiquities* 18.6.6–7). When he was eventually released by Caius Caesar, Agrippa received a gold chain, equal in weight to the iron one by which his hands had been bound (*Antiquities* 19.6.1). The word in Josephus for this chain, a model of the one by which Agrippa had been bound, is the singular *halusin* that I have been discussing. Further testimony to the practice of binding a prisoner to a soldier with a single chain comes from the poet Seneca, writing in Latin:

> Just as the same chain fastens the prisoner and the soldier who guards him, so hope and fear, dissimilar as they are, keep step together[.] (Epistle V)

The Latin word Seneca uses for "chain" (*catena*) is, unsurprisingly, singular.

Acts 28.16 says that Paul was allowed to stay by himself with a soldier who guarded him. We can put this together with Paul's demonstrative reference to "this chain" when speaking to the Jewish leaders in 28.20. The historical evidence, together with these references in Acts, indicates that Acts is implying that Paul was chained to a soldier.

All of this makes Paul's reference to himself in Ephesians 6.20 as "an ambassador in a chain" significant. It is entirely like Paul to make a vivid allusion to his own literal situation in his theological writing, and the coincidence between the wording of the two passages is highly suggestive.[23]

Any question about the independence of Acts in this coincidence almost answers itself. As I have already pointed out, Paul uses a variety of words in the epistles to describe his own imprisonment, and *halusis* is by no means the most common of them. There is no reason why a fictionalizing, later author of Acts should pick up on the isolated reference to "an ambassador in a chain" and invent both a soldier who kept Paul and Paul's somewhat dramatic reference to "this chain" in talking with the Jewish leaders in Acts 28.[24]

The far better explanation is that Paul really was confined according to this Roman method and that the author of Acts knew this independently of the epistle. This is an especially interesting confirmation that the author of Acts was Paul's companion at the time.

Conclusion

The undesigned coincidences in this chapter concern passages in the book of Acts beginning even before Paul's conversion (the establishment of the list of widows) through the last chapter of Acts. It is quite natural that the minute and circumstantial coincidences between Paul's epistles and the Book of Acts arise much more often in the parts of Acts that relate to the Apostle Paul than in the sections before Paul comes on the scene. Nonetheless, wherever they occur, they support the reliability of Acts and its authorship by someone closely acquainted with the Apostle Paul. As the cumulative case from undesigned coincidences mounts up, it becomes increasingly difficult to deny that the author of Acts knew Paul and his travels personally and reported them reliably, though not exhaustively. The picture that emerges from these coincidences is also that of someone who had a strong drive to note and record meticulously.

The author of Acts as he emerges in these chapters would have had both the opportunity and the motivation to speak with the principal characters in the earliest chapters of Acts, such as Peter and John, and with others who had witnessed events such as Pentecost. Hence, as I discussed in the introduction to Part II, the undesigned coincidences concerning Paul, his travels, his companions, and his imprisonment support the conclusion that what Acts records about the first public teaching of the apostles, the founding of the Christian movement, and the earliest persecution of the apostles is historically trustworthy. Acts is a primary historical source showing that the disciples were willing to risk death for their public proclamation, as eyewitnesses, that Jesus of Nazareth was risen from the dead.

Table 6: Coincidences Between Acts and the Other Pauline Epistles

Coincidence	Acts	Eph	Col	I Tim	II Tim	Phlm[2]
1. The roster of widows	6.1–4			5.9–10		
2. Mark, the kinsman of Barnabas	15.36–40		4.10–11			
3. Timothy's upbringing	16.1–3				1.5, 3.14–15	
4. How did Timothy know of Paul's persecutions?	13.50–51, 14.5–7, 19–20, 16.1–2				3.10–11	
5. Paul's imprisonment for the Gentiles	13.46–50, 21.18–26, 22.21–22, 26.20–21	3.1, 4–6	4:3			
6. Aristarchus	27.1–2		4.10			vv 23–24
7. An ambassador in a chain	28.16, 20	6.20				

[2] Philemon is one of the universally acknowledged Pauline Epistles, but a reference from Philemon is relevant to a coincidence that connects Acts and Colossians, which is why a Philemon reference is included in this chapter and chart. The connections between Philemon and Colossians are numerous.

CONCLUSION

Reclaiming the Forward Position

I have argued for many specific points in this book, and in conclusion I want to take a step back and look at the big picture once again. The argument from undesigned coincidences in the Gospels and Acts supports a thesis that will seem to many, even to some evangelical scholars, a radical one. That thesis is that the Gospels and Acts are very, very reliable.

Over the past several decades, an approach to arguing for Christianity and specifically for the resurrection of Jesus has gained popularity among Christian scholars and apologists. It is known as the minimal facts argument.[1] In broad terms, the minimal facts method seeks to establish certain data points that a large percentage of New Testament scholars, across the whole ideological and theological spectrum, would grant, and then to argue that the resurrection of Jesus constitutes the best explanation of these fixed points.

I do not wish to say that the minimal facts approach is valueless, by any means, and its widespread use may be in part a result of the fact that it provides a straightforward template for a debate format. However, I do want to say that it is incomplete and that its heavy promotion and near-exclusive use in Christian apologetic circles can, perhaps unintentionally, give an unfortunate misimpression. That misimpression is that we cannot establish the high reliability of the Gospels and/or Acts by neutral, historical means and therefore that we ought to eschew any argument that involves relying on a premise of reliability. A corollary error is that we cannot neutrally establish that the resurrection accounts in the Gospels and Acts came from the apostles themselves rather than being, in whole or in part, later additions by those who were not in a position to know what really happened or what the apostles claimed.

My own intention is to rehabilitate the older apologetic method of William Paley and others who argued, from the fact that the disciples made certain claims about what they saw and heard, that the resurrection of Jesus did occur and hence that Christianity is true.[2] Following this older method, one argues that the disciples must have been either deceivers, deceived, or telling the truth about the resurrection. The details and context of the disciples' claims preclude the first two options.

Again, I am not asserting that proponents of the minimal facts method *believe* or *intend* to teach that it is extremely hard to establish that the Gospels and Acts are highly reliable or that they are a close-up record of apostolic teaching. But the way that the argument is sometimes cast could be taken to imply that the reliability of these documents is something of an embarrassment. For example, if one says that the apologist should not be "saddled" with arguing for the reliability of the Gospels or need not concern himself with doing so, and if one takes it as a great virtue of a method that it does not place such a burden upon the apologist, one's audience may get the impression that it would be tough for a defender of Christianity, if pressed, to show any such thing.[3] Similarly, if one refers to a minimal body of widely agreed-upon facts as "historical bedrock," and if this definitely does not include the reliability of these documents, this could give the impression that "non-bedrock" propositions are doubtful.[4]

A similar issue arises for what is known as a "criteriological" approach, which is in some ways complementary to the minimal facts approach. This method involves applying things like (what is known as) the criterion of embarrassment, the criterion of multiple attestation, and the like to particular passages in a document. If a passage fulfills one of these criteria, and especially if it fulfills more than one, that is treated as some reason to take what it says to be part of an original tradition rather than a later accretion and some reason to take what it says to be true.[5] It is possible to use this method while emphasizing that we should not assume that a passage is "guilty until proven innocent." It does not follow from the use of criteria of authenticity that all other passages are inauthentic.[6] However, the criteriological approach is *designed* to support only specific passages rather than a document as a whole.[7] If one uses these criteria as an aid to establishing minimal facts while explicitly eschewing any intention to argue that whole documents are reliable and represent authentic apostolic testimony, then *something like* a question will understandably remain about any segments that have not been individually authenticated.

While not wishing to reject such approaches altogether, I must admit to some doubt as to whether they can support Christianity quite as strongly as their advocates believe. As I have discussed elsewhere at more length, one particular concern is the nature of the appearances to the disciples, treated as one of the minimal facts, and the relationship between the details of the appearances and Jesus' bodily resurrection.[8] Generally this minimal fact is stated in minimal terms, such as that "in some sense, the early followers of Jesus thought that they had seen the risen Jesus"[9] or that "the disciples had experiences that led them to believe and proclaim that Jesus had been resurrected and had appeared to them."[10] The limited wording and absence of detail are part and parcel of the method, presumably in order to be able to claim widespread support across the scholarly spectrum. But if we cannot be at all sure that the accounts as given in the Gospels and in the first chapter of Acts represent at least what the disciples claimed, the argument for a bodily resurrection of Jesus is considerably weakened.[11] As with any reported miracle, both God and the devil are in the details. Can we or can't we be confident that the disciples specifically claimed to have eaten with Jesus, to have been invited to touch him, to have had conversations with him while they were together in a group, to have talked with him at length and up close, and to have had such meetings repeatedly over a period of several weeks? It is these details that give such tremendous force to the apostles' testimony and to their willingness to die for it, for it is from these details that we can conclude with confidence that they were not hallucinating, experiencing some sort of non-physical, paranormal event, having visions, or merely mistaken. Yet by no means will the vast majority of New Testament scholars admit that Jesus' close friends had *these* sorts of experiences, in their crudely physical details, after his death.[12]

Moreover, as I have pointed out in the introduction to Part II, the reliability of Acts is closely intertwined with what is thought to be an early creed given by Paul at the beginning of I Corinthians 15. If we can confidently assume the reliability of Acts for purposes of deciding when Paul was converted and when I Corinthians was written, thereby establishing that Paul received the creed he gives in I Corinthians within just a few years of Jesus' death, why should we treat the accounts in Acts of the disciples' preaching and persecution with special suspicion? On the other hand, if we cannot take Acts to be unproblematically reliable for helping to date the conversion of Paul and the writing of I Corinthians, the minimal facts approach cannot place such weight as it undoubtedly does upon the earliness of the creed given in I Corinthians 15.[13]

All of this points to the great value of arguments for the reliability of the Gospels and Acts taken as whole works, which in turn should lead us to reconsider the apologetic approach of the 18th and 19th centuries. I suggest that we have such ample evidence for the reliability of these documents that we should consider ourselves privileged rather than burdened when called upon to present it. We should *welcome* the opportunity to reclaim and maintain the forward position held by the older apologists, for their arguments have been not so much refuted as forgotten in the shifts of theological fashion.

Nor do undesigned coincidences provide the only support for the reliability of whole New Testament documents. The patristic evidence for the traditional authorship of the Gospels is now sometimes considered unfashionable but is not thereby refuted.[14] There is the vast web of incidental confirmations of the authors' intimate knowledge of all manner of details, from social practices to names to geography and more.[15] There are unexplored internal arguments for reliability and eyewitness origin, including the argument from unexplained allusions,[16] the argument from unnecessary details,[17] the argument from the restraint of the Gospel authors,[18] and arguments from the unity of the characters of Jesus and Paul across various documents.[19] There are older books that have yet to be widely read in our own day and mined for their contributions to the case. These include J.S. Howson's *Horae Petrinae*, which relates the Petrine Epistles to Acts,[20] Howson's *The Evidential Value of the Acts of the Apostles*,[21] which contains among other things a fascinating discussion of the three accounts of Paul's conversion in Acts, T.R. Birks's *Horae Apostolicae*, which I have cited several times in this book,[22] James Smith's *The Voyage and Shipwreck of St. Paul*, with its fascinating confirmations of Acts concerning ships and sailing,[23] and many more.

Among these many lines of evidence, the argument from undesigned coincidences ranks high, and that is why I have chosen to focus on it in this book. I urge the reader to notice how the coincidences are distributed throughout the books. As I have already noted, there is *no* pattern in which undesigned coincidences confirm non-miraculous events but fail to support miracles. On the contrary, the coincidences concern large events and small details, non-miraculous and miraculous occurrences, early, middle, and late parts of the documents. There is every reason to think that the information substantiated by these coincidences is a representative sample of the facts and words recounted in these books. This point makes it extremely difficult to argue that there is merely an "historical core" of solid fact to the Gospels and Acts, surrounded by non-factual material. Where is the non-factual material, then? If you sample a loaf of bread on both ends and at several points in the middle and find it good, it would be caviling to say that perhaps just the parts you haven't tasted happen to be the moldy ones.

The argument from undesigned coincidences tells us something about what the authors of these documents were like. What picture of the author of the Gospel of John emerges from what we have seen? It is a picture of a careful recorder with a vivid and meticulous memory, someone with his own, independent, close access to the facts, someone who is not inventing, massaging, or exaggerating his data. Even within fairly conservative scholarly circles, it is sometimes too readily suggested that John took a loose approach to facts about time and place, redacting earlier sources to fit some agenda—that he relocated the cleansing of the Temple to early in Jesus' ministry as opposed to shortly before the crucifixion, that he altered the day of Jesus' crucifixion for theological reasons, and so forth.[24] I submit that this is not the John who emerges from the study in this book and that the argument from undesigned coincidences pulls strongly in a different direction. These authors have primarily a *testimonial* project rather than a literary or redactive one. They are honest witnesses giving their reports and honest historians relating witness reports—emphasizing and mentioning different details, to be sure, but ultimately aiming to tell what really happened. The providential provision of four Gospels gives us a three-dimensional view of the events.

Or what of the author of Acts? Given the minute, one might even say boring, details in Acts of Paul's life and travels corroborated by this study, some of which the author of Acts himself does not seem to have fully understood at the time, the idea that he was writing in any sense a work of fiction can be readily dismissed.[25] The picture of that author, who is also the author of Luke, comes shining through as exactly what Christian tradition has always held him to be—a close companion of Paul, a man who knew the apostles and had access to eyewitnesses, and a careful, conscientious historian.[26]

All that has been said so far does not imply that I am starting from the assumption of inerrancy nor even that I am arguing for that doctrine as my conclusion. I have deliberately taken no position on inerrancy at any point in this book. Obviously, high reliability and accuracy on matters of detail are *relevant* to the question of whether a book contains any errors at all, but I am far more concerned to argue what I have stated here concerning high reliability, the absence of any deliberate fictionalization, and close apostolic origin and to leave the matter of inerrancy to take care of itself. Nor am I saying that one must believe the documents to be inerrant in order to have a strong case for the resurrection and for Christianity. That is all beside the point. But if one thinks that the Gospel authors and the author of Acts had such a flexible view of historical truth that they knowingly altered facts as they redacted sources,[27] or if one is unwilling to use the premise that the resurrection accounts in these books came from those who claimed to be eyewitnesses, these concessions create unnecessary weaknesses in the argument for Christianity.

Readers who disagree with the argument of this conclusion should feel free, despite that disagreement, to glean what they find valuable in the foregoing chapters, and I certainly hope that they will do so. I simply ask them to consider that defending only an understated, stripped-down version of one's position is not always the best course. Rather, we should weigh, understand, and bring to bear all available evidence in order to set the case for Christianity in its truest and clearest light and present it to the world in all its power.

This volume is a modest contribution to that end, following in the footsteps of those who have gone before. I pray that God will use it to strengthen his church and to bring souls to Christ. It has been my great privilege to bring forward once more the evidence from undesigned coincidences hidden in plain view.

AFTERWORD

I truly believe this book by Lydia McGrew will be cherished by believers (and shared with seekers) for many years to come. Why? Because it contains important evidence demonstrating the reliability of the Gospels as eyewitness accounts. When I first investigated the claims of the Gospel authors, I wasn't doing so as an historian, biblical critic or textual expert. I was simply an unbelieving *detective*, with nearly ten years of experience interviewing and reviewing witnesses and suspects. I was a committed skeptic in my mid-thirties, and I viewed the New Testament as a collection of fables and mistruths. I certainly didn't believe they were reliable eyewitness accounts. But as I examined many of the "undesigned coincidences" in the Gospels, I changed the way I viewed the New Testament and reconsidered my perspective as a skeptic.

It's not uncommon for reliable, truthful eyewitnesses to disagree with one another when describing an event. As a detective, I've seen it happen many times, and unlike historians and textual critics who work without any confirmation or definitive resolution, I often get the chance to compare eyewitness descriptions with the confessions of suspects or with video taken at the time of the crime. As a result, I know with great certainty that two witnesses can *truthfully* describe the same event very differently. In California, we even have a jury instruction offered in criminal trials to help jurors discern between variations and "apparent contradictions":

> Do not automatically reject testimony just because of inconsistencies or conflicts. Consider whether the differences are important or not. People sometimes honestly forget things or make mistakes about what they remember. Also, two people may witness the same event yet see or hear it differently. (Section 105, Judicial Council of California Criminal Jury Instructions, 2006)

Jurors are instructed to remember the fact that witness *disagreement* doesn't necessarily disqualify witness *testimony*. I've never investigated a case in which eyewitnesses were in *complete* agreement. So, when I saw variations between the Gospel accounts, it didn't really bother me. In fact, it gave me a sense of unexpected confidence. The Gospels read like the reliable eyewitness accounts I encountered in my casework.

"Inconsistencies or conflicts" between accounts may, however, lead to serious confusion. As Lydia mentioned on page 16, I've investigated several cases in which one witness created confusion, only to have another witness unwittingly clarify the confusing issue by providing additional information. I call this kind of clarifying testimony "unintentional eyewitness support," and I consider it a true characteristic of reliable statements. So, when studying the Gospels as an unbelieving skeptic, I was surprised to see unintentional eyewitness support statements offered by the authors of the Gospels. The Gospel accounts "puzzled together" in a manner very much like the eyewitness statements I had investigated over the years. I recognized this kind of unintentional eyewitness support as a sign of reliability, not fiction. As a skeptic, this caused me to rethink what I believed about the Gospels.

Years later, I discovered I wasn't the first person to notice these hidden evidential gems in the New Testament accounts. I found the work Lydia referenced at the beginning of this book, written by J.J. Blunt. I immediately ordered the best volume I could find and eventually referenced it in my own book, *Cold-Case Christianity*. I had a hard time finding a current printing of Blunt's work, however, and realized there was a need to update this important area of research to make it accessible to people in the 21st Century. Lydia McGrew has now done that for all of us.

These undesigned coincidences and unintentional eyewitness support statements have special meaning to me, and a cherished place in my own conversion to Christianity. After reading Lydia's book, I hope they have gained an important place in your own understanding of the Gospels. The existence of many of these statements prompted me to examine the Gospels further, and that investigation ultimately led me to determine the Gospels are reliable. I came to trust what they said about *Jesus*, and even more importantly, I came to trust what they said about *me*. I decided to submit my life to God and accept Jesus as my Savior. It all started with a few ancient Gospel statements, often overlooked, but critically important to those who care about eyewitness reliability.

So, keep this book at the ready. It contains some interesting hidden gems, and God may use these overlooked pieces of evidence to persuade someone you know to take the Gospels seriously, the same way He used them in my own life.

J. Warner Wallace
Cold-Case Detective
Adjunct Professor of Apologetics, Biola University
Author of *Cold-Case Christianity*, *God's Crime Scene*
and *Forensic Faith*

NOTES

General Introduction

1. See J. J. Blunt, *Undesigned Coincidences in the Writings Both of the Old and New Testament: An argument of Their Veracity* (Birmingham, UK: The Christadelphian, 1847), pp. 287–9 and William Paley, *A View of the Evidences of Christianity, In Three Parts*. (Murfreesboro, TN: DeHoff Publications, 1952 reprint of 1859 edition), Part II, Chapter IV.

2. See J.S. Howson, *Evidential Conclusions from the Four Greater Epistles of St. Paul* (London: Religious Tract Society, 1884), pp. 406ff.

3. George Rawlinson, *The Historical Evidences of the Truth of the Scripture Records Stated Anew, With Special Reference to the Doubts and Discoveries of Modern Times* (Boston: Gould and Lincoln, 1860), p. 187.

4. J. Warner Wallace, *Cold Case Christianity: A Homicide Detective Investigates the Claims of the Gospels* (Colorado Springs, CO: David Cook, 2013), p. 187.

5. Ibid., p. 183.

6. William Paley, *Horae Paulinae, or The Truth of the Scripture History of St. Paul Evinced by a Comparison of the Epistles Which Bear His Name with the Acts of the Apostles and With One Another*. J.S. Howson, ed. (London: Society for Promoting Christian Knowledge, 1877), p. 25, note 2.

7. Paley, *View of the Evidences*, p. 336.

8. Wallace, *Cold Case Christianity*, p. 85.

9. Ibid., p. 75.

10. Some of Timothy McGrew's resources available in audio or video recording have been helpfully collected by Brian Auten of Apologetics315 and are available from http://www.apologetics315. com/2012/11/audio-resources-by-tim-mcgrew.html. See in particular "Undesigned Coincidences in the Gospels," given at First Baptist Church of Kenner, Kenner, LA, January 9, 2011, accessed June 19, 2016, http://firstkenner.org/audio/jan2011/010911A%20. mp3. See also a series of blog posts on undesigned coincidences in Acts, "Undesigned Coincidence Series," 2013, accessed June 19, 2016, http://www.apologetics315.com/2013/11/undesigned-coincidences-series-by-tim.html.

Part I Introduction

1. The last coincidence in this entire book at the end of Chapter VI is the one notable exception to this rule—that the coincidences should be accessible with minimal specialized knowledge. In other cases, even where some Greek comes up in the discussion, the relevant point is usually visible in a good modern translation.

Chapter I: The Synoptic Gospels Explain John

1. All Scripture quotations are from the English Standard Version unless stated otherwise.

2. This coincidence does not come from any other source; I discovered it independently.

3. I owe the core of this coincidence to Timothy McGrew. Thanks to Maryann Spikes for drawing my attention to it in Tim McGrew's work.

4. I owe the core of this undesigned coincidence to J.J. Blunt, *Undesigned Coincidences in the Writings Both of the Old and New Testament: An argument of Their Veracity* (Birmingham, UK: The Christadelphian, 1847), pp. 286–7.

5. This coincidence is my own discovery, independent of any other source.

6. For a summary of citations to Luther's views on this subject, see John T. Mueller, "Notes on Luther's Interpretation of John 6.47–58," *Concordia Theological Monthly* 20 (1949): 802–29.

7. Martin Luther, "Confession Concerning Christ's Supper," in *Lu-*

ther's Works, vol. 37 *Word and Sacrament III*, Robert H. Fischer, editor, Helmut T. Lehmann general editor (Philadelphia, PA: Muhlenberg Press, 1961), p. 360.

8. To be clear, I am not insinuating that Jesus' words about raising up the Temple in three days are an invention. On the contrary, in Chapter II I will show that they feature in an undesigned coincidence of their own—one related to the testimony of witnesses against Jesus before the Sanhedrin.

9. In my coding in Table 1 for this chapter, I have used the question-explanation format based on my own preferred interpretation and have coded the Synoptic Gospel passages as the explanation for John 6. Readers who disagree with that interpretation are free to class this coincidence instead with the group discussed in Chapter IV, which includes coincidences that do not follow the question-explanation form.

10. I owe this undesigned coincidence to Timothy McGrew.

11. For further discussion of Luke's independence from Matthew and Mark in this passage, see the discussion of coincidence #3 in Chapter II.

12. The core of this coincidence is found in T.R. Birks, *Horae Apostolicae*, appended to William Paley, *Horae Paulinae*, edited by T.R. Birks (London: Religious Tract Society, 1850), p. 400.

13. This entire exchange between Pilate and the religious leaders is one of many incidental historical confirmations of the historicity of the Gospels, showing in passing in the story the complex relationship of Jewish and Roman authority in Palestine at this time. This book is about internal evidence of the truth of the Gospels and Acts, but incidental external confirmations are a fertile further source of evidence that should be noted.

14. Matthew and Mark do not include the accusation of sedition and do include Pilate's question, so in a sense they raise the same question that John raises: Why did Pilate ask Jesus if he was the king of the Jews? From that perspective one might regard this coincidence as one in which a Synoptic Gospel (Luke) explains other Synoptic Gospels (Matthew and Mark) as well as John. Sometimes a coincidence can be included in more than one category. But unlike John, Matthew and Mark do not give any account of what the Jewish lead-

ers said when they delivered Jesus to Pilate. They are more evidently brief summaries and hence incomplete, so they do not raise as sharply as John does the question of why Pilate asks Jesus if he is the king of the Jews. For this reason I have not included the references from Matthew and Mark in Table 1 as "raising the question" passages.

15. I owe the core of this coincidence to Timothy McGrew. I wish to emphasize that when I use a phrase like "Luke's sources" I do not mean primarily literary or documentary sources. More often I am hypothesizing human sources.

16. I owe to Timothy McGrew the suggestion that I should emphasize the independence of detail in passages that are otherwise similar among the Synoptic Gospels.

17. In Chapter II I will show that these passages contain another undesigned coincidence in the opposite direction, where John explains Luke.

18. The core of this coincidence is found in Blunt, *Undesigned Coincidences*, pp. 304–5.

19. There is no other plausible referent for "these" in the passage. I find attempts to say that Jesus was asking Peter if he loved him more than he loved the boat or the fish to be highly questionable on their face. There is evidence of some sort of pointing gesture in the use of "these," and no abstract reference to earthly pleasures or earthly things is visible in the context. Moreover, the use of a similar Greek construction in Matthew 10.31 where Jesus says, "You are of more value than many sparrows" treats both things being compared as the subjects of the verb—"You are of more value than many sparrows [are]," which would be comparable to "Do you love me more than these [love me]." (Compare also Matt 6.25 and John 14.28.) When Jesus says that one who loves father and mother more than him is not worthy of him in Matthew 10.37, he uses a completely different construction. I am indebted to John Krivak for pointing out this information regarding the Greek constructions, though he was not making the same argument about the verse that I am making.

20. The core of this coincidence is found very briefly in Blunt, *Undesigned Coincidences*, pp. 270–1. This is one of the few coincidences that I found entirely independently; I later discovered that Blunt had found it as well.

Chapter II: John Explains the Synoptic Gospels

1. The core of this undesigned coincidence is found in J.J. Blunt, *Undesigned Coincidences in the Writings Both of the Old and New Testament: An argument of Their Veracity* (Birmingham, UK: The Christadelphian, 1847) pp. 277–8.

2. Ibid., p. 278.

3. See a relevant map at Bible History Online here: http://www. bible-history.com/maps/ancient-roads-in-israel.html, accessed June 30, 2016.

4. See George Ogg, *The Chronology of the Public Ministry of Jesus* (Cambridge, UK: Cambridge University Press, 1940), p. 19. I cite Ogg because he made inquiries into the times of year when the grass is green in the relevant region, though he himself attempts to argue that perhaps Mark's reference to green grass is not really the result of eyewitness testimony. I do not consider any of his considerations to have the slightest weight. They are all based upon bare possibilities, such as the *possibility* that some later editor or translator who had access to John, who mentions the existence of the grass but not its color, added "green" to the text of Mark, though there is no evidence in the text of Mark that the word was added.

5. One of the most interesting of the differences noted by Blunt, *Undesigned Coincidences*, pp. 264–7, is that the Greek word for "baskets," when the accounts state that there were baskets of leftovers taken up, consistently differs between the accounts of the feeding of the five thousand and the feeding of the four thousand. In the latter case the word is the same as the word used in Acts for the presumably large basket used to enable Paul to escape from Damascus. Moreover, the accounts state that fewer of these (presumably larger) baskets were filled than of the other kind. Blunt's point is that the accounts show casual, visual distinctions in their details that make it both more likely that they are real events told by eyewitnesses and less likely that one of the feedings is merely a confused account or corruption of the other story.

6. *Undesigned Coincidences*, p. 266. Although Blunt comments about the detail of the green grass, he does not note the connection with the time of Passover. I owe that connection to Timothy McGrew.

7. The core of this coincidence is found in T.R. Birks, *Horae Apostolicae*, appended to William Paley, *Horae Paulinae*, edited by T.R. Birks (London: Religious Tract Society, 1850), pp. 399–400.

8. The core of this coincidence is found in Blunt, *Undesigned Coincidences*, pp. 269–70.

9. I owe both the core of this undesigned coincidence and the approximate wording of the section header to Tim McGrew. The exposition of the coincidence is my own.

10. There is independent support for translating this response as a "yes." In Matthew 26.64 and the similar passage in Luke 22.70, Jesus gives a nearly identical answer ("You have said") to the high priest under similar circumstances, in reply to the question whether he is the Son of God, and it is clearly taken as an affirmative, since the high priest tears his clothes and says that all have heard Jesus' blasphemy. Even more significantly, in the same scene before the high priest where Matthew and Luke give "you have said," Mark gives Jesus' answer to the question literally as, "I am," an unequivocal "yes."

11. Classicist E.M. Blaiklock has this vivid note about John's visual memory in John 13.30: "...Judas opened the door to leave the tense and puzzled group. An oblong of sudden darkness seen for a second stamped itself on one mind forever; and remembering, the writer comments, 'And it was night'." E.M. Blaiklock, *Jesus Christ: Man or Myth* (Homebush West, NSW, Australia: Anzea Books, 1983), p. 69.

12. Josephus indicates that Jewish tradition forbade giving *honorable* burial to those convicted of blasphemy. Joseph of Arimathea would have been flouting this. See Josephus *Antiquities* 4.202.

13. The core of this coincidence is found in Blunt, *Undesigned Coincidences*, pp. 282–3.

14. For more on this point, see the discussion of John's supposed "alteration" of the day of the crucifixion at the end of #4 in Chapter IV.

Chapter III: The Synoptic Gospels Explain Each Other

1. See John Wenham, *Redating Matthew, Mark, and Luke.* Downers Grove, IL: Intervarsity Press, 1992.

2. Luke's list, though the names differ slightly, does the same thing if one follows the *Textus Receptus*—it groups the names into pairs using "and." If one follows the oldest texts, the pairing is not as clear in Luke as in Matthew because there are additional uses of "and." The one additional "and" in Matthew and the many additional "ands" in Luke occur in the Nestle 1904 reconstruction of the Alexandrian text but not in the *Textus Receptus* on which the King James translation was based.

3. I owe the core of this undesigned coincidence to Timothy Mc-Grew. It is also noted briefly in John Henry Burn, *The Preacher's Complete Commentary on the New Testament: Gospel According to St. Mark* (Funk & Wagnall's. 1896), p. 204.

4. If the intent is to give the disciples' names according to the actual pairs as they were sent out on the mission of the twelve, then there is a discrepancy between Matthew and Luke that cannot be resolved by means of taking Thaddeus and Judas the son of James to be the same person. This is because they are paired with different other disciples in the lists in Matthew as compared to Luke, and Luke seems to pair Simon the Zealot with James the Son of Alpheus. I do not propose any particular solution to this conundrum, but I note that the pairing of the names in Luke, if it was in the original manuscript, could have indicated Luke's knowledge *that* Jesus paired up the twelve when he sent them out even if Luke did not have specific knowledge of all of the *actual* pairings. Most of his pairings agree with Matthew's in any event.

5. J.J. Blunt, *Undesigned Coincidences in the Writings Both of the Old and New Testament: An argument of Their Veracity* (Birmingham, UK: The Christadelphian, 1847), pp. 258–9, suggests that this reversal and added title for Matthew is a sign of Matthean authorship of the Gospel, as indications of humility. The points are suggestive, but I do not press them here.

6. It might be argued that Matthew silently used the information about their being sent in groups of two from Mark 6.7 in deciding how to group his list of the disciples; this seems implausible given that Matthew does not *include* the statement that Jesus sent the disciples out in pairs in Matthew 10.1 (or anywhere else), even though Matthew 10.1 is quite similarly worded to Mark 6.7 in oth-

er respects and comes immediately before Matthew's own list of the disciples. If Matthew's decision to group his list in pairs were influenced by the statement in Mark 6.7 that the disciples were sent in pairs, one would expect to find this fact naturally included in the lead-in to Matthew's own list in Matthew 10.1. I have therefore retained the coding of this coincidence in the table for this chapter as showing Matthew's independence from Mark, though this point can be disputed.

7. In other words, this is a case where Matthew shows access to independent information not found in any other Gospel, despite the fact that in other respects Matthew might be thought to be simply taking the passage from Mark. I owe this point to Timothy McGrew.

8. This formulation—how did Matthew know what Herod was saying to his servants?—is due to Timothy McGrew. J.J. Blunt, *Undesigned Coincidences*, pp. 263ff, asks instead why Herod was discussing Jesus' ministry with his servants rather than with someone else. One can take one's choice as to which of these one considers the more noteworthy question. Either question is answered by the same point from the Gospel of Matthew.

9. The core of this coincidence is found in Blunt, *Undesigned Coincidences*, p. 263.

10. I owe the core of this coincidence to Timothy McGrew.

11. The *Textus Receptus* has "to a deserted place of/belonging to a town called Bethsaida." That it was not in the town itself is clear in any event in Luke from the disciples' statement later in the passage that they were in a desolate place.

12. The woes are considered by critical New Testament scholars to be part of so-called "Q material"—that is, passages that are nearly identical in Matthew and Luke but not found in Mark. Hence, such a scholar would say that both Matthew and Luke got the woes from the source Q. I have no intention in this book of engaging at multiple points with the minutiae of source criticism, and I have doubts about the literal existence of Q as a document. A reader who *insists* upon doing so may regard this as a confirmation of the accuracy of "Q" and Luke (remembering that the detail about the feeding's location near Bethsaida is unique to Luke) rather than Matthew and Luke.

13. Here I should note that Matthew's account of the woes comes in the Gospel *before* the account of the feeding of the five thousand. If Jesus was alluding to the feeding of the five thousand in the woes, the feeding and the woes must have actually occurred in the order as they appear in Luke—feeding and miracles at Bethsaida first, woes later, which is the opposite of the order in Matthew. However, it is widely acknowledged that Matthew in particular among the Gospels does not always relate the events of Jesus' ministry in chronological order. For example, Mark 1.21ff is arranged in a clear and explicit chronological order, but the same events are broken up, sometimes switched in comparison to Mark's order, throughout Matthew 4.23–8.16, where Matthew's order appears to be topical rather than chronological. (See Wenham, *Redating Matthew, Mark, and Luke*, pp. 102–103.) There would be nothing remarkable about Matthew's relating the woes before his account of the events in Bethsaida to which one of the woes referred, especially since Matthew does not mention that the feeding of the five thousand took place near Bethsaida at all and may not even have remembered that detail. It is one aspect of eyewitness testimony that some details are left out of one account simply because they are forgotten while another witness remembers them.

14. This claim of an undesigned coincidence is my own, independent of other sources.

15. There are three coincidences which I have left out of my discussion for this very reason: The "who struck you" coincidence between Luke 22.63–64 and Matthew 26.67–68, since Matthew and Luke could have each been merely including one piece of information from all the information contained in Mark; the "waiting until evening" coincidence between Matthew 8.16 and Mark 1.21, since Matthew may have merely included incomplete information from Mark; the coincidence concerning the command to the disciples to tell no one about the Transfiguration until after the resurrection, from Matthew 17.9 and Luke 9.36, since all of the information may be found in Mark 9.10, depending upon one's translation of the Greek in Mark. My careful exclusion of coincidences that could plausibly be a result of mere incomplete copying from Mark is part of the explanation for the relative shortness of this chapter. This does not mean that I think these coincidences are valueless, since

the arguments for Matthean priority (such as Wenham's) deserve, in my opinion, more attention than they usually receive. But I am deliberately taking care that the evidence brought forward in this book does not depend in any way on *denying* Markan priority in the order of the Synoptic Gospels or on *denying* the presence of any literary dependence among the Gospels, since I anticipate that critics of the argument from undesigned coincidences will mistakenly attempt to dismiss the argument on that basis.

Chapter IV: Still More Undesigned Coincidences in the Gospels

1. The core of this coincidence is found in J. J. Blunt, *Undesigned Coincidences in the Writings Both of the Old and New Testament: An argument of Their Veracity* (Birmingham, UK: The Christadelphian, 1847), pp. 260–1.

2. The Greek phrase translated "family" in Mark 3.21 is more literally "those who were from him" and is rather unusual. The King James translates it "friends," which could include one's family in older English. Modern translators seem agreed in taking it to mean "family."

3. Occasionally skeptics will imply that this passage in Mark contradicts the infancy narratives in Luke and Matthew where it is made clear that Jesus is the promised Messiah. How could Mary have thought that Jesus was out of his mind if she had the evidence of the Annunciation and virgin birth? But Mark does not actually say that *Mary herself* thought that Jesus was out of his mind, only that she went with his brothers to confront him. Common experience tells us how often different family members agree that "We need to have a talk with so-and-so" while not all sharing exactly the same perspective. Mary may have wanted to warn Jesus to tone down inflammatory statements that were antagonizing his own people. Or she and/or his other family members may have been consternated by the failure of his ministry thus far to live up to the Messianic expectations they had in mind—expectations actually encouraged, given the account of the Annunciation, by the angel's own words that the coming child would reign on the throne of David. In any event, what this passage shows is that an account used in the attempt to manufacture a contradiction can actually participate in an undesigned coincidence that confirms the passage. If Joseph was indeed dead, this passage in Mark and the parallels in Matthew and Luke

are part of a pattern showing the Gospel writers' knowledge of who was and was not present on particular occasions.

4. I will have many occasions in this chapter to refer to Jesus' brothers. I am of course aware of the view of the Roman Catholic Church that Mary retained her virginity after the birth of Jesus and hence that these could not have been Jesus' biological half-brothers by his mother Mary. For purposes of the conclusion that Joseph was dead, if readers prefer to substitute the concept of step-brothers or other near kinsmen in the relevant passages, it will make little difference to the argument. They were in any event close enough family members to be mentioned repeatedly with Mary as Jesus' family, yet Joseph does not appear with them. See further discussion in #7 in this chapter.

5. The Greek word for "know" is the verb οἶδα, which is used in expressions such as, "Teacher, we know that you are true" in the lead-in to the Pharisees' question in Matthew 22.15–16 or Jesus' statement to the woman at the well, "We know what we worship" in John 4.22. It therefore does not usually refer (by itself) to acquaintance with a person.

6. See Stanley Leathes, *The Religion of the Christ: Its Historic and Literary Development Considered as an Evidence of Its Origin* (London: Rivingtons, 1874), pp. 257–258.

7. The core of this coincidence is found in Blunt, *Undesigned Coincidences*, pp. 279–80.

8. I owe this formulation to Timothy McGrew.

9. The core of this coincidence is found in Blunt, *Undesigned Coincidences*, pp. 266–7.

10. Ibid., p. 280.

11. The core of this coincidence is found in Blunt, *Undesigned Coincidences*, pp. 294–98. I have significantly altered Blunt's argument for the coincidence, since he overstates and implies that *Mark* clearly takes Jesus to have arrived in Bethany the day before the triumphal entry. In fact this is an assumption based on *John* and is needed to start the sequence, as I have made clear.

12. Mark 14.12 begins the description of Jesus' activities with his disciples on the day of the Last Supper, which Mark says was "on the

first day of Unleavened Bread, when they sacrificed the Passover lamb." Since there has been no time note in Mark since 14.1, which says that it was two days before the Feast of Unleavened Bread, one might wonder if Mark has skipped a day in his daily log between 14.1 and 14.12. This takes us into a variety of questions concerning the meaning of Mark 14.12 and its relationship to 1st-century Passover practices. It also introduces certain alleged problems raised by other statements in John about the "preparation" and the Passover (e.g., John 13.1, 18.28, and 19.31). These issues lie outside of my purpose in arguing for this coincidence, though they certainly illustrate the independence of the accounts. It would in any event be surprising if Mark skipped a day in the last week of Jesus' life at this point given that he has been ticking off each day rather carefully. One reason not to assume that Mark has left out a day is the known Jewish practice of reckoning parts of days as days. If we take Mark 14.1 to refer to a Wednesday as "two days before the Passover," and if the Passover meal was actually eaten after sundown on Thursday, then Mark 14.1 can be counting both Wednesday and Thursday (daytime) in the reckoning, yielding "two days before Passover," while 14.12 describes the Thursday when the lamb was killed more broadly as "the first day of Unleavened Bread." My purpose here, however, is to point out the connection between John and Mark concerning how long before the Passover Jesus came to the Jerusalem region. This is accomplished by my reasoning concerning Mark's notes of time *through Mark 14.1*, regardless of how one interprets Mark 14.12.

13. See, for example, John Gill's commentary on John 18.28 (in loc.) It is particularly noteworthy that the claim that John changed the day of the crucifixion shows a lack of understanding of Jewish customs, for the Passover Seder was eaten after sundown in any event, so any ritual uncleanness of the Jews (as mentioned in John 18.28) would not have extended from the morning into the evening to prevent their eating a Passover Seder. It would, however, have prevented their eating the *chagigah* in the middle of the day. I am indebted to Tim McGrew for pointing this out to me. See R.C.H. Lenski, *The Interpretation of St. John's Gospel 11–21* (Minneapolis, MN: Augsburg Fortress, 2008 reprint), pp. 1213–14.

14. The core of this coincidence is found in Blunt, *Undesigned Coincidences*, pp. 301–3.

15. Edmund Bennett, *The Four Gospels from a Lawyer's Standpoint* (Boston: Houghton, Mifflin and Company, 1899), p. 17.

16. Richard Bauckham, *Jesus and the Eyewitnesses: The Gospels as Eyewitness Testimony* (Grand Rapids, MI: Eerdmans Publishing Company, 2006), p. 52.

17. This coincidence is fairly widely known, as illustrated by its being addressed by Bauckham in a recent work. One older source in which it is found is Bennett, *The Four Gospels From a Lawyer's Standpoint*, p. 30.

18. Bauckham, *Jesus and the Eyewitnesses*, p. 52, note 49.

19. See John Wenham, *Redating Matthew, Mark, and Luke* (Downers Grove, IL: Intervarsity Press, 1992), pp. 136–142, for a summary of the patristic evidence.

20. As implied throughout and in note 4, above, concerning coincidence #1, I do not accept the view that Mary was ever-virgin. In this coincidence the assumption that these brothers were actual sons of Mary, who normally would have been responsible for her care, plays a somewhat larger role than it does in #1. It seems to me that it is simplest to take the textual evidence at its face value that these were, in fact, Jesus' brothers (half-brothers) in the ordinary, biological sense, the sons of Mary and Joseph, born after Jesus. Absent independent theological reasons to think otherwise, the matter would not even come into question. Again, however, in the interests of the ecumenical intent of this book, I will point out that there is still force to the argument for coincidence #7 even if one takes the other brothers to be near kinsmen or children of Joseph by an earlier marriage. They certainly appear repeatedly in the same scenes with Mary, and the question still arises as to why she was committed to John rather than being left to their care.

21. Acts 1.14, Acts 12.17, Acts 15.13ff, I Corinthians 15.7.

22. I owe this coincidence to John Wenham, *Easter Enigma: Are the Resurrection Accounts in Conflict?* (Eugene, OR: Wipf & Stock Publishers, 1992), p. 62. Wenham expressly uses the phrase "undesigned coincidence" for this connection and mentions J.J. Blunt's and William Paley's development of the concept (p. 152, note 16).

23. William Paley, *Horae Paulinae, or The Truth of the Scripture History of St. Paul Evinced by a Comparison of the Epistles Which Bear His*

Name with the Acts of the Apostles and With One Another. J.S. Howson, editor. (London: Society for Promoting Christian Knowledge, 1877), p. 25, note 2.

24. This coincidence is my own discovery. My thanks to Timothy McGrew for urging me to include it in this book and for suggesting that I stress the fact that it might seem to some scholars to be "transferred" from Luke and yet is, in fact, not well explained by that hypothesis.

25. It's also worth noting that any intentional connection of this miracle with the earlier miracle could, if both occurred, be attributed to Jesus himself. Presumably Jesus would have remembered the earlier event and its connection with Peter and his boat. He could have been attempting to connect the two in the disciples' minds by standing on the shore, asking if they had caught anything (knowing that they had not), and performing this miracle. In real life we often see that people deliberately create parallels to earlier actions or events that have occurred among friends; doing so is even considered somewhat humorous. It's important not to assume that, if there are resemblances between two events in the Gospels, this automatically implies a *literary* parallel created by the author. Taking seriously the reality of the events as an hypothesis means realizing that there could be other people involved (in this case, Jesus) who have something to say about what happens.

26. I am not unaware of attempts to give some mystical or theological meaning to the number of fish here and thereby to cast doubt on its literalness. I am not going to pause to evaluate these fanciful theories, because I think it is clear that the number fits into a pattern of vivid, literal detail in the story as a whole. Also, anyone who knows fishermen knows that they count their fish. The disciples would have had to deal with the fish by hand in any event, taking them out of the net, and it would have been entirely natural to attempt to count them after the miracle.

Part II Introduction

1. A.N. Sherwin-White, *Roman Society and Roman Law in the New Testament* (Oxford: Oxford University Press, 1963), p. 189.

2. An invaluable resource on the subject of external confirmation of Acts is Colin J. Hemer, *The Book of Acts in the Setting of Hellenis-*

tic History, Conrad H. Gempf, ed. (Tübingen: J.C.B. Mohr, 1989). Chapters 4, 5, and 6 of Hemer (pp. 101–243) contain a wealth of information on this subject, listing detail after detail. Here is just one passage that I cannot resist describing, to give a taste of the kind of thing I am talking about. Hemer (p. 170) notes the passage (Acts 22.28) in which a Roman commander, surprised that Paul is a Roman citizen, says that he himself bought his freedom (citizenship) at a great price. Hemer first points out (a fact that makes it into some Bible footnotes) that the sale of citizenship was a well-known feature of the reign of the Emperor Claudius. (By Hemer's chronology, this scene in Acts took place about three years after the end of Claudius's reign.) This is interesting in itself, but there is more. The commander's name is Claudius Lysias (Acts 23.26) which Hemer says may well attest to his attaining his citizenship under Claudius. Most striking of all, the Roman historian Dio Cassius records that the cost of purchasing citizenship *went down* in the course of the reign of Claudius. Says Hemer, "This man … had presumably gained his rights early in the reign, and had seen his pride reduced by Claudius' later practice, and his remark reflects this." Such a wealth of indirect historical confirmation of a single remark in Acts is truly remarkable. See also Timothy McGrew, "The Evidential Value of Acts," lecture at Calvary Bible Church, April 17, 2016, accessed June 19, 2016, http://calvarybible.org/sermons/2016/4/2016apr17-the-evidential-value-of-acts-dr-tim-mcgrew.

3. I owe this point and wording about Acts and "the larger Roman world" to Timothy McGrew.

4. An extremely brief account of the ascension is found in Luke 24.51. The long ending of Mark, which was probably not written by the author of the rest of the Gospel of Mark but which is quite ancient, gives a brief account of it as well in Mark 16.19.

5. Bart Ehrman, *Forged: Writing in the Name of God—Why the Bible's Authors Are Not Who We Think They Are* (New York, Harper-Collins, 2011), p. 93.

6. The difference between my argumentative emphasis and Paley's is also evident in my organization. Paley organizes the *Horae Paulinae* according to the order of the Pauline Epistles as they appear in the New Testament. In contrast, in this chapter and the next I will dis-

cuss undesigned coincidences according to the approximate order in which they come up in Acts and confirm events or claims made there. I go through the coincidences in this chapter while going through Acts and then, in the next chapter, start again near the beginning of Acts with my first coincidence. This will sometimes mean going back and forth among the epistles; the order is roughly chronological in each chapter if one follows the narrative order in Acts.

Chapter V: Coincidences Between Acts and the Universally Acknowledged Pauline Epistles

1. The core of this coincidence is in William Paley, *Horae Paulinae or The Truth of the Scripture History of St. Paul Evinced by a Comparison of the Epistles Which Bear His Name with the Acts of the Apostles and With One Another*. J.S. Howson, editor. (London: Society for Promoting Christian Knowledge, 1877), pp. 149–150. Though the *Horae Paulinae* was originally published in 1790, my references will be to the edition by J.S. Howson published in 1877 unless otherwise noted.

2. Similar, though not identical, Greek phrases to the phrase "many days" in Acts 9.23 are used in the Septuagint Old Testament for considerable lengths of time, up to and even greater than three years (Exod 2.11, I Kgs 1.18). The Hebrew expression "many days" is used to refer to a period of three years in I Kings 2.38–39, a point noted by Paley, *Horae Paulinae*, pp. 145–146, note 2.

3. This point about independence is in Paley, *Horae Paulinae*, p. 145.

4. This coincidence is found in Paley, *Horae Paulinae*, p. 101.

5. See Robert Jamieson, A.R. Faussett, and David Brown commentary on II Corinthians 11.32–33 (1871), in loc.

6. Paley, *Horae Paulinae*, p. 101.

7. Ibid., p. 9.

8. Colin J. Hemer mentions this coincidence and uses the phrase "most famous Old Testament member of his tribe" in Colin J. Hemer, *The Book of Acts in the Setting of Hellenistic History*, Conrad H. Gempf, ed. (Tübingen: J.C.B. Mohr, 1989), p. 183.

9. This coincidence is also found in F.F. Bruce, "Is the Paul of Acts the Real Paul?" (*Bulletin of the John Rylands University Library*, 1976), p. 285.

10. The coincidence concerning the Thessalonians' knowledge of Paul's mistreatment in Philippi comes up briefly in Paley, *Horae Paulinae*, pp. 268–9.

11. I owe these points about differences between Acts and I Thessalonians to Paley, *Horae Paulinae*, pp. 276ff.

12. This coincidence is found in Paley, *Horae Paulinae*, pp. 243–4.

13. *Horae Paulinae*, p. 244.

14. Bruce, "Is the Paul of Acts the Real Paul?" p. 294.

15. This is an instance where the core of one part of the undesigned coincidence is found in Paley, *Horae Paulinae*, pp. 274ff, but where I have gone somewhat farther than Paley. Paley discusses the connection with the phrase "your own countrymen" but does not note the correspondence between Acts and Paul's reference in I Thessalonians to the Jews' having "driven [him] out." F. F. Bruce notes the connection between Paul's harsh language in I Thessalonians about the Jews and Acts 17.5–9 but does not note that the passage in I Thessalonians also alludes to Gentile complicity in the persecution. F.F. Bruce, "Is the Paul of Acts the Real Paul?" (*Bulletin of the John Rylands University Library*, 1976), p. 294. This, somewhat like the next coincidence I discuss, may be a case where Paley's exclusive use of the King James Version is the cause of his overlooking useful evidence. The KJV has the statement in I Thessalonians 2.15 that the Jews "have persecuted us" rather than "drove us out," but "drove us out" is a more accurate translation of the Greek. I will not always note precisely how I have expanded upon Paley's discussions.

16. This coincidence is entirely my own. I discovered it when reading Acts 18 in the NASB.

17. See #13.

18. Notice again the implication from the passage in Philippians that he was in Thessalonica for some time. As I have emphasized above, if the author of Acts were deliberately attempting to write his book based on the epistles, he would have made it clearer that Paul stayed in Thessalonica for more than three or four weeks.

19. Paley does not note the naming of Paul's craft as a separate coincidence, but he does note that Paul gave a good example of personal labor by working at his craft. *Horae Paulinae*, p. 195.

20. H.D.M. Spence-Jones, *The Pulpit Commentary*, volume 18: *Acts and Romans*.

21. I do not insist on the hypothesis that the money came from Philippi, specifically, though it is quite plausible. Paley argues compellingly (*Horae Paulinae*, pp. 271–274) that Timothy and Silas were at this time coming to Paul from Thessalonica (which is also in Macedonia), and there is no indication that they had gone back along Paul's previous route as far as Philippi. It is possible that by now the Thessalonians had also decided to contribute to Paul's work, or the Philippians may have sent money to Thessalonica to be delivered to Paul in Greece as soon as a trustworthy messenger was available. In any event, the main point is the correspondence between II Corinthians 11.7–9 and Acts 18.1–5.

22. This point about Titus is emphasized by Paley, *Horae Paulinae*, p. 128, and at more length by his editor, Howson, in a footnote (*Horae Paulinae*, p. 120–1, note 7).

23. The coincidence between Paul's expression, "I planted, Apollos watered," and Acts is found in Paley, *Horae Paulinae*, pp. 73–75. Paley notes, further, that Paul's comment in the epistle implies that Apollos was at Corinth not only after himself but, of course, before the writing of I Corinthians. This fits with Paley's (and my) further argument concerning the time of the writing of I Corinthians. Paley also notes the connection I will discuss later concerning Apollos and letters of reference (*Horae Paulinae*, pp. 129–130).

24. This sub-coincidence concerning Apollos's eloquence and Paul's defensiveness about his own lack of personal eloquence and impressiveness is my own.

25. The verb for "comes" is in the subjunctive aorist, and the word ἐάν ("if" or "when") is translated "if" more often when it precedes a subjunctive aorist verb. (Thayer's Greek lexicon, entry on ἐάν.)

26. The core of this especially lovely coincidence is found in Paley, *Horae Paulinae*, pp. 71–73, though my discussion expands and supplements his a great deal.

27. *Horae Paulinae*, p. 73, note 4.

28. This sub-point concerning Paul's anxiety recorded in II Corinthians and the probability that I Corinthians was sent by sea is my own.

29. Colin Hemer, *The Book of Acts in the Setting of Hellenistic History*, p. 188, does not explain why he interprets the references in I Corinthians to sending Timothy as referring to some *previous* visit by Timothy to Corinth rather than to his being sent at the end of Paul's stay in Ephesus. Hemer mentions these verses only very briefly. Hemer's later conclusions that I Corinthians was written "near the end of an Ephesian residence" (p. 258) and that Paul's sending Timothy and Erastus into Macedonia in Acts 19.22 "is to be placed near the end of his Ephesian residence" (p. 256) seem to *agree* with my argument that the sending of Timothy referred to in I Corinthians is the very journey of Timothy referred to in Acts 19.22. Since Hemer does not discuss at any length the references in I Corinthians to Paul's sending Timothy, I am unable to make any further conjecture about his position on this point.

30. My conclusions in this undesigned coincidence are consistent with my agreement with Paley (*Horae Paulinae*, pp. 131ff) that Paul did not actually make three visits to Corinth and that his allusion to "coming" a third time in II Corinthians 13.1 is a reference to his having intended and decided against an additional visit (II Cor 1.15–16), but I will not attempt to spell out the arguments that convince me that Paley is right on this point. My reconstruction of the timeline here places the time of the writing of II Corinthians closer to that of I Corinthians than does Colin Hemer's reconstruction. See Hemer, *Acts in the Setting of Hellenistic History*, p. 261. I think the time period between the two epistles was approximately seven to eight months. This timing takes account of the coincidence between Paul's statement in I Corinthians that he may spend the next winter with the Corinthians and the statement in Acts that he stayed three months in Greece. Hemer's placement (p. 261) of an entire additional winter, unmentioned in Acts, in Macedonia and in general his lengthening of the time represented by Acts 20.1–3 would require him to treat this as a more or less meaningless coincidence, since on Hemer's timeline Paul did not spend the next winter in Corinth after all. His estimate of the time represented by Acts 20.1-3 appears to be motivated by his confidence (for reasons that I do not have space to go into) that Paul eventually arrived in Jerusalem in Acts 21 in AD 57, approximately five years after the end of the proconsulship of Gallio, mentioned in Acts 18 (p. 256). Assuming Hemer to be correct about

that five-year period, in my opinion the necessary time to fill out the five years can be better accommodated by the indefinite time indications in Acts 18.18 and/or 18.23.

31. As mentioned earlier, Titus, though prominent in II Corinthians, is mentioned nowhere in Acts, which further supports the conclusion that Acts was not based on the epistles.

32. The core of this coincidence comes from Paley, *Horae Paulinae*, pp. 19–27. Paley casts it as a confirmation of the genuineness of the epistles (especially Romans), and that is true as well. My discussion recasts it as a confirmation of Acts; I therefore bring in considerations that Paley does not use in his discussion.

33. I also note that Paul's wording in this passage implies that the Corinthians already knew about the collection prior to his writing this epistle. He mentions that the collection is for Jerusalem but in a manner that strongly suggests that they knew this already. These instructions appear to be telling them more specifically *how* to take up a collection that had already been discussed with them. If I Corinthians was written between the end of a winter and Pentecost (possibly in AD 56), and if II Corinthians was written from Macedonia just before the next winter (which was spent in Corinth), then the gap between I and II Corinthians is, as I have suggested above, something on the order of seven to eight months. This does not contradict, however, Paul's statement in II Corinthians that, as he brags, they were "ready since last year" (II Cor 9.2). A comparison with II Corinthians 8.10 shows that a year previously the Corinthians had been ready *in mind*, desiring to take up the contribution, not that they had had it put together. Indeed, Paul clearly says even at the writing of II Corinthians that he is not sure that they will have the collection put together yet. The allusions to "last year" and "a year ago" in II Corinthians should therefore not be taken to refer to the time of the writing of I Corinthians. They can instead refer to a time *prior* to the writing of I Corinthians when (as we can tell from I Corinthians itself) Paul had had some communication with them that we do not possess on the subject of the collection and they had expressed eagerness to participate. Paley (*Horae Paulinae*, pp. 97–98) seems to take the reference to "a year ago" to refer to their having begun to take up the collection based upon Paul's instructions in I Corinthians, but my reconstruction fits better with Paley's own ideas

elsewhere (e.g., see pp. 88–89) about the timing of I Corinthians and II Corinthians. My chronology, placing I and II Corinthians somewhat less than a year apart, agrees with that of T. R. Birks, another of Paley's editors. See T.R. Birks, *Horae Apostolicae*, appended to William Paley, *Horae Paulinae*, edited by T.R. Birks (London: Religious Tract Society, 1850), pp. 232–3.

34. Paley, *Horae Paulinae*, pp. 24–25.

35. The core of this coincidence is found in Paley, *Horae Paulinae*, pp. 43–46.

36. Since I Timothy 3.4 implies that Timothy was located in Ephesus, the greeting to Priscilla and Aquila in II Timothy 4.19 may mean that they were at that time in Ephesus. That would have been a number of years after the writing of Romans (years comprising Paul's first Roman imprisonment, his release, and his re-imprisonment), so they easily could have decided to go back from Rome to Ephesus, where they had, according to Acts, lived for a time.

37. This point is noted by Birks, *Horae Apostolicae*, pp. 234–235. Birks emphasizes that the greeting from Priscilla and Aquila to the church at Corinth is said to be especially hearty.

38. This point is noted by Paley, *Horae Paulinae*, p. 32.

39. Besides Paul's explicit discussion in Romans of his imminent departure for Jerusalem to take the collection from the churches of Macedonia and Achaia, there are several other indications placing Romans at this specific point in Acts. Paul makes it clear in Romans that he is staying in a city of some size, with a settled church (Rom 16.23). This would fit with his writing from Corinth. Several of the names of people *from* whom Paul sends greetings to the Romans are also the same. He names Timothy, whom evidently he had caught up with at Corinth, Sosipater, and Gaius (Rom 16.21–23). Acts 20.4 expressly states that Paul was accompanied as he set out from Greece to travel to Asia and from there to Jerusalem by a group of people among whom Timothy, Gaius of Derbe, and Sopater are named. (This point is noted by Paley, *Horae Paulinae*, p. 29.) It is *possible* that the latter two are not those referred to in the epistle, but I think at least one of them is the same. The Gaius named in Romans is said to be the host of the church meeting in Corinth, which might be an argument that he would not leave the city to travel with Paul, and

one could question whether "of Derbe" would be appended to the name of a person who is now well-settled in Corinth. But neither of these considerations tells very strongly against the conclusion that it is the same Gaius, and the identification of Sosipater with Sopater has nothing at all against it.

40. Hemer, *Acts in the Setting of Hellenistic History*, p. 261.

41. Paley, *Horae Paulinae*, p. 33. As this quotation indicates, the core of the coincidence concerning the movements of Priscilla and Aquila comes from Paley (pp. 32–34), though his emphasis is more upon the confirmation this offers to the Pauline authorship of Romans than upon the confirmation of the reliability of Acts.

42. Birks, *Horae Apostolicae*, p. 252, thinks that they may have been among those who restrained Paul from going into the theater in Ephesus during the riot (Acts 19.30). But Birks is incorrect to say that "we know … that they were then at Ephesus," though they do appear to have been with Paul when he wrote I Corinthians. Acts states that Paul stayed in Ephesus for a time after sending Timothy and Erastus. We do not know how long it took Paul to write the epistle of I Corinthians or exactly how soon thereafter Priscilla and Aquila might have left. He alludes fairly early in the epistle (I Cor 4.17) to having sent Timothy already, so it seems that most of it was written after Acts 19.22, but it is by no means certain that Aquila and Priscilla were still in Ephesus when the riot occurred.

43. The core of the coincidence concerning the speech to the elders of Miletus is found in Paley, *Horae Paulinae*, pp. 77–79). My digression on the unity of Paul's personality in Acts and the epistles is my own, not Paley's. Despite the fact that it bears some similarities to the discussion by J.S. Howson, my discussion here is independent of his and is actually rather different, not only in content but also in my somewhat less positive impression of Paul's personality. Nonetheless, Howson's reflections are well worth reading. See Howson's appendix to *Horae Paulinae*, pp. 406ff and J.S. Howson, *Evidential Conclusions from the Four Greater Epistles of St. Paul* (London: Religious Tract Society, 1884), pp. 28–32.

44. J.S. Howson, in an appendix to his edition of the *Horae Paulinae* (pp. 400ff) has a fascinating discussion in which he compares Paul's two accounts of his conversion given in Acts—one to the mob at the

Temple in Acts 22 and the other to Agrippa in Acts 26. Howson argues that these accounts, in comparison with the account in Acts 9, show many subtle evidences of Paul's rhetorical skill in tailoring the message to a specific audience while presenting the same facts.

Chapter VI: Coincidences Between Acts and Other Pauline Epistles

1. William Paley, *Horae Paulinae or The Truth of the Scripture History of St. Paul Evinced by a Comparison of the Epistles Which Bear His Name with the Acts of the Apostles and With One Another*, J.S. Howson, ed. (London: Society for Promoting Christian Knowledge, 1877), pp. 219ff. Bruce M. Metzger, et. al. *A Textual Commentary on the Greek New Testament* (London: United Bible Societies, 1975), p. 601, raise genuine textual doubts about the phrase "at Ephesus" in 1.1. That phrase is the strongest, and as far as I am aware the only, reason for the traditional ascription of destination.

2. It is indirectly helpful to the confirmation of Acts if we can support the Pauline authorship of these epistles independently. For example, the connections between Philemon and Colossians make it extremely difficult to argue that Philemon is unproblematically Pauline while Colossians is dubiously Pauline. See *Horae Paulinae*, pp. 334ff. Those connections therefore strengthen the value of the coincidences in this chapter between Colossians and Acts. I encourage the interested reader to read the sections of the *Horae Paulinae* that I do not make use of, including those arguing for the Pauline authorship of all of the epistles, both because the question of Pauline authorship is intrinsically important and because of such indirect confirmation of Acts.

3. Colin Hemer, *Acts in the Setting of Hellenistic History*, Conrad H. Gempf, ed. (Tübingen: J.C.B. Mohr, 1989), p. 176.

4. The core of this coincidence is found in Paley, *Horae Paulinae*, pp. 299–301.

5. *Horae Paulinae*, pp. 300–301.

6. The core of this coincidence is found in Paley, *Horae Paulinae*, pp. 257–59.

7. Paley, *Horae Paulinae*, pp. 314–16, treats this as two coincidences between II Timothy and Acts—one concerning Timothy's father's ethnicity and the other concerning his mother's.

8. This coincidence comes from Paley, *Horae Paulinae*, pp. 318–323.

9. The "Antioch" in question is clearly Pisidian Antioch in Asia Minor, not the Antioch north of Damascus on the east coast of the Mediterranean Sea.

10. J.S. Howson, *Evidential Conclusions from the Four Greater Epistles of St. Paul* (London: Religious Tract Society, 1884), p. 27 notes that Paul's rising up after being stoned and going on immediately with his travels manifest his characteristic "alacrity and courage."

11. *Horae Paulinae*, p. 320.

12. Ibid., p. 322.

13. Thus far in this section I follow Paley's reasoning closely (*Horae Paulinae*, pp. 252–53) and would not have noticed the coincidence independently. But my argument in the rest of the discussion, though in agreement with Paley's and indebted to it, is more extensive and somewhat different in emphasis.

14. The core of the undesigned coincidence concerning Aristarchus is taken from Paley, *Horae Paulinae*, pp. 257–58. Paley for some reason does not discuss here the reference to Aristarchus in Philemon.

15. *Horae Paulinae*, pp. 262–64, 335–38.

16. Ibid., p. 259.

17. Ibid., p. 228.

18. Ibid.

19. The case of the noun is different in Acts and in Ephesians, but both are singular.

20. Ibid., pp. 229–30.

21. *Horae Paulinae*, p. 229. Paley apparently thinks that in Acts 26.29 *desmōn* does refer to the literal shackling of Paul's two hands, perhaps because Paul seems to be making a demonstrative gesture in his speech to Agrippa.

22. This is a particularly interesting example, since it is a kind of parallel passage to Ephesians 6.20. (There are many such parallels between Ephesians and Colossians.) In Ephesians, Paul says that he is "an ambassador in a chain" for the mystery of Christ. In the similar passage in Colossians, he says that he "has been bound" for the

mystery. The ESV translates the Colossians phrase as "am in prison." Paul also frequently refers to himself as "a prisoner" using the noun *desmios* (Eph 3.1, 4.1, Philem v 1, v 9, II Tim 1.8).

23. Paul uses the singular *halusin* in II Timothy 1.16 when he calls down a blessing upon the house of Onesiphorus, who, he says, sought him out in Rome and "was not ashamed of my chain." (Once again, for some reason, the ESV translates this as plural "chains," but the word is singular.) I do not wish to place much weight upon this verse, because there is good evidence that the II Timothy period of Roman imprisonment is different from that described in Ephesians, Colossians, and the end of Acts. It does, however, provide additional reason to believe that this mode of shackling was applied to Paul in Rome.

24. Because I am trying to support Acts on the basis of the epistles, I have made it my practice not usually to discuss the opposite skeptical conjecture—that the epistle was forged on the basis of Acts. Paley deals with that type of conjecture repeatedly in the *Horae Paulinae*. In this case, Paley makes the particularly nice point that, since Ephesians and Colossians were quite evidently written by the same person, it is evidence against the claim that they were forged that the phrase "for which I am an ambassador in a chain" (using the specific Greek word I have been discussing in this section) is used in Ephesians and the more generic phrase "on account of which I am bound" in the almost identical passage in Colossians. "A real prisoner might use either general words, which comprehended this among many other modes of custody; or might use appropriate words which specified this, and distinguished it from any other mode. It would be accidental which form of expression he fell upon. But an impostor, who had the art, in one place, to employ the appropriate term for the purpose of fraud, would have used it in both places." (p. 230)

Conclusion: Reclaiming the Forward Position

1. For a detailed discussion, see Gary Habermas, "The Minimal Facts Approach to the Resurrection of Jesus: The Role of Methodology as a Crucial Component in Establishing Historicity," *Southeastern Theological Review* 3:1 (2012), pp. 15–26.

2. A classic example of this older method is found in William Paley, *A View of the Evidences of Christianity in Three Parts* Richard What-

ely, editor (Murfreesboro, TN: Dehoff Publications, 1952 reprint of 1859 edition).

3. William Lane Craig, *Reasonable Faith*, 3rd edition (Wheaton, IL: Crossway Books, 2008), pp. 11–12, 298.

4. See Michael R. Licona, *The Resurrection of Jesus: A New Historiographical Approach* (Downers Grove, IL: IVP Academic, 2010), pp. 56–57, 393–94, 485 note 64, 542.

5. See Gary Habermas, "Recent Perspectives on the Reliability of the Gospels," *Christian Research Journal* 28:1 (2005). Available online at Liberty University Digital Commons, http://digitalcommons. liberty.edu/cgi/viewcontent.cgi?article=1105&context=lts_fac_pubs, accessed June 19, 2016. Page number references in these notes refer to the on-line version.

6. William Lane Craig, *Reasonable Faith*, pp. 292–293.

7. Ibid., p. 298, Habermas, "Recent Perspectives," p. 5. I note, too, that the "multiple attestation" criterion as normally used for the Gospels refers to attestation by multiple "sources," where only Mark and John among the canonical Gospels are treated as sources. The remaining "sources" are the purely hypothetical entities Q, M, and L (Habermas, "Recent Perspectives," p. 6, note 22). The design of this criterion as usually used therefore incorporates some of the dubious suppositions of source criticism, such as that Matthew and Luke are to be treated as dependent upon Mark except in the separate passages considered to come from Q, M, and L. My own study here at various points has shown an important degree of independence even in those places where it would otherwise be assumed that Matthew and Luke are merely dependent upon Mark.

8. Lydia McGrew, "Minimal Facts vs. Maximal Data," at *What's Wrong With the World*, February 21, 2015, accessed April 5, 2016, http://whatswrongwiththeworld.net/2015/02/minimal_facts_are_not_enough.html.

9. Gary Habermas, "Resurrection Research from 1975 to the Present: What Are Critical Scholars Saying," *Journal for the Study of the Historical Jesus*, 3:135 (2005), p. 151.

10. Licona, *The Resurrection of Jesus*, p. 303.

11. Sometimes scholars will argue for Jesus' bodily resurrection in

other ways, such as by pointing out that Paul would have believed in a bodily resurrection and would have meant that in the creed in I Corinthians 15, given Jewish ideas of resurrection. See N.T. Wright, *The Resurrection of the Son of God* (Minneapolis, MN: Fortress Press, 2003) and Licona, *The Resurrection of Jesus*, pp. 406–407, 601. Research such as Wright's into Jewish ideas of resurrection provides extremely useful information and adds to the cumulative case, as well as refuting poor exegesis of Paul, but I think it is important *not* to give the impression that the argument for the resurrection must always be in some way or other "routed through" the ideas of Paul, the creed given by Paul, etc. Another strategy is to point out that all of the canonical Gospel accounts are most naturally read as portraying Jesus as physically alive and to argue that this unanimity would be difficult to explain if a physical resurrection were not the view of the apostles (Craig, *Reasonable Faith*, p. 383). Again, this argument is not worthless, but it is roundabout. I contend that there is no more reason to doubt that the resurrection *accounts themselves*, even the most physically detailed, are apostolic in origin (written either by apostles or by associates of the apostles) than to doubt this about any other part of the Gospels and Acts. Therefore, given the defense we can make of the Gospels and Acts as wholes, these passages should be treated as *prima facie* apostolic.

12. A good example of this point is Gerd Lüdemann. Craig (*Reasonable Faith*, p. 381) mentions Lüdemann as someone who acknowledges the minimal fact of the appearances to the disciples. But in fact Lüdemann considers all of the appearance scenes in the Gospels *not* to be ancient in the form that we currently have them and to be almost entirely unhistorical in their details. Concerning most of the appearances he makes statements (in this case about Luke 4.36ff) such as, "The historical yield is virtually nil" (*What Really Happened to Jesus: An Historical Approach to the Resurrection*, in collaboration with Alf Özen, trans. by John Bowden, Louisville, KY: Westminster John Knox Press, 1995, pp. 46–78). The most he concedes is that the appearance to the disciples in Galilee in Matthew 28.16–20 has an "historical nucleus" in some sort of vision (p. 60) and that Mary Magdalene, the disciples, and Peter appear to have been witnesses to an appearance experience of Jesus "in some form" (pp. 66, 76–77). Lüdemann explicitly says that the physical "objectification" of Jesus

in the appearance accounts in the Gospels "is a secondary addition and unhistorical" and that "the original seeing … was a seeing in the spirit" (p. 69). The very sentence that Craig quotes (from Lüdemann, p. 80) to illustrate Lüdemann's acknowledgement of the appearances as "historically certain" initially occurs four pages earlier in the midst of Lüdemann's insistence that the meal scene in John 21 on the shore of Galilee is late and unhistorical (p. 76). Craig seems to acknowledge that the scholarly consensus cited by the minimal facts approach does not extend to the detailed nature of the appearance experiences when he says, "[I]t must be admitted that skepticism concerning the appearance traditions in the Gospels persists," William Lane Craig, "Jesus' Resurrection," accessed April 5, 2016, http://www.reasonablefaith.org/jesus-resurrection.

13. See for example Craig, *Reasonable Faith*, pp. 362ff and Craig, "Jesus' Resurrection."

14. See Thomas Nicol, *The Four Gospels in the Earliest Church History* (Edinburgh and London: William Blackwood and Sons, 1908). See also Timothy McGrew, "Who Wrote the Gospels," lecture at St. Michael Lutheran Church, January 23, 2012, accessed June 19, 2016, http://www.apologetics315.com/2012/02/who-wrote-gospels-audio-and-video-by.html.

15. Colin Hemer's magisterial work on Acts is extremely important in this regard: *The Book of Acts in the Setting of Hellenistic History*, Conrad H. Gempf, ed. (Tübingen: J.C.B. Mohr, 1989). See also Timothy McGrew, "The Evidential Value of Acts," lecture at Calvary Bible Church, April 17, 2016, accessed June 19, 2016, http://calvary-bible.org/sermons/2016/4/2016apr17-the-evidential-value-of-acts-dr-tim-mcgrew. On names in the Gospels, see Richard Bauckham, *Jesus and the Eyewitnesses: the Gospels as Eyewitness Testimony* (Grand Rapids, MI: Eerdmans Publishing, 2006), Chapters 3 and 4. On incidental external confirmations see also George Rawlinson, *The Historical Evidences of the Truth of Scripture Records, Stated Anew* (Boston: Gould and Lincoln, 1860); E.M. Blaiklock, *Compact Handbook of New Testament Life* (Minneapolis, MN: Bethany House, 1979); Jefferson White, *Evidence and Paul's Journeys* (Hilliard, OH: Parsagard Press, 2001); Lydia McGrew, "The Annotated Rawlinson," *Extra Thoughts*, April 29, 2015, accessed April 5, 2016, http://lydiaswebpage.blogspot.com/2015/04/the-annotated-rawlinson.html.

16. Lydia McGrew, "Unexplained Allusions: The Sons of Thunder," *What's Wrong With the World*, November 1, 2014, accessed April 5, 2016, http://www.whatswrongwiththeworld.net/2014/11/unexplained_ allusions_the_sons.html.

17. See the discussion in Chapter IV, #8, of the vivid details in John 21. Countless such theologically pointless details are found throughout the Gospels and Acts, giving them enormous realism.

18. See the discussion of restraint at the end of Chapter IV, #1.

19. J. J. Blunt, *Undesigned Coincidences in the Writings Both of the Old and New Testament: An argument of Their Veracity* (Birmingham, UK: The Christadelphian, 1847), pp. 287–9; William Paley, *A View of the Evidences of Christianity*, Part II, Chapter IV; J.S. Howson, *Evidential Conclusions from the Four Greater Epistles of St. Paul* (London: Religious Tract Society, 1884), pp. 406ff; F.F. Bruce, "Is the Paul of Acts the Real Paul?" (*Bulletin of the John Rylands University Library*, 1976, pp. 282–305); see also my discussion of the unity of the character of Paul in Chapter V, #13.

20. J.S. Howson, *Horae Petrinae: or, Studies in the Life of St. Peter* (London: Religious Tract Society, 1883).

21. J.S. Howson, *The Evidential Value of the Acts of the Apostles* (London: Wm. Isbister, Ltd., 1880), pp. 94–104.

22. T.R. Birks, *Horae Apostolicae*, appended to William Paley, *Horae Paulinae*, edited by T.R. Birks (London: Religious Tract Society, 1850).

23. James Smith, *The Voyage and Shipwreck of St. Paul, With Dissertations on the Life and Writings of St. Luke, and the Ships and Navigation of the Antients* (London: Longman, Brown, Green, Longmans, and Roberts, 1856).

24. Licona, *The Resurrection of Jesus*, pp. 592, 594 notes 440 and 443. Licona also expressly considers *unknown* "the amount of liberty the Evangelists may have taken in their reports [of the resurrection]," p. 542.

25. The thesis that the genre of Acts is ancient novel is advocated by Richard Pervo, *Profit With Delight: The Literary Genre of the Acts of the Apostles* (Philadelphia: Fortress, 1987).

26. Contrast this picture with the casual suggestion that Luke deliberately has all of the post-resurrection appearances and the ascension "occur on Easter," though this is not how they actually happened (Licona, *The Resurrection of Jesus*, p. 596 note 449). If the author of Luke really believed that the events did not all take place on Easter and yet deliberately made them all take place on Easter in his Gospel, for us to dub this a literary trope of "telescoping" does nothing to remove the problem: This theory implicates Luke in deliberately falsifying the data. In contrast, I would argue that it is an overreading of the end of Luke to take it to be saying that these events all occurred on Easter Sunday. Moreover, a practice of deliberately altering facts is not characteristic of the author of Acts and Luke as he emerges in this study. Similarly, Licona gives the thesis that the speeches in Acts reflect "the teaching of the Jerusalem apostles" only a rating of "possible" (p. 220), while I see no reason to doubt that at all, given the overall reliability and care of the author of Acts and his placement in time as a contemporary of the apostles. Licona also says that the accounts of Paul's conversion in Acts have only "limited historical value," basing this conclusion apparently on nothing more than ideas about genre (see note 27) and on the lack of "strong agreement" about them among scholars (pp. 393–394).

27. Licona, *The Resurrection of Jesus*, pp. 592–94, see also references in notes 24 and 26. Licona seems confused here on the matter of genre, stating that the genre to which he considers the Gospels to belong "offered biographers a great deal of flexibility to rearrange material...[and] invent speeches" (p. 593). But what he has actually said earlier about the genre in question (e.g., pp. 127, 202–204) does not at all support this statement on p. 593. On p. 593 (and in a similar statement on p. 34), Licona seems to conflate the claim that a genre designation is broad and flexible, including both more and less strictly historical documents, with the far more controversial claim that, if a document belongs (in some sense or other) to a broad genre, the author would have considered himself *inherently licensed by the genre* to fictionalize, invent speeches, etc., to at least some degree and that his readers would have expected him to do so. The two claims are *not* the same and must be kept sharply distinct, even if we grant the genre designation of Greco-Roman *bioi* that Licona, following Richard Burridge (*What Are the Gospels: A Comparison with Graeco-*

Roman Biography, Grand Rapids, MI: Eerdmans, 2004), wishes to make. That last question about genre (whether the Gospels and/or Acts actually "are" something so specific as Greco-Roman *bioi*) is one that I do not have leisure to address here; but even if this genre designation were correct in some sense, it would be entirely compatible with as high a degree of meticulous reliability and the absence of invention in a *particular* document, and with the audience's expectation of that historical meticulousness, as one could wish. Nor does Burridge himself argue to the contrary. Indeed, one point of defining a *broad* genre in this regard is that the alleged genre includes some documents that hold themselves to a high standard of historical factuality and accuracy as well as others that do not.

WORKS CITED

Bauckham, Richard. *Jesus and the Eyewitnesses: The Gospels as Eyewitness Testimony.* Grand Rapids, MI: William B. Eerdmans Pub., 2006.

Bennett, Edmund H. *The Four Gospels from a Lawyer's Standpoint.* Boston: Houghton, Mifflin and Company, 1899.

Birks, T. R. *Horae Apostolicae.* In *Horae Paulinae*, by William Paley. Edited by T.R. Birks. London: Religious Tract Society, 1850.

Blaiklock, E.M. *Compact Handbook of New Testament Life.* Minneapolis, MN: Bethany House, 1979.

_____. *Man or Myth.* Homebush West, N.S.W.: Anzea Books, 1983.

Blunt, John J. *Undesigned Coincidences in the Writings Both of the Old and New Testament, an Argument of Their Veracity.* Birmingham, UK: The Christadelphian. 1965 reprint of 1847 edition.

Burn, John Henry. *The Preacher's Complete Commentary on the New Testament: Gospel According to St. Mark.* New York: Funk & Wagnalls, 1896.

Burridge, Richard A. *What Are the Gospels? A Comparison with Graeco-Roman Biography.* Grand Rapids, MI: William B. Eerdmans, 2004.

Bruce, F. F. "Is the Paul of Acts the Real Paul?" *Bulletin of the John Rylands University Library*, 1976, 58:282–305.

Craig, William Lane. *Reasonable Faith.* 3rd ed. Wheaton, IL: Crossway Books, 2008.

_____. "Jesus' Resurrection." ReasonableFaith. Accessed April 5, 2016. http://www.reasonablefaith.org/jesus-resurrection.

Ehrman, Bart D. *Forged: Writing in the Name of God: Why the Bible's Authors Are Not Who We Think They Are.* New York: HarperOne, 2011.

Exell, Joseph, and H.D.M. Spence-Jones. "The Pulpit Commentary." StudyLight. Accessed June 20, 2016. https://www.studylight.org/commentaries/tpc.html.

Gill, John. "John Gill's Exposition of the Bible Commentary." Bible Study Tools. Accessed June 19, 2016. http://www.biblestudytools.com/commentaries/gills-exposition-of-the-bible/.

Habermas, Gary. "Recent Perspectives on the Reliability of the Gospels." *Christian Research Journal* 28, no. 1 (2005). Liberty University Digital Commons. Accessed June 19, 2016. http://digitalcommons.liberty.edu/cgi/viewcontent.cgi?article=1105&context=lts_fac_pubs.

_____. "Resurrection Research from 1975 to the Present: What Are Critical Scholars Saying." *Journal for the Study of the Historical Jesus* 3, no. 135 (2005): 135–53.

_____. "The Minimal Facts Approach to the Resurrection of Jesus: The Role of Methodology as a Crucial Component in Establishing Historicity." *Southeastern Theological Review* 3, no. 1 (2012): 15–26.

Hemer, Colin J. *The Book of Acts in the Setting of Hellenistic History.* Edited by Conrad H. Gempf. Tübingen: J.C.B. Mohr, 1989.

Howson, J.S. *The Evidential Value of the Acts of the Apostles.* London: Wm. Isbister, Ltd, 1880.

_____. *Horae Petrinae; Or, Studies in the Life of St. Peter.* London: Religious Tract Society, 1883.

_____. *Evidential Conclusions from the Four Greater Epistles of St. Paul.* London: Religious Tract Society, 1884.

Jamieson, Robert, A. R. Fausset, and David Brown. *Bible Commentary Critical and Explanatory.* Bible Study Tools. Accessed June 19, 2016. http://www.biblestudytools.com/commentaries/jamieson-fausset-brown/.

Leathes, Stanley. *The Religion of the Christ: Its Historic and Literary Development Considered as an Evidence of Its Origin.* London: Rivingtons, 1874.

Lenski, R. C. H. *Interpretation of St. John's Gospel.* Minneapolis, MN: Augsburg Fortress, 2008.

Licona, Michael R. *The Resurrection of Jesus: A New Historiographical Approach.* Downers Grove, IL: IVP Academic, 2010.

Lüdemann, Gerd, and Alf Özen. *What Really Happened to Jesus: A Historical Approach to the Resurrection.* Translated by John Bowden. Louisville, KY: Westminster John Knox Press, 1995.

Luther, Martin. "Confession Concerning Christ's Supper." In *Luther's Works.* Vol. 37, *Word and Sacrament III.* Edited by Robert H. Fischer and Helmut T. Lehmann, Philadelphia, PA: Muhlenberg Press, 1961.

McGrew, Lydia. "Unexplained Allusions: The Sons of Thunder," *What's Wrong with the World* (blog), November 1, 2014. Accessed April 5, 2016. http://www.whatswrongwiththeworld.net/2014/11/unexplained_allusions_the_sons.html.

_____. "Minimal Facts vs. Maximal Data," *What's Wrong with the World* (blog), February 21, 2015. Accessed April 5, 2016. http://whatswrongwiththeworld.net/2015/02/minimal_facts_are_not_enough.html.

_____. "The Annotated Rawlinson," *Extra Thoughts* (blog), April 29, 2015. Accessed April 5, 2016. http://lydiaswebpage.blogspot.com/2015/04/the-annotated-rawlinson.html.

McGrew, Timothy. "Who Wrote the Gospels? Audio and Video by Tim McGrew." Apologetics 315. January 23, 2012. Accessed June 19, 2016. http://www.apologetics315.com/2012/02/who-wrote-gospels-audio-and-video-by.html.

_____. "Undesigned Coincidences Series." Apologetics315. 2013. Accessed June 19, 2016. http://www.apologetics315.com/2013/11/undesigned-coincidences-series-by-tim.html.

_____. "Undesigned Coincidences in the Gospels." First Baptist Church of Kenner. January 9, 2011. Accessed June 19, 2016. http://firstkenner.org/audio/jan2011/010911A%20.mp3.

_____. "The Evidential Value of Acts." Calvary Bible Church. April 17, 2016. Accessed June 19, 2016. http://calvarybible.org/sermons/2016/4/2016apr17-the-evidential-value-of-acts-dr-tim-mcgrew.

Metzger, Bruce Manning. *A Textual Commentary on the Greek New Testament: A Companion Volume to the United Bible Societies' Greek New Testament*, 3rd ed. London: United Bible Soc., 1975.

Nicol, Thomas. *The Four Gospels in the Earliest Church History*. Edinburgh: W. Blackwood and Sons, 1908.

Ogg, George. *The Chronology of the Public Ministry of Jesus*. Cambridge: University Press, 1940.

Paley, William. *A View of the Evidences of Christianity: In Three Parts*. Edited by Richard Whately. 1859 ed. Murfreesboro, TN: Dehoff Publications, 1952.

_____. *Horae Paulinae, or The Truth of the Scripture History of St. Paul Evinced by a Comparison of the Epistles Which Bear His Name with the Acts of the Apostles and With One Another*. Edited by J. S. Howson. London: Society for Promoting Christian Knowledge, 1877.

Pervo, Richard I. *Profit with Delight: The Literary Genre of the Acts of the Apostles*. Philadelphia: Fortress Press, 1987.

Rawlinson, George. *The Historical Evidences of the Truth of the Scripture Records: Stated Anew, with Special Reference to the Doubts and Discoveries of Modern times.* Boston: Gould and Lincoln, 1860.

Sherwin-White, A. N. *Roman Society and Roman Law in the New Testament.* Oxford: Oxford University Press, 1963.

Smith, James. *The Voyage and Shipwreck of St. Paul: With Dissertations on the Life and Writings of St. Luke, and the Ships and Navigation of the Antients.* London: Longman, Brown, Green, Longmans, & Roberts, 1856.

Thayer, John Henry. "A Greek-English Lexicon of the New Testament." Bible Hub. Accessed June 19, 2016. http://biblehub.com/.

Wallace, J. Warner. *Cold-Case Christianity: A Homicide Detective Investigates the Claims of the Gospels.* Colorado Springs, CO: David C. Cook, 2013.

Wenham, John William. *Easter Enigma: Are the Resurrection Accounts in Conflict?* Eugene, OR: Wipf and Stock, 1992.

_____. *Redating Matthew, Mark & Luke: A Fresh Assault on the Synoptic Problem.* Downers Grove, IL: InterVarsity Press, 1992.

White, Jefferson. *Evidence and Paul's Journeys: An Historical Investigation into the Travels of the Apostle Paul.* Hilliard, OH: Parsagard Press, 2001.

Wright, Nicholas Thomas. *The Resurrection of the Son of God.* Minneapolis: Fortress Press, 2003.

AUTHORS AND MODERN NAMES

SCRIPTURES

SUBJECTS

ABOUT THE AUTHOR

Dr. Lydia McGrew is a widely published analytic philosopher who specializes in classical and formal epistemology, probability theory, and philosophy of religion. She is the co-author (with Timothy McGrew) of *Internalism and Epistemology: The Architecture of Reason* (Routledge, 2007) and of the article on the argument from miracles in *The Blackwell Companion to Natural Theology* (2009). Her articles have appeared in such journals as *Erkenntnis, Theoria, Acta Analytica, Philosophia Christi,* and *Philosophical Studies,* and she is the author of the entry on historical inquiry and theism in *The Routledge Companion to Theism* (2012). She home schools, and in her spare time, she blogs about apologetics, Christianity, culture, and politics. She lives in southwest Michigan with her husband and children.

*For a full listing of DeWard Publishing
Company books, visit our website:*

www.deward.com

CPSIA information can be obtained
at www.ICGtesting.com
Printed in the USA
BVHW080132171221
624155BV00003B/125